Communication Skills

Stephen Daunt

Gill & Macmillan

Gill & Macmillan Ltd

Goldenbridge

Dublin 8

with associated companies throughout the world
www.gillmacmillan.ie

© Stephen Daunt 1996

0 7171 2389 8

Designed by Graham Thew Design

Print origination by Graham Thew Design

All rights reserved. No part of this publication may be copied, reproduced or transmitted in any form or by any means without permission of the publishers.

CONTENTS

Preface	vii
Acknowledgments	x
Part 1: Making and Taking Meaning	
1. Breaking Down Communication: Theory	1
2. As I See It: Perception	12
3. Actions Speak Louder?: Non-Verbal Communication	22
Part 2: Words We Speak	
4. Talking Heads: Oral Skills	40
5. Stand and Deliver!: Making an Oral Presentation	62
6. Getting an Earful: Listening	72
7. Between Ourselves: Interactive Skills	87
Part 3: Words We Write	
8. In My Own Write: Personal Writing	105
9. Doing the Right Thing: Formal Writing	122
10. 'Business English'	135
11. The Project: Process and Product	150
12. Brush Up Your Basics: Writing Skills	163
Part 4: Words We Read	
13. Reading for a Purpose	187
14. Reading for Pleasure	202
Part 5: Mass Communication	
15. The Mass Media	210
Bibliography	236

Preface

Communication Skills is designed for those following a communications course such as the mandatory General Studies module in Communications prescribed for National Vocational Certificate Level 2.

Fundamental to *Communication Skills* is the belief that 'communication is too often taken for granted when it should be taken to pieces' (John Fiske, *Key Concepts in Communication*, p. x. Full details of books cited will be found in the bibliography, p. 236.) We tend to take it for granted that we are satisfactory communicators in the various roles we play in our adult daily lives. Yet in the home, in school, in the work-place and in the community, most of us communicate less effectively than we might. We regularly fail to make our meaning plain to others, or else we fail to understand fully the messages that others send us. Only when a crisis occurs do we stop to assess our own performance.

Educational systems, in Ireland and elsewhere, are starting to acknowledge what as individuals we are slow to admit: *the ability to communicate effectively in our professional and private lives may not come naturally and cannot be taken for granted.* It is a skill—perhaps the *core* life skill—that must be learned and may be taught like any other.

Skills improve through constant practice and so this book contains a great many tasks to develop and refine students' competencies. Few groups are likely to have time to attempt all tasks set in a chapter; in picking and choosing, a group may suit the interests of its members. Some tasks are of practical relevance to areas of vocational specialisation, while others may be adapted by the group leader to suit the demands of a particular course. None of the tasks as set requires the student to have specialised vocational knowledge.

In keeping with the increasing emphasis on the spoken word at all levels of education, many tasks encourage oral participation and may be carried out in pairs or small groups. This should provide valuable training in interactive skills and help prepare the student to face the challenge of an oral presentation, now a vital element of most communication courses.

A number of the oral tasks use terms that may require clarification. **Brainstorming** is an activity that is intended to produce as many ideas as possible in a short time. A time limit (say, five minutes) is usually an essential stimulus. The hope is that one idea will 'spark off' another. The 'rules' of brainstorming are simple:
- *All* ideas are acceptable
- *Quantity* is the goal
- *Discussion* is forbidden
- All ideas must be *recorded.* Whether working in the full group or as sub-groups, a recorder must be appointed. When the time limit has expired, recorded items may be evaluated.

Rounds are best conducted with the group seated in a circle. The aim is to get, fairly rapidly, everybody's one-line opinion on the subject under discussion. Rounds are usually based on starters supplied by the teacher or group leader. The starter is an incomplete sentence, which each participant in turn is asked to repeat and complete—e.g.

A: 'I think hypochondria is ...'
B: 'I think hypochondria is the one disease I haven't got.'

Consensus is listed as an objective in a number of tasks. It means reaching agreement through discussion, negotiation and concession rather than by straight vote (majority 'victory'), bullying, or any other means! The search for consensus is usually helped if the group or sub-group has a firm chairperson.

Communication Skills is divided into five parts, with a logical sequence.

Part 1 deals with the **theory** of communication. Isn't it a fact that when we fully understand how something is made or works we become much better at using it? If we take the communication process to pieces and understand its workings, we may become better communicators. A grasp of *theory* may benefit *practice*. In this instance, theory takes us back to communication's origins, which lie in the realm of **perception**. For now, perception may be defined as what each of us makes of the world around us. When we want to let others know what we as individuals register in our senses and minds, we draw on the most basic means at our disposal, **non-verbal communication**, that huge resource of signals which we send, consciously or unconsciously, using body, face, sound, clothes etc.

However, it is **language** that sets us apart as a species, allowing us to dominate this planet through our astonishing ability to transfer complicated ideas from one human mind to another across vast tracts of time and space. Language belongs at the centre of any communications course. Parts 2, 3 and 4, all dealing with *verbal* communication, begin with the **spoken** word, because 'the real engine of verbal communication is the spoken language we acquired as children' (Steven Pinker, *The Language Instinct*, p. 16).

In human evolution, the *spoken* word came long before the **written**. It's easy to forget that many millions of people today still can't write or read the words they freely speak. **Speaking** and **listening** belong together—as children, we *listen* in order to learn to *speak*—and are accordingly paired in part 2.

Writing and **reading** (parts 3 and 4) are also closely related. Together, these two Rs occupy, it is estimated, a mere 25 per cent of our adult communication time. Yet they receive far more attention than speaking and listening in most second-level English programmes.

Many of the words we read are supplied by the mass media. **Mass communication**, the subject of part 5, is such a comparatively recent phenomenon that even the definition of the term still causes experts to argue. What nobody disputes is that the already significant role played by the media in our lives is certain to increase in the future.

Each of the five parts is divided into chapters, which in turn are mostly sub-divided into sections that might be covered in a briskly paced forty-minute session. Thus chapter 1, containing three sections (1.1, 1.2, and 1.3), might be delivered over three periods. In certain chapters (e.g. chapters 5 and 12) this arrangement is suspended and a different approach is recommended.

Overall, the text assumes a minimum allocation of three forty-minute sessions per week throughout the academic year. A fourth weekly session would be extremely useful for consultations between teacher and students to discuss projects, oral presentation, problem areas etc. At many points in the course the teacher's role is envisaged as one of organising, facilitating and advising, rather than of lecturing to the full group.

Taking communication to pieces can be a demanding and frustrating business but because it is so closely bound up with interpersonal relationships it can also be enjoyable and even exhilarating. I hope that in seeking answers to the problems set in these pages you gain enjoyment and satisfaction, even if you don't always emerge with a solution. Perhaps to some of the questions there are no clear-cut answers. At the end of each part, look back and ask yourself:
- What have I learned?
- Was it worth learning?

You might like to include a review of this textbook in your evaluation. Feedback on whether or not it met your needs and those of the group would be appreciated.

A note on personal pronouns

In the absence of consensus on a non-sexist formula, I have kept options open by random use of 'she' and 'he'.

Acknowledgments

For permission to reproduce copyright material, grateful acknowledgment is made to the following:

Penguin Books Ltd for an extract from *The Language Instinct* by Stephen Pinker;

David Wilkinson Associates for extracts from *The Complete Fawlty Towers* by John Cleese and Connie Booth;

Faber and Faber for an extract from 'Trouble with the Works' by Harold Pinter in *Harold Pinter: Plays Two*;

Hamish Hamilton Ltd for an extract adapted from *The Mother Tongue* by Bill Bryson;

The Agency (London) Ltd for an extract from *The Communication Cord* by Brian Friel;

Faber and Faber for 'Good Taste' by Christopher Logue and 'A Study of Reading Habits' by Philip Larkin;

James MacGibbon for 'Not Waving but Drowning' from *The Collected Poems of Stevie Smith*;

Institute of Public Administration for an extract from *The IPA Yearbook and Diary*;

Blackstaff Press for 'Tullyvoe: Tête à tête in the Parish Priest's Parlour' by Paul Durcan;

A.M. Heath & Co. Ltd for an extract from 'Down the Mine' from *Inside the Whale and Other Essays* by George Orwell (copyright © The estate of the late Sonia Brownell Orwell and Martin Secker and Warburg Ltd);

Peters, Fraser and Dunlop for an extract from 'A Public-House Man' from *Excursions in the Real World* by William Trevor;

Harper Collins Ltd for an extract from 'Popular Mechanics' from *The Stories of Raymond Carver*;

Cordon Art for the illustration 'Another World' by M.C. Escher;

Universal Press Syndicate for one 'Far Side' cartoon by Gary Larson.

Photos are reproduced by permission of RTE, *Cork Examiner*, Frank Spooner Pictures, Camera Press, Paul Popper (Popperfoto).

PART 1

MAKING AND TAKING MEANING

 BREAKING DOWN COMMUNICATION: THEORY

THREE PERIODS

1.1 WHAT IS COMMUNICATION?

When you enter a classroom to study French or biology or economics, you know pretty much what to expect—both *what* you will be taught and *how* you will be taught it.

Does the same hold true for the study of a subject called 'communication'? Let's put it to the test.

TASK 1.1 A

Communication defined

Divide a blank sheet into a top and bottom half. Head the upper section *Communication (self)*, and write a definition of what the word means to you. If it seems to have more than one meaning, give a number of definitions—words or phrases will do. Resist the temptation to use a dictionary.

Now, using a board or flip-chart, pool your definitions. As a group, try to reach consensus on a single definition or set of short definitions to cover *all* forms of communication. When you have consensus, head the bottom half *Communication (group)*, and write down the agreed definition (or definitions). Preserve them carefully!

Evolving a group definition may not have been easy but you will all agree that 'communication', 'communicate' and 'communicator' are familiar, everyday words. You probably use them yourself and you're so used to hearing them in some contexts that they're in danger of becoming clichés. Think of

- Television serials: 'Maybe you should *talk* to Greg—just open the lines of *communication!*'
- Industrial relations: '*Communication* breakdown threatens plant closure.'
- Problem Page letters: 'My boy-friend and I just don't seem to *communicate* any more.'

Are there other areas of human interaction with which we associate the words?

The words are commonplace because the activity to which they refer is central to all our lives. It is as fundamental a part of our existence as breathing or eating. We humans, it is sometimes said, 'cannot *not* communicate.'

1.1.1 HUMAN AND ANIMAL COMMUNICATION

Animals also need to communicate, both among themselves and to us. How do they send and receive messages without the benefit of humankind's most valuable asset—language?

Language works though *sound*, and many animals use this important channel for messages. The locust rubs its legs against the sides of its body, and the resulting noise (or 'stridulation') conveys simple messages to other locusts. How do your household pets use *sound* to warn of danger, to assert territorial rights, to mate, or to call young?

Bees use *sight* and *smell* to pass information. The waggle-dance by which the honeybee tells her fellow-workers where a good supply of a particular bloom may be found is one of nature's communicative marvels but even it is severely restricted in dealing with distance (or *space*) and *time*. The movements can 'speak' only of what lies within her own personal experience in the very recent past. Imagine how frustrating it would be if in all your dealings with other people you could only talk about what you had experienced within the past couple of hours or were experiencing at the time of interaction!

A few minutes spent discussing the ways animals communicate and the limits of their powers should help to make us aware of the extraordinary value of *language* to the Naked Ape.

TASK 1.1.1 A

What makes language special?

Form groups of four or five, each with its own chairperson and recorder. As groups, study the five statements below, which try to pin down what makes language special. Which statement best captures human language's edge over animal communication?

Reach consensus in the groups on how the five statements should be ranked, from 1 (top) to 5 (bottom). At the end of ten minutes ask each recorder to give his or her group's ranking and to explain briefly the group's choice of number 1.

(1) The distinctive characteristic of human language is that in both speaking and listening there is virtually *no expenditure of energy* and it is possible to do other things at the same time.

(2) Human language's most vital distinction is its *capacity for constant self-renewal*, dropping old words and inventing new ones.

(3) What sets human language apart is its

ability to refer to things that may be far distant in either time (past or future) or place.

(4) The most striking feature of human language is its *international currency*—any human can learn any other human's language.

(5) Whereas animal 'language' consists of *fixed systems of signals* conveying quite primitive information—

The song of canaries
Never varies (Ogden Nash)—
human language is distinctive in that *it can communicate anything the communicator wishes* to put into words, even pure nonsense.

In discussion, don't overlook some of the less obvious animals and how they communicate: chimpanzees, dolphins, parrots, bats, fish, ants, and the various circus animals.

1.2 COMMUNICATION IN THEORY

When we're faced with the need to take something to pieces, we often enlist the help of an expert. Here is Tim, an expert on verbal communication, explaining to his barrister friend Jack exactly what happens in the process of communicating:

JACK: But your thesis is nearly finished, isn't it?
TIM: I don't know. Maybe.
JACK: What's it on again?
TIM: Talk.
JACK: What about?
TIM: That's what the thesis is about—talk, conversation, chat.
JACK: Ah.
TIM: Discourse Analysis with Particular Reference to Response Cries.
JACK: You're writing your thesis on what we're doing now?
TIM: It's fascinating, you know. Are you aware of what we're doing now?
JACK: We're chatting, aren't we?
TIM: [*Warming up*] Exactly. But look at the process involved. You wish to know what my thesis is about and I wish to tell you. Information has to be imparted. A message has to be sent from me to you and you have to receive that message. How do we achieve that communication?
JACK: You just tell me.
TIM: Exactly. Words. Language. An agreed code. I encode my message; I transmit it to you; you receive the message and decode it. If the message sent is clear and distinct, if the code is fully shared and subscribed to, if the message is comprehensively received, then there is a reasonable chance—one, that you will understand what I'm trying to tell you—and two, that we will have established the beginnings of a dialogue. All social behaviour, the entire social order, depends on our communicational structures, on words mutually agreed on and mutually understood. Without that agreement, without that shared code, you have chaos.

JACK: Chaos. Absolutely. Why?

TIM: Because communication collapses. An extreme example: I speak only English; you speak only German; no common communicational structure. The result?—Chaos ... But let's stick with the situation where there is a shared context and an agreed code, and even here we run into complications.

JACK: So soon?

TIM: The complication that perhaps we are both playing roles here, not only for one another but for ourselves ...

Brian Friel, *The Communication Cord*, p. 18–19.

TASK 1.2 A

A model of communication

Since this is quite a difficult passage, at least two readings are recommended: a preliminary, silent skim to get the general drift, followed by a reading-aloud using two expressive volunteers.

When Tim writes up his thesis he will want to include a *model* to complement and reinforce his written explanation of the communication process. A model in this sense is a way of representing complex ideas, relationships or issues with diagrams or simple graphic forms. It is a *visual aid* to clarification, and there are in existence many models illustrating communication at work.

Using Tim's explanation as your guide, devise your own model to demonstrate the communication process. Compare the completed models. Which express the process most clearly?

TASK 1.2 B

Feedback

As a group, spend a few minutes discussing answers to the following questions:

1. Tim and Jack are talking about communication. How effectively are they communicating to each other? Do you notice any breakdowns?
2. As an audience, we watch here two people in face-to-face interaction, which is the simplest form of interpersonal communication. What do the two men communicate to *us* about themselves? Does, for example, *the way they use words* send us signals about the kind of people they are?
3. Does this passage make you want to alter in any way the group definition you negotiated in task 1.1 A?

1.2.1 TOP TWENTY COMMUNICATION CONCEPTS

Brian Friel's Tim is one of an ever-growing army studying communication as an academic discipline. Courses in communication are becoming popular further education choices.

Like any academic subject or occupation, communication has acquired its specialised vocabulary. Here are some terms that you may find useful:

1, 2. Person and Another

They stand for any two people: you and me, A and B, Tim and Jack, Romeo and Juliet, Beavis and Butthead. This book couldn't exist without them, since communication is a *social* activity, requiring two or more players.

3. Intrapersonal communication

Immediately we need to revise that last sentence, because the most limited form of communication is carried on *within* Person, in the privacy of his or her own head—the ceaseless monologue we all carry on within ourselves.

4. Interpersonal communication

What this book is mostly about—Person(s) making meaning(s) to Other(s), such as Tim chatting to Jack, or Romeo declaring undying love for Juliet. At its simplest it is the classic face-to-face encounter, involving most of the senses: mother and baby, doctor and patient, teacher and pupil, interrogator and suspect, priest and penitent.

5. Medio-communication

Small-scale interaction with the vital addition of technology—for example, Person speaking to Another over a mobile phone. This is an increasingly extensive form of communication, as the technology of phone, fax and computer becomes ever more sophisticated and widespread.

6. Mass communication

Another growth area and, as the name indicates, the most expansive (and expensive) form of communication, involving, typically, a huge audience receiving information or entertainment via a sophisticated technology. You'll recognise in this description television, radio, cinema, advertising, newspapers, books, and popular music. How many people watched the 1994 soccer World Cup final?

7. Sender

Person wishing to send a message to Another, thereby starting up the communicative process.

8. Receiver

Another interpreting Person's message, thereby completing a stage of the process.

9. Message

Whatever thought, feeling, information or request for information Person chooses to send to Another—in short, the *content* of communication. As you read this sentence, you are the *receiver* of a *message* that I, the *sender*, have written for you.

10. Code

Person, in deciding to send a message, must choose a *code* in which to send it, a code that will make sense both to her and to Another. The code most often selected is spoken or written *language*, which is an agreed system of sounds or symbols to help us make meanings to each other. Other codes include the presentational (dress, gesture, head nods, facial expression etc.), music and dance, sign language, numbers, heraldry, logos, pictograms, and Morse code.

11. Encode

Any message has to be organised or 'translated' into a form or *code* in which it can be sent or transmitted to Another with a reasonable chance of being received as intended.

12. Decode

Having received Person's encoded message, Another must now *decode* it—work out what it was that Person intended.

13. Feedback

The response Another *feeds back* to Person in reply to Person's original message—including blank-faced incomprehension. Feedback is Person's way of knowing how his message has been received. In face-to-face communication, Person can send a message by his voice and simultaneously receive Another's non-verbal facial feedback with his eyes.

14. Language

See *code* above.

15. Channel

The *physical* means of sending messages, such as the sound waves that carry Person's voice to Another's ear or light waves that carry Another's smile to Person's eye.

16. Noise

The word is used in a specialised sense to mean anything that interferes with or distorts the message intended. Noise may originate in the Sender (e.g. strong accent, speech impediment), in the Message (e.g. regional dialect), in the Channel (e.g. nearby pneumatic drill), or in the Receiver (e.g. too drunk to understand).

17. Medium

In the singular, this refers to a particular *means* of sending a message—Person's voice, for instance. The plural form, 'media', is much more common, referring to the mechanical or technical media, especially the mass media.

18. Context

Person and Another always interact in a particular *place* at a particular *time* and in some form of *relationship* to each other—social, psychological etc.

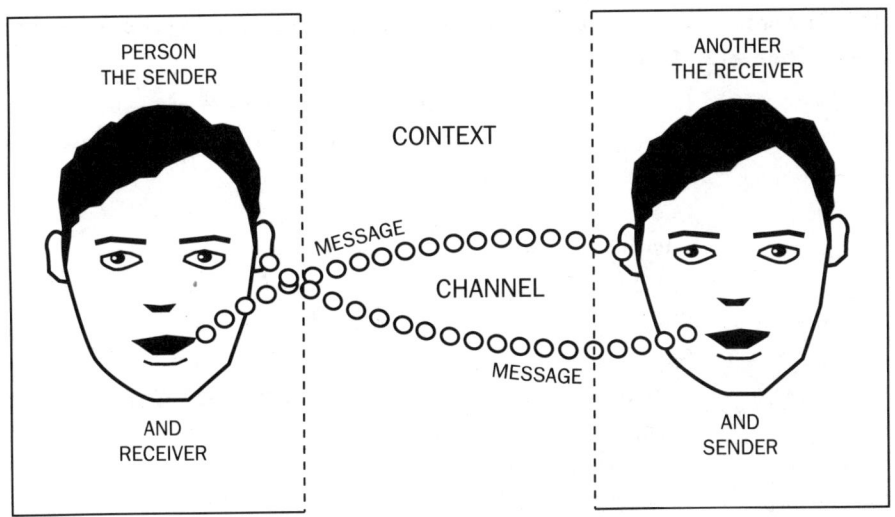

19. NVC

Non-verbal communication, which is such an important medium for transmitting and receiving messages that it demands a chapter to itself (chapter 3).

20. Communication

Review these statements:
(1) We cannot *not* communicate.
(2) Communication is essential to human survival.
(3) Communication is always undertaken with some purpose or aim in mind.
(4) Communication is social interaction through messages.
(5) Communication always happens on more than one level: even when Person says 'Good morning' to Another, she is making multiple meanings.

 TASK 1.2.1 A

True or false?

Write a short paragraph (8–12 lines) explaining why, in your view, any *one* of the statements in no. 20 above is either true or false. Feel free to support opinion with example.

1.3 COMMUNICATION IN PRACTICE

So far we've been dealing with the *theory* of communication. Sadly, theory and practice don't always match. Between source and destination, all sorts of accidents happen to messages. Emergencies arise, the communication cord is pulled, and the process grinds to a halt.

Communication breakdown is brilliantly demonstrated in the following three extracts from an episode of the classic television comedy series *Fawlty Towers*:

1. Mrs Richards (who wears a hearing aid but doesn't like turning it on) confirms her reservation with Manuel:

MRS RICHARDS [*to Manuel*] Now, I've reserved a very quiet room, with a bath and a sea view. I specifically asked for a sea view in my written confirmation, so please be sure I have it.
MANUEL Qué?
MRS RICHARDS ...What?
MANUEL ...Qué?
MRS RICHARDS K?
MANUEL Sí.
MRS RICHARDS C? [*Manuel nods*] KC? [*Manuel looks puzzled*] KC? What are you trying to say?
MANUEL No, no—Qué—what?
MRS RICHARDS K—what?
MANUEL Sí! Qué—what?
MRS RICHARDS C. K. Watt?
MANUEL ...Yes.
MRS RICHARDS Who is C. K. Watt?
Manuel Qué?
Mrs Richards Is it the manager, Mr Watt?
MANUEL Oh, manager!
MRS RICHARDS He is.
MANUEL Ah ... Mr Fawlty.
MRS RICHARDS What?
MANUEL Fawlty.
MRS RICHARDS What are you talking about, you silly little man. [*turns to Polly,*] What is going on here? I ask him for my room, and he tells me the manager's a Mr Watt and he's aged forty.
MANUEL No. No. Fawlty.
MRS RICHARDS Faulty? What's wrong with him?
POLLY It's all right, Mrs Richards. He's from Barcelona.
MRS RICHARDS The manager's from Barcelona?

2. Basil warns Manuel to say nothing:

BASIL Manuel, Manuel.
MANUEL Your horse, it win, it win!
BASIL Ssh!! ... Manuel ... [*putting his head close to Manuel*] You know nothing. [*Manuel is puzzled*] You know nothing.
MANUEL You always say, Mr Fawlty. But I learn.

BASIL	What?
MANUEL	I learn, I learn.
BASIL	No, no, no, no ...
MANUEL	I get better.
BASIL	No, you don't understand.
MANUEL	I do.
BASIL	No, you don't
MANUEL	I do understand that.
BASIL	Shh ... you know nothing about the horse.
MANUEL	[*doubtfully*] I know nothing about the horse.
BASIL	Yes.
MANUEL	Ah ... which horse?
BASIL	What?
MANUEL	Which horse I know nothing?
BASIL	My horse, nitwit.
MANUEL	Your horse, 'Nitwit'.
BASIL	No, no. Dragonfly.
MANUEL	It won!
BASIL	Yes, I know.
MANUEL	I know it won, too.
BASIL	What?
MANUEL	I put money on for you. You give me money. I go to vetting-shop, I put money on ...
BASIL	I know, I know, I know.
MANUEL	Why you say I know nothing?
BASIL	Oh. Look ... look ... look ... you know the horse?
MANUEL	Witnit? Or Dragonfly?
BASIL	Dragonfly. There isn't a horse called Nitwit. You're the nitwit.
MANUEL	What is witnit?
BASIL	[*puts his hand round Manuel's throat*] It doesn't matter ... look ... it doesn't matter ... Oh ... I could spend the rest of my life having this conversation. Please try to understand before one of us dies.

3. Basil begs a favour of the Major:

Basil	Major ... could you do me a favour?
The Major	Well, I'm a bit short myself, old boy.
Basil	No, no, no, could you look after some money for me. [*he takes it out*] I won it on that horse, only Sybil's a bit suspicious you see, and she goes through my pockets some nights ...
The Major	Oh, absolutely. Which horse?

Basil	... Dragonfly. [*gives the Major the money*]
The Major	When's it running?
Basil	No, no. It ran today. I won that on it.
The Major	Oh! [*starts to give the money back*] Well done, old boy.
Basil	No, no, could you keep it.
The Major	Oh, no, no, I couldn't do that. No, it's very decent of you.
Basil	No, no, could you keep it just for tonight? It's Sybil, you see. Secret?
The Major	Ah. Present.
Basil	Sort of, yes. Don't mention it.
The Major	Mum's the word.

John Cleese and Connie Booth, *The Complete Fawlty Towers*, p. 162-3, 171-2, 177-8.

TASK 1.3 A

Fawlty connections

Best of all, start by viewing the relevant extracts on video. Otherwise, persuade volunteers to reproduce the three passages as authentically as possible. Then, individually, make notes in response to the following questions:

1. Has the Sender in each case encoded his or her message in terms that he or she can confidently assume will be received?
2. Has the Sender taken account of the Receiver's personal situation or circumstances (e.g. physical, mental, emotional or social state)?
3. Is the Receiver fully prepared to accept the message?
4. Does the Sender seek feedback?

Now, as a group, share your responses to the questions. Try to establish the *main* cause of communication breakdown in each of the extracts.

Interpersonal communication isn't usually as chaotic as it is in *Fawlty Towers*. Nevertheless, in all our lives there are times when we despair of reaching mutual understanding. Confusion may arise just at the point where we most need to transmit and receive unambiguous messages, with results that are far from funny. For example, those in the caring professions sometimes speak of risks of serious misunderstanding in communicating information that a patient may not wish to know.

TASK 1.3 B

Communication needs

You have now spent some time thinking and talking about communication, in theory and practice. This would be a good point at which to establish some of the communication needs of the group. One way to achieve this is through a short brainstorming session.

Spend five minutes brainstorming answers to the following questions:

1. Every occupation sets its own communication problems, and values some skills more than others. Which communication skills are particularly desirable in the vocation for which your group is training? List at least five.
2. In which areas of your chosen vocation are interpersonal communication skills most likely to be tested?
3. You may wish to extend the brainstorming session to include the listing of specific communication skills that people see as *personal* needs and would hope to acquire over the course.

Keep copies of all lists compiled. It may be instructive to review them at various stages of the course!

Supplementary tasks

1. 'Lack of communication' is often cited as a reason for poor performance, bad relationships, or an unpleasant atmosphere in the work-place. Might there also be dangers in over-communication?
2. Within an agreed period (e.g. a week) collect at least *three* good examples of communication collapse that you personally witnessed. Share the examples with the group.
3. Make *five* practical recommendations for better communications in the institution where you are studying.

Chapter review

1. Give a short, clear definition of 'communication'.
2. Summarise briefly the advantages of human speech over animal means of communication.
3. In your own words, supply definitions and examples of each of the following concepts:
    noise
    encode
    medio-communication
    intrapersonal communication
    feedback
4. 'Genuine communication is always a two-way process.' Explain.

As I See It: Perception

THREE PERIODS

2.1 DEFINING PERCEPTION

Perception is where the story of any act of communication starts.

Surrounding us all is an external world full of stimuli. We register those stimuli through our senses of sight, hearing, smell, touch, and taste. We *take in* sense impressions, and inside our heads we *make* our own individual meanings from them. Person and Other might take in the same distant rumble and make quite different meanings from it, Person interpreting it as thunder while Other thinks it is Concorde passing overhead. In making these meanings, Person and Other might be influenced by *other stimuli* (such as thick cloud or a preceding flash of lightning) or by *knowledge* (of, for example, Concorde's daily flight path and schedule).

In making a meaning for a sense impression we draw on *memory, knowledge*, our *experience, values* and *feelings*, and the *context* in which the impression is received.

Look at the door. Light waves are being

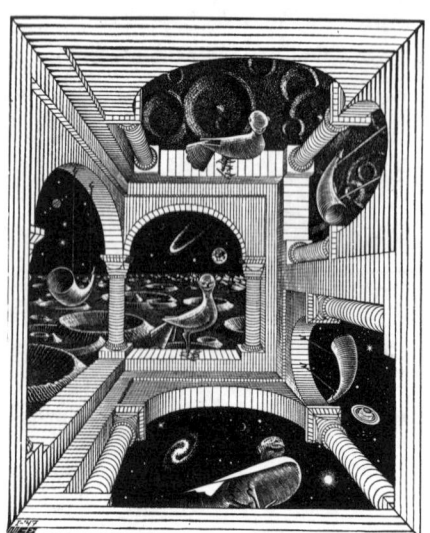

© M.C. Escher/Cordon Art – Baarn Holland. All rights reserved

reflected off it. Some of them are falling on the retina of your eye and stimulating cells at the back of the retina. These cells, once stimulated to a certain threshold, send impulses along the optic nerve to the visual cortex. There the image is turned right side up and interpreted.

This is merely the first stage. Your brain now takes over and processes the information fed to it. It does this by matching the sensory input with stored internal concepts, sorting through memory, experience etc. in a trice.

- In your *experience*, shapes of that dimension set into walls in that position with fittings and frame such as those you see have *usually* been hinged to swing open and shut.
- *Memory* informs you that you entered the room by that route recently.
- Your social, geographical and intellectual *background*, everything with which you are familiar, your *culture*—all remind you of countless doors that fall into the same category. (Are there people in today's world who might *not* be familiar with the concept 'door'?)
- In the *context* of a room you *expect* a door: *expectations* feature largely in the perceptual process—for rooms always have doors, haven't they?

Perceiving the door is an unproblematic exercise. When asked to look at it, nobody gazed up at the ceiling. You *share* a perception of 'door'. Yet when you looked at it, each person perceived a slightly different door from her neighbour. Physically, no two people saw it from precisely the same *angle*. Some saw it more *clearly* than others. Perceptions of its *colour* might vary within a general category of, say, brownness. Moving into a trickier area, perception is affected by *feelings*: could this account for different versions of the same door? Why is it that, if everybody wrote fifty words on 'The door', it is most unlikely that any two accounts would be the same?

TASK 2.1 A

Hearing things

Seeing a static object is a relatively easy way of receiving information. Hearing noises that may be faint, irregular or fleeting tends to be more problematic.

Observe *two* minutes' silence, during which note down *all* the sounds you hear. At the end, compare notes.

As a group, you may have disagreed about some of the sounds listed. If you were a group of spectators or supporters at a football match and an 'off-the-ball' incident occurred at the other end of the pitch, would there be more likelihood of agreement? Or witnesses of a cycling accident that was 'over in a flash'? Or participants at a heated meeting about the siting of a rubbish dump?

2.1.1 TESTING PERCEPTION

Perception doesn't always proceed smoothly. It is possible to trip even where no obstacles are visible!

Here is a short series of tests of your ability to perceive correctly:

TASK 2.1.1 A

The eye beguiled?

1. How many complete, stacked cubes does the diagram contain?

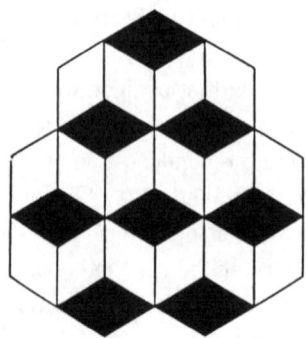

2. Which of the following are films?

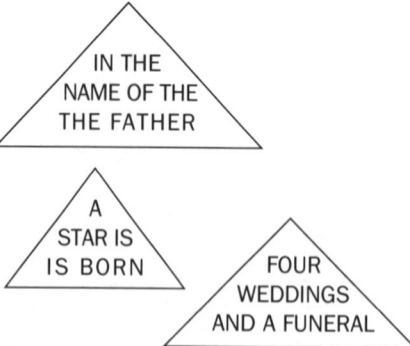

3. Which part of the human body do you see in the photograph below?

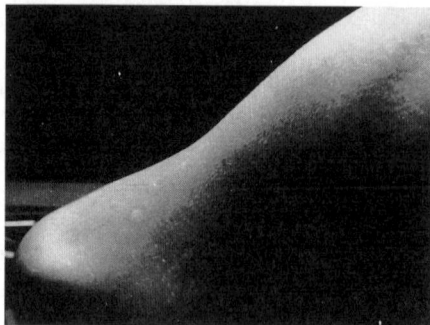

Study it this way up and you may see a chin in the top right corner and a neck stretching down to the bottom left corner.

4. Which of the three cats in this diagram is the biggest?

5. The next diagram shows two separate sets of seven circles. Each set contains a central circle. Which is the bigger— A or B?

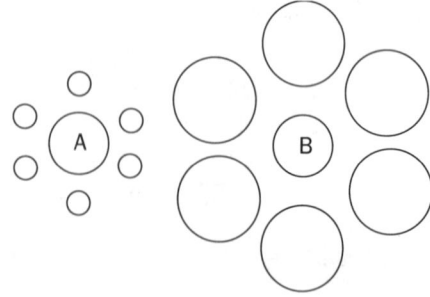

6. The object pictured below is a blivit. How many prongs are on a blivit? (Make sure you look at both ends!)

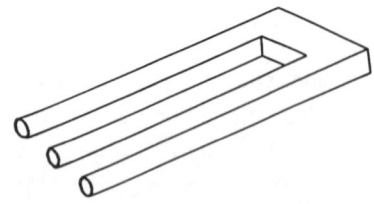

Each of the questions you have answered illustrates a common type of *optical illusion*. It is surprisingly easy for the eye to be deceived; it's not only our eyes that let us down ...

TASK 2.1.1 B

Timed teasers

Sticking closely to the suggested time limits, answer the following questions:

1. The Dublin–Cork train leaves at 7:05 a.m. and travels at a speed of 125 km/h, while its counterpart, the Cork–Dublin train, leaves thirty minutes later and travels at 135 km/h. When they meet, which is the closer to Dublin? (20 seconds)
2. Starting from opposite ends of a 30 km stretch of road, two cyclists, each travelling at 15 km/h, cycle to meet each other. A fly, travelling at the rate of 30 km/h, proceeds without stopping from one cyclist's nose to the other. What distance will the fly have covered when the two cyclists meet? (20 seconds)
3. Which weighs more, a dead fish or one that is alive? (3 seconds)
4. A cowboy called Tex rode into Dry Gulch, the roughest town in the West, at noon on Thursday. He left on Sunday at 6:10 p.m. Yet he only stayed two days. How do you explain this? (5 seconds)
5. Two Danes walk out of a house. One is the father of the other's son. What relation are they to each other? (2 seconds)
6. Tony's mother has three sons—Tom, Dick, and ... (2 seconds)
7. A pet-shop owner had forty-six gerbils. All but fourteen of them caught a disease and died. How many had he left? (5 seconds)
8. Two Russians played chess. In a series of five games, each woman won three. Can you explain this? (2 seconds)

A group of students who had been 'teased' by these questions discussed their performances afterwards. Here are some of their comments. Do they tell us anything about perception?

A: 'I freaked because I thought they were all maths questions, and I'm awful at maths!'
B: 'I could have done better if I'd had more time.'
C: 'I got nervous because I thought it was like a proper exam.'
D: 'As soon as I realised what sort of questions they were I got the hang of them and got right answers.'
E: 'They're a bit like conjuring tricks: your attention is distracted by unimportant things.'
F: 'They were fun but I don't see what they've got to do with perception.'

2.1.2 SELECTION AND FILTERING

Perception precedes communication. Being social animals, when we have taken in our individual sense impressions and made our meanings from them, we wish to *share* those meanings. The common definition of 'communication' is 'achieving one-ness or union, bridging a gap between two minds.' How often have you heard

'I'm freezing.'

'This milk's off.'
'Am I hearing right?'
'Something's burning ...'?

As soon as we start to send messages, confusion is always a possibility. Why? For a start, because no two people duplicate sensory experiences. Exposed to the same external stimuli, we *filter* and *select* differently to suit our individual tastes, needs, aptitudes, expectations etc.

At this moment you are exposed to a variety of external stimuli. Your eyes may be fixed on this page (out of the corners of your eyes, what are you aware of?) and at the same time your ears may be listening to a voice reading these words. Those perceptual acts of seeing and listening may, if you are an attentive student, *dominate* your consciousness, but a moment's thought will reveal that they are far from the *sum* of your total perceptual awareness.

- What tastes linger in your mouth?
- What smells is your nose picking up?
- What sensations is your body experiencing: stiffness through sitting, pressure from tight clothing, unwelcome heat or cold?

It is only when you make a deliberate *selection* and bring a sensation to the front of your mind that you realise you can still taste the tuna sandwich you enjoyed for lunch. It had been *filtered out* of your awareness.

Throughout our waking lives we are *filtering and selecting*. Our sensory apparatus bombards us with sense impressions that would threaten to overwhelm us if we didn't *filter*, *selecting* what meets our needs or is of particular interest and ignoring the rest. A teacher in a full classroom may be seeing far more than the students suppose!

We should remember that processes of perception can be trained. Skill in perceiving clearly can be developed. A person deprived of one sense may, to compensate, develop one or more of the remaining senses to an unusual degree: for instance, acute hearing may to some extent compensate for loss of sight. Certain occupations require a particular sense to be highly trained: tea and wine tasters need 'educated' noses and palates. Can you think of other examples?

While it's possible to improve perceptual skills, it's also possible for perception to be coloured or clouded by *emotion*. Feelings of insecurity in the dark cause us to see and hear things if we wake alone in the middle of the night. In the context of daylight, with full vision available, we select different meanings for shapes and sounds!

2.2 PERSON PERCEPTION

Of all the forms of perception we daily engage in, the most fascinating, important and challenging is our perception of other people. The rest of this chapter considers the nature of that challenge, highlighting such complicating factors as *role-playing*, *stereotyping*, and *prejudice*.

TASK 2.2 A

Not waving but drowning

Nobody heard him, the dead man,
But still he lay moaning:
I was much farther out than you thought
And not waving but drowning.

Poor chap, he always loved larking
And now he's dead
It must have been too cold for him his heart gave way,
They said.

Oh no no no, it was too cold always
(Still the dead one lay moaning)
I was much too far out all my life
And not waving but drowning.

Stevie Smith

Feedback (oral or written)
1. Is this poem about person perception?
2. How useful are the following concepts in thinking about the poem?—

message
code
NVC
medium
channel
noise
feedback

3. Do selection and filtering play any part in this sad story?

'Not Waving But Drowning' illustrates the importance of perceiving and interpreting signals correctly. It demonstrates how our perceptions of people may be wildly inaccurate, how we may fail to receive each other's most urgently transmitted signals.

How could the drowning man's despairing gesture for help be perceived as 'larking'? Part of the answer may lie in a game that engages us every day of our lives: role-playing.

2.2.1 ROLE-PLAYING

One barrier to clear person perception and hence to good communication is the fact that, as Tim pointed out in *The Communication Cord* (see p. 4 above), we spend our everyday lives playing *roles*, 'not only for one another but for ourselves.'

In any one day we each act out a variety of roles and role relationships and sometimes behave very differently from one to another. Who hasn't heard of 'house angel, street devil'? On an ordinary day, Person may enact the roles of female, wife, mother, lover, employer, colleague, friend, nurse, neighbour, cook, hostess, daughter, parishioner, and only have dipped into her repertoire. Think for a moment about the roles you yourself have already played today: could you list at least five?

Roles are *patterns of expected behaviour* that are built in to social situations, positions, and occupations. As 'actors' of roles, we know we are expected to behave in certain ways: a nurse might try to conform to the expectation that he or she will be calm, organised, efficient, compassionate and patient. A student does not *expect* the teacher to tell her to tear pages out of an expensive textbook and throw them away. No hotel guest expects to be abused by the manager, for isn't the customer always right?

We perceive each other in roles and communicate on that basis. Occasionally we cause ourselves embarrassment by mistaking roles—for example, addressing another customer as if he were the shop assistant.

The pressure of playing a role that is in conflict with our *real* needs and feelings brings about *role strain*. The blame may lie with ourselves, if we have misunderstood our own natures (faulty self-perception) and cast ourselves in unsuitable roles. A shy, highly strung or introverted person, for example, might suffer role strain if asked to run a creche.

2.2.2 STEREOTYPING AND PREJUDICE

When Person meets Another for the first time, a huge quantity of information passes back and forth. Person registers Another's sex, approximate age, height, weight, colour, physical attractiveness etc. He uses the incoming data to *categorise* Other, fitting her into a role.

This may be convenient, but categorisation has drawbacks:
- 'He's a psychiatrist? That makes sense: aren't all psychiatrists nutty?'
- 'Oh, one of the Ballygobackwards Daunts? Say no more: we know the type!'

Stereotyping is an extension of categorising. It means classifying people (individuals, groups or entire races) using indicators that may be very simple and highly generalised. We hold in our heads stereotypes of races, skin colour, occupations, classes, the sexes, age groups, religions, intelligence levels, body shapes, even of those whose hair is a certain colour or style.

The risks of stereotyping aren't hard to see. Three members of one family have jobs in the same firm and have proved themselves conscientious, reliable and hard-working employees. Isn't it likely that a fourth member of the family who applies for a job in the firm will benefit from the so-called 'halo effect'? Had the other members of the family proved unsatisfactory employees, mightn't she have encountered *prejudice* (i.e. pre-judging), even though she possessed all the virtues in the world?

Clearly, we ought at all times to reserve judgment, guarding against easy pigeon-holing. Stereotyping is often an indicator of an underlying *ideology*, a concept we'll be examining in relation to the mass media (chapter 15).

TASK 2.2.2 A

Stereotypes

Here is a list of some familiar stereotypes. After each one, jot down a selection of adjectives that describe your image—e.g. 'Stockbroker: male, middle-aged, dark-suited, boring, well-off, conservative.'

A redhead
An only child
A middle child
A spoilt brat

A Protestant
A mother-in-law
The Japanese
A football star
A traveller (male or female)
A Kerryman
A Dub
People whose first name is ...
A tomboy

Discuss a selection of your descriptions. Where do we get these stereotypes?

2.3 PERSON PERCEPTION: THREE TASKS

TASK 2.3 A

Who's Who?

The four girls pictured below come from the Netherlands, Norway, Cyprus — and Kerry. Match each girl with her place of origin. Be prepared to explain your reasons to the group.

TASK 2.3 B

First Impressions

Here are some photographs of persons who are probably strangers to you. Jot down your first, immediate impressions of each person: age, class, occupation, personality, background etc. Share your first impressions. Is there consensus?

Task 2.3 C

As I was Saying ...

If the persons in the following photographs suddenly began to speak, what kinds of things would they talk about and how would they express themselves?

Write a short monologue for each person. Share the results and discuss any significant variations of perception.

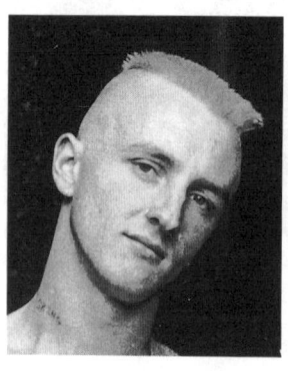  

Supplementary tasks

1. Orally or in writing, describe an occasion in your own experience when relying on the evidence of your senses led you astray or proved unwise
2. Bring to your next session a selection of photographs from your family albums or personal collections. Working in pairs, exchange the photographs and discuss your first impressions of those photographed. Those who own the photographs can reveal how accurate the impressions were!

Chapter review

1. 'Perception = sensation + meaning.' Could you explain this proposition?
2. List some reasons, either physical or psychological, why human perception is sometimes at fault.

3. Describe the part played by *filtering* and *selection* in the perceptual process.
4. Write brief explanatory notes on *role strain* and *stereotyping*.

Answers

Task 2.1.1 A: The eye beguiled?

1. It depends. There are six black-topped cubes (1:2:3) or, alternatively, there are seven black-bottomed cubes (2:3:2).
2. Only one: *Four Weddings and a Funeral*. Look again!
3.
4. The cats are all the same size.
5. The inner circles are the same size. A is made to look bigger because it is surrounded by *small* circles, while B is made to look smaller by being surrounded by *bigger* circles.
6. Depending on which end you're looking at, either two or three. The problem is to find where the change comes!

Task 2.1.1 B: Timed teasers

1. When they *meet*, they must logically be the *same* distance from Dublin.
2. 15 km.
3. The same. (Question the question!)
4. His horse was called Thursday (or perhaps Sunday).
5. Husband and wife.
6. Tony.
7. Fourteen.
8. Who said they were playing each other?

21

 # ACTIONS SPEAK LOUDER?: NON-VERBAL COMMUNICATION

FOUR PERIODS

3.1 NVC: AN ALTERNATIVE CHANNEL

Non-verbal communication (NVC) refers to communication between people that doesn't involve words. NVC covers a wide range of ways by which Person and Another send and receive messages.

NVC is often said to be more *powerful* (to 'speak louder') than words. Not that we actually speak very many words: it is estimated that on average we spend only ten to eleven minutes each day speaking. Even allowing a very fast rate of talking (180 words a minute), that adds up to a mere 1,980 spoken words a day.

You may be surprised at how little we speak. It doesn't mean that we spend the bulk of each day alone or ignoring one another. The fact is that much of our daily communication is *non-verbal*.

Even when we use words we don't show great confidence in their power. It is generally reckoned that in any face-to-face encounter, NVC carries at least *two-thirds* of the meaning conveyed. That is why reference is often made to the *primacy* of NVC.

In everyday life we demonstrate this primacy by trusting the evidence of our eyes rather than of our ears. Person opens the door to find Another swaying on the doorstep.

- Public—the distance at which a lecturer might address an audience.

What estimates (in metres) would your own experience lead you to place on the four distances? Do the same measurements apply to *seated* interactions?

Nationalities differ in relation to personal space. Swedes and Scots are said to be notably 'stand-offish' in their spatial requirements, while Latin-Americans and Arabs will comfortably chat at elbow length, a distance that most Irish would regard as invasive.

The distance at which we see two people interact can communicate to the onlooker something about national origins, their relationship, class, and sex. It is sometimes argued that in our society the middle class require *more* personal space than the working class, and that men demand *more* personal space than women. These class and sex differences, some believe, may be attributed to the inferior status that the working class and women have in the past been afforded in our culture.

Ask yourselves how human competition for power, status and dominance makes itself apparent in the management of territory and personal space. You might start with your school or college environment!

TASK 3.1.2 A

Seating plan

A doctor's waiting-room has seven seats placed in a row. Person is already seated as indicated. Six Others arrive singly. In what order do they fill the remaining seats?

Come to an individual decision, numbering the spaces. Then explain your sequence to others in the group. (Begin by asking yourself: where would I sit in this situation, and why?)

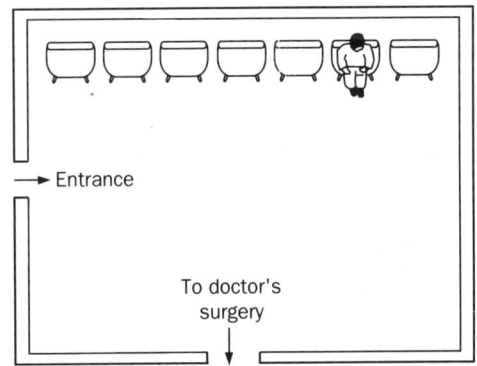

3.1.3 ORIENTATION

We send messages to others not only by our *distance* from them but also by <u>the way we angle</u> or <u>orient our bodies towards them</u>. 'Giving the cold shoulder' is an obvious example. The action's significance is stronger in female interaction than in male, since women in pairs generally communicate face-to-face, while males are more comfortable shoulder-to-shoulder (as, for instance, spectators or fellow-workers).

TASK 3.1.3 A

Guess the relationship

Our body position in relation to others may be unconsciously selected, but it usually signifies something to an observer. What do you imagine is the relationship between the people in the photographs below? Justify your guess!

A context where orientation is particularly important is the classroom. A traditional classroom might have thirty single desks (or fifteen double) arranged in rows to face a teacher behind his desk. What kinds of interaction and practical purpose does this arrangement facilitate? Is it the layout you would choose if you wished to promote group discussion? What difficulties arise if Person and Another, seated at a double desk just in front of the teacher, have a heated disagreement? In your experience, is this traditional seating arrangement equally suitable for all the subjects you've studied?

3.1.4 BODILY CONTACT

The amount of body contact made varies greatly from one culture to another. Universally, there is frequent, intimate body contact between parent and child, but once adulthood is reached, cultures display considerable variation. It would be unusual to find Irish students greeting one another outside the school gates in the morning with *handshakes*; in France, it would be commonplace.

The handshake is just one of 457 varieties of social body contact available to us and it is used mainly in our society as a formal way of greeting and parting. Other cultures use different methods: sniffing, sticking out the tongue, rubbing noses. But even so innocuous a form of contact as the handshake can be seen as highly symbolic and can make world news.

before the Revolution could give herself almost an extra metre in stature by donning a wig! We still use the term 'big-wig' for somebody of high standing, even though outside the legal profession wigs are no longer fashionable.

TASK 3.2 A

Hairstyles

Study the four photographs. The man is wearing four different wigs. How does hair alone help the man to create a new personality?

Most of us enjoy experimenting with the different ways in which *clothes* can suggest the personality underneath. Endlessly we disagree over, laugh at, covet, discard, are shocked by, admire, envy and change clothes.

TASK 3.2 B

What to wear

Use one or more of the following questions or statements as starters for general discussion:

1. In the twentieth century the female skirt has risen during booms and lengthened in depressions—though you would imagine the *opposite* to be the case. Can you suggest reasons for the phenomenon?
2. What styles of dress do you associate with the twenties, fifties, sixties, seventies, eighties? *Why* do you make these associations?
3. Compared with women's fashions, men's seem to change hardly at all. Why is this?
4. How do we use the *colour* of clothes to send messages?
5. 'The young complain bitterly when asked to wear an institutional uniform, yet, given the freedom to choose casual dress, they rush into what is in effect another uniform!'
6. Our choice of clothes sends messages. Which of the following considerations rate highly when you buy clothes?
   They look expensive.
   They'll be 'different'.
   They're the latest fashion.
   They're what everybody's wearing.
   They're practical and comfortable.
   They're sexy.
   They'll wear well.
   They project a particular image.

   Rank them 1 to 8 in order of importance. Does any *pattern* emerge from the group's responses?

3.2.1 Gesture

Gesture is movement by any part of the body that sends a visual message. Most such messages are sent by our heads (*head nods* need a separate section), shoulders, arms, and hands, but legs and feet are also brought into play, often without our being aware of it.

Each of us has a huge repertoire of gestures, learned as we learn language: we toss our heads, cup our hands, wag and cross our fingers, shrug our shoulders, tap our feet, clap our hands, stick out our tongues, wave our arms, wrinkle up our noses, smack our lips, waggle our hips. Our European neighbours from Mediterranean countries are even more likely to employ gestures—not always the ones we use!

Consciously and unconsciously we use gestures to replace, to support, to illustrate, to emphasise and to complement verbal communication.

In a normal conversation we make constant use of our bodies; if we saw ourselves on film we'd probably be quite surprised by our energetic movements. Watching the 'Rose of Tralee' interviews you sense the contestants' discomfort as they stand unnaturally *still* speaking to the microphone and camera, with hands usually tightly clasped in front of the body.

To gesture is *natural* and helps us make our meaning clearer to others. We even use gestures when speaking on the phone! In delivering an oral presentation, care must be taken to ensure that gestures are *purposeful*. A lot can be learned by observing practised communicators (politicians on television, your teachers etc.). Watch especially how *hands* are used.

Two aspects of gesture deserve attention:
- Gesture used to replace speech
- Non-verbal 'leakage' (i.e. *unconscious* gestures that transmit messages we might prefer not to send!)

Gesture has a surprising capacity to replace speech. The garda on point duty using hand and arm signals is sending simple messages in a context where speech would be impossible. The contestants in 'Play the Game', admittedly with the benefit of feedback, relay difficult concepts. A trained mime artist may even convince us that language is inadequate.

TASK 3.2.1 A

Excuses with a difference

Three students are late for the first period of the day. Individually they enter, in a sequence to be decided by the three volunteers. A fourth volunteer takes the teacher's role. Each latecomer offers an inventive excuse for lateness but, because he has lost his voice, must do so by *gestures* alone. The 'teacher' may use speech and is welcome to interrogate.

At the end of the exercise, consider the following questions:
- What difference would it have made if the *teacher* was also voiceless?
- Is it possible to categorise gestures in any way?
- In what kinds of interpersonal communication would we be particularly disadvantaged by having to rely on gesture?

Our involuntary, unconscious gestures 'leak' information about our thoughts and feelings to an observant onlooker. Nervousness leaks from Person in foot-tapping and hand-wringing, even though she may be fixedly smiling in an effort to convey self-confidence. Our bodies can betray us and if preparing for an interview, for example, we should be aware of how leakage may occur.

Some occupations demand skill in concealing. Show business people, politicians, diplomats and barristers are some of those who have to practise concealment, if only to appear relaxed and confident when in reality they may be under intense pressure.

The common belief is that lies leak out through blushing, stammering, and reluctance to meet Other's eye. Those whose futures may involve deliberate deception (e.g. the nurse concealing the gravity of an illness from an anxious patient, or the secretary concealing the boss's whereabouts) should know what research reveals: primarily, that the frequency of our hand-to-face movements increases. Apparently, we stroke chins, press lips, rub cheeks, scratch eyebrows, pull earlobes, and groom hair. Most telling of all, we cover the mouth and touch the nose. Can you suggest *why* these two actions in particular seem to accompany deception?

Finally, we should be aware that gestures carry different meanings between one country or culture and another. Unfamiliarity with another culture's gestures can cause grievous misunderstanding. In Ireland the slow hand-clap expresses strong disapproval; elsewhere in Europe it's a compliment. Can you think of further examples?

3.2.2 POSTURE

In gesturing, we use *parts* of our body. Posture involves the *whole* body and its way of *standing, sitting*, or *lying*. Some would include the way we *walk* or *run*.

The meanings, intended or otherwise, conveyed by posture are usually seen as falling under three headings:

Mood

Feelings towards others

Status

(1) Mood: The way we stand, sit or walk may give a very clear picture of our emotional state. A good actor can show with her *back* what the character is going through.

> **TASK 3.2.2 A**
>
> **What's my mood?**
>
> Individually, select a mood from the list below. Don't reveal your choice to the others. Spend a minute in silence thinking about your selected mood. The teacher will then ask a member of the group to walk to a designated 'hot seat' and sit in it, expressing, through the way of walking and the seated posture, the mood chosen. When the student asks 'What's my mood?', others guess.
>
> If you want to add to the list below, do so—but make sure everyone is aware of the additions.
> Angry
> Nervous
> Sexy
> Depressed
> Joyful
> Frustrated

(2) Feelings towards others: Person's posture signals her attitude towards Another. It is usually possible to tell from a distance whether a group of people is on friendly terms or is composed of people who feel hostile or aggressive towards one another.

If you observe groups, particularly groups of friends, you will sometimes see examples of *postural echo*. Have you ever found yourself unconsciously mirroring the posture of the person you're talking to? Sitting with legs crossed the same way, both sets of arms folded, both heads inclined at the same angle? Even a faint echo can make an amusing photograph!

(3) Status: Many of the postures we adopt signal views of relative status. With those whose status we perceive to be superior to our own we adopt submissive postures: people *kneel* to pray, even superbrat tennis stars *bow* to Wimbledon's royal box, and some pupils still *stand* when the teacher enters the room (though few now bow out of the room backwards when leaving his presence).

3.3 Facial expression

The face: an open or a closed book? On the one hand
   'There's no art
   To find the mind's construction in the face'
and on the other
   'Your face, my thane, is as a book where men
   May read strange matters.'

Judging by these photos, which bits of the human face are most expressive of our feelings?

It is generally accepted that the *face* is Person's best guide to Another's feelings—in expressiveness, almost the equal of language itself. It is hard to fake facial expressions, to divorce the look from the feeling. Foreheads sweat, cheeks go scarlet or white, lips twitch, jaw muscles tighten—and all *involuntarily*.

When a film director wants us to understand a character's innermost feelings, she shows us a close-up of the character's *face*, allowing us to decode the signs of forehead, eyebrows, eyelids, eyes, nose, cheeks, lips, tongue, chin. If Others could have seen Person's face in close-up when he got into difficulties they'd have grasped immediately that Person was drowning.

What is more, a close-up of an actor's face will be understood as readily in Calcutta as in Cork. Facial expressions have universal currency. An example: people the world over momentarily raise and lower their eyebrows when meeting a friend or acquaintance.

TASK 3.3 A

The face

1. What do we mean by the following?
    Poker face
    Two-faced
    Ashen-faced
    Stony-faced
    Blue in the face

    Blank face
    A straight face
    Putting on a brave face

2. Using just the given area of the face in each of these drawings, can you say what the person is feeling?

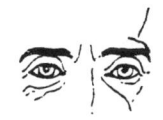

3.3.1 Eye contact

Eyes rove, dance, narrow, sparkle, dull, widen, burn, glint, glisten, glitter, grow round ... and much more! In all this activity, they send unmistakable non-verbal messages.

If the face is almost as expressive as language, the bit of the face that works hardest and most successfully to communicate is ... well, the *eyes* have it (sorry!).

When our director has shown the actor's face in close-up, she will often intensify further by filling the screen with eyes, perhaps in extreme close-up just the pupils, dilated in (say) terror.

At times of heightened feeling we make extra demands on our eyes. So, flirting or in love we 'make eyes' at the object of our desire. In a display of hostility or aggression, such as at the boxers' weigh-in or during the All-Blacks' fearsome *haka*, the fixed, bulging eyes say it all.

In common with animals, we find stares challenging, often intimidating. In the struggle for dominance, the person of inferior status usually 'submits' by dropping his eyes. Even among equals we find it hard to sustain eye contact indefinitely.

TASK 3.3.1 A

Eyeball-to-eyeball

Revive memories of childhood by having a staring match with a partner. How long before one of you looks away?

When we look at faces, we target the mouth and eyes. In the latter we look for a glimpse of the 'soul' and for feedback. A listener's dull, glazed eyes send the speaker messages she would do well to heed. Regular eye contact is a *must* for the public speaker.

One of the ways in which we use eye contact is to regulate the flow of conversation between two or more people. Before your next session, closely observe a casual conversation and see if you can reach any conclusions about the *pattern* or *code* of eye contact that governs turn-taking. Do we maintain 100 per cent eye contact when talking? Does the speaker look more often at the listener than vice versa? How do eyes signal our intention to interrupt? Is it possible to formulate some 'rules'?

3.3.2 Head nods

Head movements, of which there are many, work together with eye contact in refereeing turn-taking among speakers. The head nod is the commonest head motion in everyday use and is almost universally understood to mean 'yes', just as the shake means 'no'.

When listening, we feed back encouraging nods to the speaker. The nod means 'Yes, I'm interested; please continue.' Interviewers on television keep speech to a minimum and encourage interviewees by nodding—hence the technical term 'noddie' for cutaway shots to a nodding interviewer, which can be inserted to cover joins in the tape.

When we wish to take a turn at speaking we signal our intention sometimes by a series of rapid head nods. Or the current speaker may show he is ready to pass the conversational baton by a single nod—'Your turn!' A model classroom transaction has the student waiting quietly with hand up until given the nod by the teacher.

3.3.3 Paralanguage

If language is *what* we say, **paralanguage** (a term that refers to non-verbal aspects of speech) is *how* we say it—and sometimes the *manner* is the *matter*. Very common words such as 'yes', 'no', 'really', 'never', can be said in all sorts of ways to convey a range of meanings. 'Very clever' said with a long drawn-out 'Veeeery …' may usually be taken to mean the opposite of its face value.

Paralanguage refers to aspects of speech such as
- pitch
- speed
- volume
- tone
- accent
- use of pause.

All these aspects (which will be considered in more detail in chapter 4) may provide the listener with information about the speaker's *mood* (a very fast speed might signal rage), *personality, social class, country or region of origin* ('Amferoffni' would signal which English-speaking country of origin?), *level of education*, and more.

Very often we choose to communicate feelings through noises rather than through speech. Take, for example, the sound that novelists reproduce as 'tsk-tsk'. What sound is this? What head movement tends to accompany it? And together what do they signify?

It is possible to hold a meaningful conversation using nothing but paralinguistic noises.

TASK 3.3.3 A

Eh?

1. In pairs, devise a short restaurant scene where the 'dialogue' consists *entirely* of vocal but non-verbal signals. To start you off:
   Person [reading menu]: Mmm!
   Other [also reading]: Ah-ha!
2. Further proof of the frequency with which we emit noise signals is contained in clichés such as 'a *gulp* of fear'. Can you complete the following?
   (1) A … of dismay

(2) A … of relief
(3) A … of pain
(4) A … of joy
(5) A … of rage
(6) A … of surprise
(7) A … of satisfaction
(8) A … of ecstasy
(9) A … of grief
(10) A … of nervousness
(Remember that there may be acceptable alternatives!)

3.4 OTHER SYSTEMS AND CODES OF NVC

We have seen how humans using their bodies can communicate non-verbally. We send and receive messages by other non-verbal means. Intentionally or not, we communicate through the **physical environments** we create, through the spaces we design and fill, through the choice and arrangement of **objects**, **colours**, and **textures**. It's easy to forget that our houses, flats and work-places were once empty spaces requiring human selection of paint, fabric, floor covering, furniture, lighting, etc. In making these choices, we communicate.

As we saw in section 3.1, when groups or professions resort to devised codes, substituting signs or signals for language, there are practical reasons. You would have little difficulty explaining why at various times **smoke**, **drum** and **beacon** have been employed, though you probably couldn't decode their signals. Members of your group might understand **semaphore** or **Morse** 'language'; and everybody will interpret **traffic lights** and **road signs** correctly.

Is there a case to be made for more widespread use of codes? What arguments would you put for or against the use by English-teachers of a standard code by which to correct technical errors—e.g. 'Start a new paragraph here' or 'This should be a capital letter'? Does such a code already exist?

In our heads we carry the codes of **flags**, **logos**, **colours**, and **badges**. The colours on flags are often symbolic, as with our own Irish flag. Sometimes a flag will have an emblem (sun, moon, star, bird, cross) that will non-verbally say something about the country. Switch on the television; a football game is in progress. Without sound, you recognise that a Swedish team is playing a Spanish team. How? Carry out a very simple test: in one minute, how many flags can you jot down?

Who could fail to recognise the significance of a cross, dove or swastika on a banner or badge? You may not know *why* the pelican symbolises the Blood Transfusion Service, but you know *what* it stands for. The penguin is an emblem of what product?

In times past, the 'language' of **heraldry** had a currency it doesn't enjoy today. Coats of arms and crests on carriages and household articles carried messages about the families they represented.

Music and **dance**, like heraldry, are devised languages. They enable the composer or choreographer to send messages to performers about what sounds or movements to produce. The sounds send messages to listeners: 'Greensleeves' wafting through a housing estate on a hot summer afternoon carries what meaning? Can the group come up with ten signature tunes in one minute? If you want to know in what manner to play a piece of classical music, you need to learn certain words from what language? There may in your group be somebody familiar with musical notation or one of the common ways of writing dance: ask for a brief demonstration!

Other humanly devised systems that carry meanings include **numbers** (which, like words, are symbols), the various languages made up to accompany the relatively recent computer technology (Basic, Fortran, Cobol etc.), and the secret codes used mainly in times of war. To somebody unfamiliar with its signs and symbols, **shorthand** will look like a secret code.

The only certainty about the meanings we take from the physical environment (including colour) is that they will vary hugely from Person to Another. Individual perception and personal taste are major factors in the way we respond to the spaces in which we live, work, and play.

TASK 3.4 A

A room of my own

What does each of these rooms communicate to you about its owner or occupier? Brainstorm ideas and then ask for some of the more interesting or unusual ideas to be explained.

Since NVC is such a powerful, direct and efficient way of sending messages, you might wonder why humans felt it necessary to invent language. Try a small experiment: rely on NVC to make all your meanings over a lunch break. At the end of it, ask yourself: is there a role for words in human communication?

Supplementary tasks

1. Devise a mnemonic to help remember the ten ways of communicating non-verbally listed on page 24.

2. Use a combination of research and personal observation in providing written answers to the following questions:
   (a) Does overcrowding in cities produce aggression?
   (b) 'Women invade; men evade.' Is this true?
   (c) Is there anything to be learned about territory from gang behaviour?
   (d) Clothes preserve our modesty; they provide comfort in temperature extremes; they signal status. In your view, which is the most important of the three functions?
   (e) It seems to be a fact that women make more eye contact than men and also smile more often. How might this imbalance be explained?
3. To produce a textbook such as this in full colour is very expensive but increases the range of communicative possibilities. Take *any* page of this book and show how the availability of colour might have helped to get the message across more clearly, powerfully, or attractively.
4. Arrange for a volunteer from the group to videotape from television or some other source three short extracts in which a person (*not* somebody famous) speaks either directly to camera or to an unseen interviewer. The extracts might last approximately one minute each.

   Play the extracts to the group *without sound and without explanation*. What conclusions can the group reach about the speaker's age, social status, occupation, personal circumstances, emotional state, topic etc.?

   Replay *with sound*. Does the group wish to revise its opinions?
5. Describe a room you particularly admire and explain what features of the room appeal to you.

   or

   Describe a room in which you feel uncomfortable and try to account for your feelings.
6. Colour has a profound effect on our moods and well-being. It has the power to create atmosphere, to expand or contract space, to suggest coolness or warmth, to evoke memories. Colour is always considered in relation to light. For example, very bright colours work in the strong, bright sun of a hot climate; tweeds seem to suit softer Irish light.

   How do you feel about the colour scheme in this classroom? Given a free hand, what changes (if any) would you make? Does the present scheme take sensible account of natural and artificial light sources and intensity? Spend ten minutes discussing proposed changes.
7. Here are five possible ways of organising seating for a face-to-face interview:

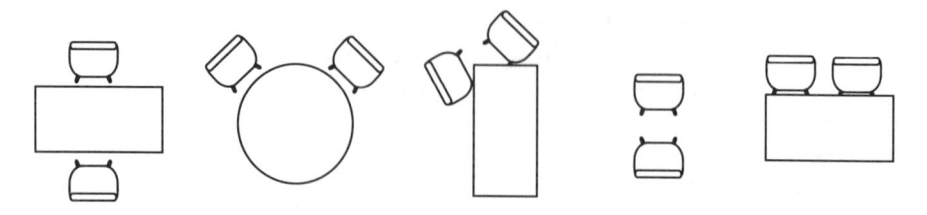

What effects might each arrangement have on human interaction? Spend ten minutes discussing the layouts.

Chapter review

1. Write brief explanatory notes on: the primacy of NVC; postural echo; non-verbal leakage; paralanguage.
2. Explain the part played by head nods in everyday interaction.
3. Describe ways in which posture can communicate status.
4. Compile a list of at least ten common signals we make with our hands: e.g. thumbs-up sign = success.

PART 2

WORDS WE SPEAK

TALKING HEADS: ORAL SKILLS

TEN PERIODS (MINIMUM)

4.1 FOUR LANGUAGE ARTS

Language is unique to our species on this planet. According to Steven Pinker it is 'one of the wonders of the natural world. For you and I belong to a species with a remarkable ability … simply by making noises with our mouths, we can reliably cause precise new combinations of ideas to arise in each other's minds' (*The Language Instinct*, p. 15).

Note, 'reliably'; not 'infallibly' because, as we all know, words can be slippery and cause confusion. If you were each asked to produce a meaning for a very short, common word such as 'love', is it likely that you would all agree? But what is language if it isn't an *agreement* between people that a particular sound should stand for or symbolise a particular thing?

You have in your hand this book. 'Book' is a short, monosyllabic sound which we represent in English writing with four marks on paper. There is no physical relationship or connection between the *sound* you make in pronouncing those letters and the object you are holding. Nor is there any connection between the *letters* and that object. If you wanted to refer to the same object in Irish you'd make a different noise in your throat, and you'd use more letters to represent that sound on paper ('leabhar'). Only one of those letters is found in 'book'—but in our country both sounds and both groups of letters refer to or symbolise 'a set of sheets of paper bound in a cover'.

The wonder of language, which is still such a comparatively recent arrival in the 4,600-million-year life of the Earth, is made still more marvellous by modern technology. An

American president can sit at his desk in the White House in Washington making noises with his mouth and simultaneously send messages via those noises to all corners of the globe. Increasingly, his listeners, who might number thousands of millions, will understand his particular brand of language—American English—even if their mother tongue is some quite different brand. There are, for example, more students learning English in China than there are people in the United States.

What's equally marvellous is that language puts us in touch with those who lived centuries ago in countries far distant from our own. Through marks on stone, parchment and paper we can connect over the millenniums with the greatest minds of the past almost as easily as we can say hello to a friend in the street.

For the purposes of study, language is normally broken down into
- speaking
- listening
- writing
- reading

and these are known as the four language arts.

4.1.1 TALKING AND LISTENING

In practice, most of our daily communication needs are met by the first two arts: speaking and listening. For many people,

talking + listening = communicating.

The statistics provide some support for this view: the average adult's 'communicating day' consists of

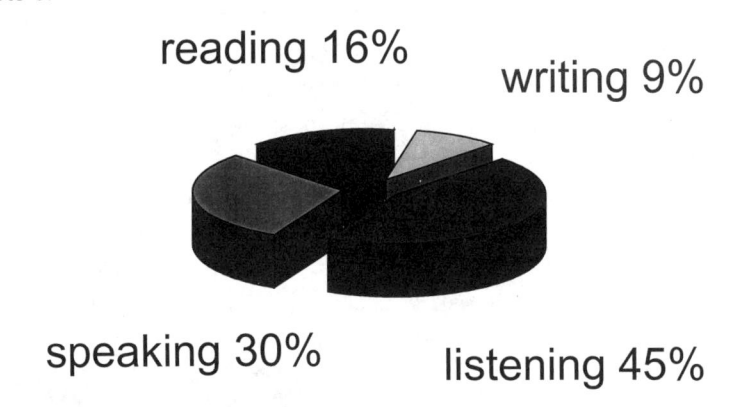

reading 16%
writing 9%
speaking 30%
listening 45%

Can you guess why the massive imbalance between the paired activities of speaking and listening (75 per cent) and reading and writing (25 per cent) may become even more marked in the future?

In part 2 we concentrate on *spoken* language, from which it follows that we must also think about *listening*. This chapter offers a crash course in good speaking practice. Chapter 5 shows how the techniques and skills you have acquired may be used to advantage in an oral presentation. Chapter 6 focuses on good listening practice.

One of the best situations in which to test listening skills is at a meeting, and chapter 7 gives you the chance to participate in meetings of various kinds, including an interview, when skills in listening and speaking are thoroughly tested.

4.1.2 TALKING HEADS

For better or worse, we humans are talking heads. At work and in leisure, on top of Mount Everest or in mines deep underground, in outer space and in prison, asleep in bed, to our reflections in the mirror, to pets, to a lover whose face is only inches away or to a relative on the other side of the world, we *talk*. It's a strain to be silent in libraries, classrooms, churches, or backstage during a performance. Being 'sent to Coventry' is a punishment. The child *threatens*, 'I'll never speak to you again!'

TASK 4.1.2 A

Jaw, jaw

How many words or phrases do you know that refer to the sending and receiving of messages by *speaking*? Here are five to start your list:

abuse
accuse
argue
articulate
assert

Spend three minutes brainstorming.

Mostly when we open our mouths to talk, the circumstances are informal and we don't pick our words with too much care. Our everyday talk is full of false starts to sentences, incomplete sentences, fillers such as 'um' and 'er', redundant words or phrases such as 'well,' 'like,' 'like I mean,' and 'y'know,' and gaps. Spoken sentences are short, the average one lasting a mere 2.5 seconds. One reason is that in speech we *contract* words. 'Did you go out last night?' becomes in speech, 'Jew gout lass night?'—six syllables contracted to four.

The tape-recorder can cruelly expose our everyday speech deficiencies. Even highly experienced speakers may be caught sounding foolish. Here is Senator Edward Kennedy on the campaign trail in 1994, when asked if he had a fight on his hands to hold onto his seat:

'I look at it as a wonderful, interesting, challenging time in terms of running for the US Senate. Most challenging time. Let me answer it in this way: in many respects not so. Why I take a moment is because ... what I find is, in terms of, you know, the challenging, is when you're not, you don't know where, where, what you're about ... You're, you don't have a viewpoint and that you're a believer in and you don't, er, you're questioning what your basic kinds of value systems and outlook are about ...' (quoted by Russell Miller, *Sunday Times Magazine*, 2 October 1994).

In cold print our day-to-day speech practices don't look very impressive but mostly we get our message across. Occasionally, of course, we encounter problems ...

> TASK 4.1.2 B

Communication breakdown!

This cartoon shows communication failure. Orally, explain what precisely has happened, avoiding hesitations, gaps, fillers, repetition, etc.

Suddenly, a heated exchange took place between the king and the moat contractor.

There are times when we exercise unusual care in our spoken language. For example, what changes in our habits do we make when talking to someone whose mother tongue is not English?

We take extra care when we're being interviewed, when we're with those of higher status than ourselves, when we're trying to impress, or when we find ourselves addressing a number of others formally.

Almost everybody is required at some stage in his or her life to make a speech: making or acknowledging a presentation, being best man at a wedding, introducing or thanking a guest speaker, addressing a meeting, debating, appealing for funds etc.

Large numbers of people daily address groups as a routine part of their jobs: teachers, lecturers, trade unionists, barristers, those working in the media, national and local politicians, churchmen and churchwomen, team trainers and captains, and many more.

Given the numbers who daily face an 'ordeal by the spoken word', it's hardly surprising that clubs and societies exist to give instruction and practice in the skills of public speaking (e.g. Toastmasters). Banks, trade unions, charitable organisations, businesses and newspapers try to foster the skills by sponsoring speaking competitions for schools and colleges.

The rest of this chapter concentrates on speech tasks. The short-term aim is to help you lay the groundwork for an oral presentation (chapter 5). In the long term, the skills you acquire will help you to become a better communicator in all areas of your life.

4.1.3 A WORD OF ADVICE ...

(1) Participate fully: It is absolutely *natural* to be worried and nervous about formally speaking to even quite a small group of people one knows. The most experienced public speakers confess to feeling nervous *every* time they get to their feet. In fact, they would be worried if they weren't! Recognise that everybody is going through the same ordeal—and give it a lash!

(2) Learn from experience: Very few are *born* good speakers. The skills are gained by trial and error, by experimenting and learning from mistakes. There will be regular opportunities to learn from the criticisms of your peers and teachers. Take to heart their comments, and adjust your performance next time.

(3) Build self-confidence: Self-confidence is possibly the most important asset of any public performer. It comes through practice and experience, and having it means that, although nervous, you know, underneath the anxiety, *you can do it!* The most difficult assignment is the very first; from then on it becomes progressively easier.

(4) Take it step by step: The programme of tasks leads from relatively simple demands at the start to much more complex requirements. Tasks may be adapted to suit the group's vocational interests and expertise.

(5) Avail of technology: Throughout the graduated programme it would be extremely useful to have at the group's disposal a video camera, so that you could learn by watching yourselves. If borrowing isn't possible, consider hiring equipment. Almost as invaluable for the feedback it provides is a tape-recorder.

(6) Warm-ups: It's always advisable to start a session of oral work with a warm-up exercise or two, if only to warm up the vocal cords and to loosen inhibitions. Here is a selection of basic routines, most of which could be used in a conventional classroom without undue disturbance to others:

Friend and foe

The group divides into pairs. For one minute the pairs role-play being guests at a crowded party, meeting each other for the first time, introducing themselves, and quickly becoming great friends.

It is now some hours later at the same party. In the same pairs, role-play a serious falling-out. Perhaps A has gone off with B's partner or spilt drink on B's dress. However heated the exchange, *no physical contact* is permissible. If noise is a problem, play the scene in whispers or hisses so that it won't attract the attention of other guests.

Change partners and repeat the exercise.

Variations might include stipulating different kinds of party (diplomatic reception, kiddies' birthday party etc.).

Sound circle

This very versatile exercise explores the capacity of the human voice to produce (and reproduce) different sounds.

Begin simply. Going round the circle, each person produces *any* non-verbal sound with the voice.

Next round, each person produces an *animal* sound. In succeeding rounds, the circle could try:
- sound effects (door creaking open, wind sighing)
- sounds mechanical (bus stopping, computer bleeps)
- sounds peculiar to a particular location (classroom yawns and chalk scratching)
- sounds funny or sad (varieties of laughing and crying)
- sounds expressive (varieties of intonation producing different meanings for the same word or phrase: 'Yes,' 'No,' 'Never,' 'Really,' 'Hello,' 'Goodbye,' 'Excuse me,' 'I've got it,' 'You never did,' 'I believe you,' 'I love you').

In each of these rounds you might like to try the *echo effect*: Person's sound is imitated by Another, Another's by Other etc.

Pass the story

This exercise may be done in a large circle but is probably more successful when the group sub-divides into smaller circles of four to six people.

Each circle's aim is to tell a story, the difficulty being that each person is allowed to add only one word at a time. The story may begin slowly, with contributors allowed time to think of their words. The pace can become faster, and those who fail to make an instant contribution can be eliminated until just two are left.

To start with, circles might pass full sentences, or people may be allowed to keep the story for a specified period (e.g. one minute).

To increase the difficulty, 'and' and 'very' could be banned!

Beat the clock

It is possible to read aloud the passage below within twenty seconds. It should be read so that it makes *sense* to listeners! Imagine it's a radio piece; *one* stumble is one too many. You'll improve your chances if you *stand* when reading:

'I bought a batch of baking-powder and baked a batch of biscuits. I brought a big basket of biscuits back to the bakery and baked a basket of big biscuits. Then I took the big basket of biscuits and the basket of big biscuits and mixed the big biscuits with the basket of biscuits that was next to the big basket and put a bunch of biscuits from the basket into a box. Then I took the box of mixed biscuits and a biscuit mixer and biscuit basket and brought the basket of biscuits and the box of mixed biscuits and the biscuit mixer to the bakery and opened a tin of sardines.'

Group readings

In groups of four or five, study 'Good Taste' below. Decide how it might be read aloud to maximum effect using all the voices in the group.

Take into account the differing qualities of the voices at your disposal; remember that it is possible to use more than one voice at the same time, and as you rehearse your reading think of *pace* (fast v. slow bits), *volume* (loud v. quiet bits), and *pause*.

Good Taste

Travelling, a man met a tiger, so ...
He ran. The tiger ran after him
Thinking: How fast I run ... But

The road thought: How long I am ... Then,
They came to a cliff, yes, the man
Grabbed at an ash root and swung down

Over its edge. Above his knuckles, the tiger.
At the foot of the cliff, its mate. Two mice,
One black, one white, began to gnaw the root.

And by the traveller's head grew one
Juicy strawberry, so ... hugging the root
The man reached out and plucked the fruit.

How sweet it tasted!

Christopher Logue

If you find this an effective warm-up, other poems could be given similar treatment.

Solo readings

The following passages call for expressive delivery in a variety of styles. Try to find a voice that suits the words. Deliver them standing.

(i) Now, children, I want you all to sit quietly on the floor in a big circle and when you're all ready and nice and comfy—no, Aisling, the floor's really clean, it was swept this morning—I'm going to tell you all a really, really exciting story—there's no need to push, Fiachra, there's lots of room for everybody—about a very, very bad magician and a handsome young prince—Fiachra, I told you not to push! Now, when I can hear a teeny tiny pin drop ... Fiachra!

(ii) Good evening, sir. I am speaking to Mr Dan O'Dowd, am I not? Well, now, you'll be wondering who I am. Thought so! The name's O'Connor, Don O'Connor, and I represent Inisfree Financial Services. I'm sure you've seen our ads in the press recently. Yes? Well, I'm here to offer you the unique opportunity to avail of our once-off absolutely free offer of a financial check-up service. May I step inside for a moment?

(iii) What sort of time do you think this is to arrive home? Eh? Well? Oh, you thought. You thought! And your mother and me nearly demented with worry about you. Did I or did I not tell you to be home by midnight? And what time is it now? That's right, 2 a.m. 2 a.m.! Hey! Where do you think you're going? Look at the state of you! Come here till I get a good look at you.

(iv) Aaaah! Now wouldn't that make anyone feel better? Oisín O'Shaughnessy there with a track from his latest album bringing us almost up to the hour here on the 'DD Show', your favourite teatime listening. But enough of the oul' blather! Just time, yes, just time to tell all you crazy Smooch fans to mosey on down to Blip's tonight—last chance to catch your heroes before they take off on their first-ever Continental tour. Join us after the news for our absolutely fabulous autumn competition!

(v) Good afternoon, ladies and gentlemen. On behalf of Captain O'Shea and his crew I'd like to welcome you aboard flight PQ 207 from Farranfore to Frankfurt. We shall be taking off shortly and expect to arrive in Frankfurt at 16:45 hours. Light refreshments will be served during the flight. Please fasten your safety belts, and there will be no further smoking until we are in the air. Once again, we are pleased to have you with us and wish you a pleasant flight.

4.2 Stage 1: Describing, explaining, informing

Much of the speaking we do each day is *explaining*: giving information, instructions, our reasons, or opinions. *Describing* and *informing* really come under the umbrella of explaining. To carry out all three processes successfully—

(1) Aim for clarity: Above all, your listeners must understand your explanation. This will only happen if you make yourself clear.

Tips
(i) Be clear *in your own mind* exactly what you want to say.
(ii) Consider your listeners: their existing knowledge of your subject, their level of understanding, maturity etc. Pitch your talk within their range: neither too complicated nor too simple.
(iii) Be brief. Keep the whole explanation simple and opt for short, precise sentences. Stick to the point!
(iv) Provide signposts to let your listeners know where you're taking them. Signposts are like paragraphs in writing. 'That's stage 2 completed. Now let's look at stage 3 ...'
(v) Speak loudly enough to be heard by *all* without strain.

(2) Aim for fluency: You will make it hard for listeners to follow your explanation if your speech is full of 'er' and 'um' or of phrases such as 'Likelmeantosay.' Eventually, noise will enter the channel. The ideal is smooth continuity.

Tips

(i) Resolve that whatever happens, your explanation won't begin 'Ehrm, well ...' Have a fluent opening sentence prepared.
(ii) As you talk, don't be afraid to pause and think out your next sentence; just don't fill the pause with 'ehrm'!
(iii) The best guarantee of fluency is a thorough knowledge of your subject.

TASK 4.2 A

Ice-breakers

Many groups when assembling for the first time use this exercise. At some time in the future you may find yourself called upon to introduce yourself—at a group interview, for example. Method B is a variation on the theme.

Method A
Prepare for the next session a *one*-minute speech introducing yourself to a group that doesn't know you. Alternatively, give yourselves the next ten minutes to work out what you'll say. No notes should be used when you introduce yourself.

You are very familiar with your subject! You know so much you'll have to be highly *selective*. Passport-style information is unlikely to interest your listeners, and *any* oral presentation ought to be interesting.

Method B
Divide into pairs. Each pair has five minutes to share autobiographical information. When the full group reassembles, Person introduces Another to the group. At the end of Person's introduction, Another may point out errors or significant omissions. Another then introduces Person, who also has the 'right of reply'.

Seated delivery is acceptable in this exercise.

Feedback discussion questions:
- Which introductions captured and held interest, and why?
- What are the difficulties in carrying out the task?
- If you were given the chance to repeat the task, what would you be keen to improve?
- How did speakers rate in terms of *clarity* and *fluency*?

TASK 4.2 B

How to ...

Here is a list of common processes. You may wish to add to it from your area of vocational specialisation. Distribute titles at random to members of the group. Allow three minutes to think about describing the process; then start the explanations. Each speaker has *one* minute. Stand to explain—
- How to brush teeth
- How to knot a tie
- How to tie shoelaces
- How to scramble eggs
- How to cover a book
- How to wire a plug
- How to erect a tent
- How to set a fire
- How to put hair in a bun
- How to make a toasted sandwich
- How to change a baby's nappy

- How to mend a bike puncture
- How to make a 999 call
- How to make chips
- How to play Snap
- How to use a call card
- How to do a crossword puzzle
- How to apply lipstick
- How to open a bottle of champagne
- How to polish shoes
- How to wash windows

Assess performances by keeping individual records on a simple mark sheet such as that below.

The mark sheet illustrated has five columns. Criteria may therefore be adjusted to suit the task: you may wish to assess interest level, voice quality, originality etc.

Allow a brief pause between speakers for assessors to complete records. A simple rating is:

5—excellent
4—very good
3—good
2—fair
1—poor

A brief comment may be helpful. Aim to be constructive: treat the efforts of others with the consideration you would expect for your own efforts.

After the final speaker, circulate the mark sheets. To round off, discuss as a group what the best explanations had in common.

TASK: *ICEBREAKER*						DATE: *10 October 1996*	
ASSESSOR: *Seán Doherty*						CLASS: *Meat 3*	
SPEAKER:	1	2	3	4	5	TOTAL	COMMENT
	Clarity	*Fluency*					
Niamh	4	2				6	*Tendency to pause, use fillers. Amusing and original*

TASK 4.2 C

The name of the game

In pairs, devise an ingenious game with the following materials: a packet of balloons; a bodhrán; a reel of thread; some coloured markers; a drawing pad; two scarves; a plank of wood; two plastic buckets; several bars of soap; and one additional ingredient of your own choice.

When you have clarified the rules to your own satisfaction, explain to the rest of the group how to play your game, sharing the explanation between you. If a blackboard or flip-chart is available, you may support your explanation with visual aids. Don't forget to *name* your game.

Assess using *applause*; when *all* presentations have been made, list them in order of delivery and invite applause for each named game. Loudest and longest applause wins. (You may not applaud yourself.)

An element of *persuasion* may be added to description in the following pair of exercises:

TASK 4.2 D

Going, going ...
Divide into pairs (A and B). The scene is a Roman slave market in AD 100. A is a greedy owner, determined to get the top price for his or her slave. The owners describe slaves (B) to maximum advantage for the benefit of prospective buyers (the group). When the As have finished displaying their wares, the roles are reversed.

TASK 4.2 E

Head to toe
Divide into pairs (A and B). The As are models at a fashion show. Unusual adjustments may be made to dress and original accessories added. B's task is to supply the commentary as A parades the catwalk. Commentaries should describe clearly and also 'sell' the look.

If you wish to assess performances, try a bidding system. The 'slave' for whom most bids are made has the most persuasive owner, and the look for which most buyers compete has the most persuasive sales pitch.

4.3 Stage 2: Instructing, expressing opinions, narrating

These are three further forms of speech activity we engage in daily—for example, when we direct someone to a particular location, give an opinion on last night's television, or tell an anecdote about something that happened at work.

How can we improve our practice?

(1) Aim for clarity and fluency (as always).

(2) Aim for structure: It will help your listeners if you provide a *logical sequence*, making them aware of *stages* by which a conclusion is reached. A narrative, for example, has a beginning, middle, and end. An opinion is the result of a chain of reasoning. A set of instructions will often be numbered to ensure ease of understanding.

A formal talk will usually consist of an **introduction**, **body**, and **close**. Sentences that mark the transition from one stage to the next are called 'links'. It's standard practice to write the introduction and close *after* the body (when you've seen what it is you've said!).

(3) Aim to know your stuff: To instruct others you need to know what you're talking about. Opinions should be based on knowledge. There is no surer way to spoil a good story than by being unsure what happened next, making false starts, and repeating yourself unnecessarily.

Tips

(i) Research your subject thoroughly so that you are in complete command of your material. Know more than you will use.

(ii) Plan your talk carefully and be clear in your own mind how one stage leads into the next. Make sure the links are in place.

(iii) Use *notes* rather than writing out your speech word for word. Notes are best done on small **cue cards** (e.g. 100 × 100 mm), which should be clearly *numbered*. Often the notes are written in clear capital letters. The shorter they are the better. Best of all are single **keywords**—just enough to guide you from stage to stage or from point to point. Sometimes link sentences are included. Don't be tempted to scribble additions to each card. Rehearse with the cards.

(4) Aim for eye contact: Eye contact with your audience is essential. Making a speech to a group is really just an **expanded conversation**, and when talking to others we always make eye contact.

Regular eye contact will

- make your listeners feel *personally* involved
- make you, the speaker, seem more open, friendly, and sincere
- make your listeners less inclined to switch off
- make you aware of your listeners' reactions and give you the chance to change your tactics if need be.

Tips

(i) Know your material so well that your eyes aren't tied to your cards.

(ii) Letting your eyes roam quickly over your audience is not making effective eye contact: focus on individual listeners for a few seconds each, picking your targets at random.

(iii) Don't fall into the trap of addressing everything to the teacher if he or she is in the audience.

(iv) Remember that listeners tend to mirror the speaker's facial expression and even mannerisms, so if your audience looks worried and nervous, try to smile or look cheerful!

(5) Aim for appropriate body language: As we've seen in chapter 3, up to 80 per cent of our meanings may be made non-verbally. Getting your message across to a group must involve your whole body. *You are yourself a visual aid!* It is *natural* to use arms and hands when instructing: your hands can describe size, shape, kind of movement, number, and location. Gestures *support* your words, helping to *clarify* and *emphasise*.

Tips

(i) When talking to a group, make gestures slightly bigger than you would in talking to a friend. Exaggerate a little, as you would for a mime.

(ii) Learn from watching others, particularly practised public speakers on television. It can be instructive to turn down the sound and see if you can follow the speaker's message from body language alone.

(iii) If possible, watch yourself on video. Failing that, try a mirror.

(iv) Don't *overdo* body language: you may 'drown out' your own words.

(v) Cut out purposeless movement and gestures—shifting weight from foot to foot, swaying from side to side, tossing hair out of the eyes, fiddling with small objects.

An audience can become so fascinated by the speaker's mannerisms that it ignores the message.

TASK 4.3 A

Instructing

Working in pairs, A instructs B how to make a journey from one place to another, choosing a route B will not be familiar with. B then *retraces* the route, guiding A back to the starting point.

Good listening is almost as important as clear instructing in this task. If all the pairs work at the same time, you could use this exercise as a warm-up for the following one.

TASK 4.3 B

Two students stand back-to-back in front of the class. Each is supplied with a set of identical materials (e.g. pack of playing cards and box of paper clips, or pieces of card cut out in assorted shapes, or a selection of Lego pieces). A makes a construction out of the materials, instructing B on how to follow suit. The aim is to produce *identical* constructions using oral instruction *without* feedback. Use two or three pairs, and after each discuss briefly the pair's strengths and weaknesses.

TASK 4.3 C

Demonstrating

This is a more advanced version of task 4.2 B. Each member of the group, given adequate notice, puts on a short *practical* demonstration for the others. Ideally the demonstration should be related to the group's vocational area: how to use or service an appliance, how to carry out an essential routine, how to practise a technique, etc. Acceptable alternatives might include how to tie complicated knots, how to do a card or conjuring trick, how to juggle, how to create a hairstyle, how to perform a first aid operation, how to create a dish, how to make a paper hat etc. It is important to use actual materials and to set a time limit on each demonstration.

Assess demonstrators with a mark sheet whose criteria include structure, command of subject, eye contact, and body language. Circulate the mark sheets.

4.4 EXPRESSING OPINIONS

A useful (if rather noisy) group warm-up exercise is to have a short 'street corner soapbox' session. If the group is large, divide into sub-groups of five or six. Using one sub-group at a time, put all its members standing on chairs facing the rest of the group. For *one* minute, those on 'soapboxes' harangue the group about *any* bee they may have in their bonnets. Try to keep up an unstoppable flow, exchanging banter with imaginary passers-by or trading insults with imaginary hecklers.

TASK 4.4 A

In my opinion ...

In carrying out this task, remember that, first and foremost, the listeners must know what your opinion is and, secondly, why you hold it. Use the task to practise effective techniques for *opening* and *closing*, and for *linking* points.

Talk for two minutes, either impromptu or, if you prefer, using cue cards, on one of the following themes:

(i) Books have no future.
(ii) Patriotism is out of date.
(iii) Pubs should have unrestricted opening hours.
(iv) All education should be completely free.
(v) The Land of Saints and Scholars is now a Land of Sinners and Scroungers.
(vi) There is only one quality newspaper in Ireland today ...
(vii) It's now time for male liberation.
(viii) Fashion is pure folly.
(ix) There ought to be more women TDs.
(x) Dole queues are full of work-dodgers.
(xi) The Irish are the clowns of Europe.
(xii) The Government should resign.
(xiii) Our countryside is being ruined by insensitive development.
(xiv) Voting should be made compulsory.
(xv) This course needs the following improvements ...
(xvi) Prison is no longer a deterrent.
(xvii) Chat shows should be banned from television.
(xviii) Heavy lorries should be taken off the roads.
(xix) Meat is murder.
(xx) All zoos should be abolished.
(xxi) Boxing is a blood sport and should be banned.
(xxii) RTE is too Dublin-based.
(xxiii) Live exports should be banned.
(xxiv) It's time to bring back radio licences.
(xxv) There are too many days in the week.

If there are topical controversial issues within your vocational area, add them to the list.

Assess speakers with a mark sheet whose criteria include opening, close, links, and interest level. Circulate the mark sheets.

4.5 NARRATING

A good story may be ruined in the telling; a mediocre story may become highly entertaining in the hands of a skilled storyteller.

Much of the art in telling a story well lies in the teller's use of the *voice*. This section's tasks focus on the voice; discovering the qualities of your own through the comments of the group. How do others react to your voice? What are the characteristics of a good speaking voice? Are there ways in which, without becoming too technical, you could improve your voice?

To help you assess the voices in the group, use the four gauges below. Remember, it just isn't possible to hear your own voice objectively: you will have to trust the estimates of others. Complete the gauges as part of task 4.5 A.

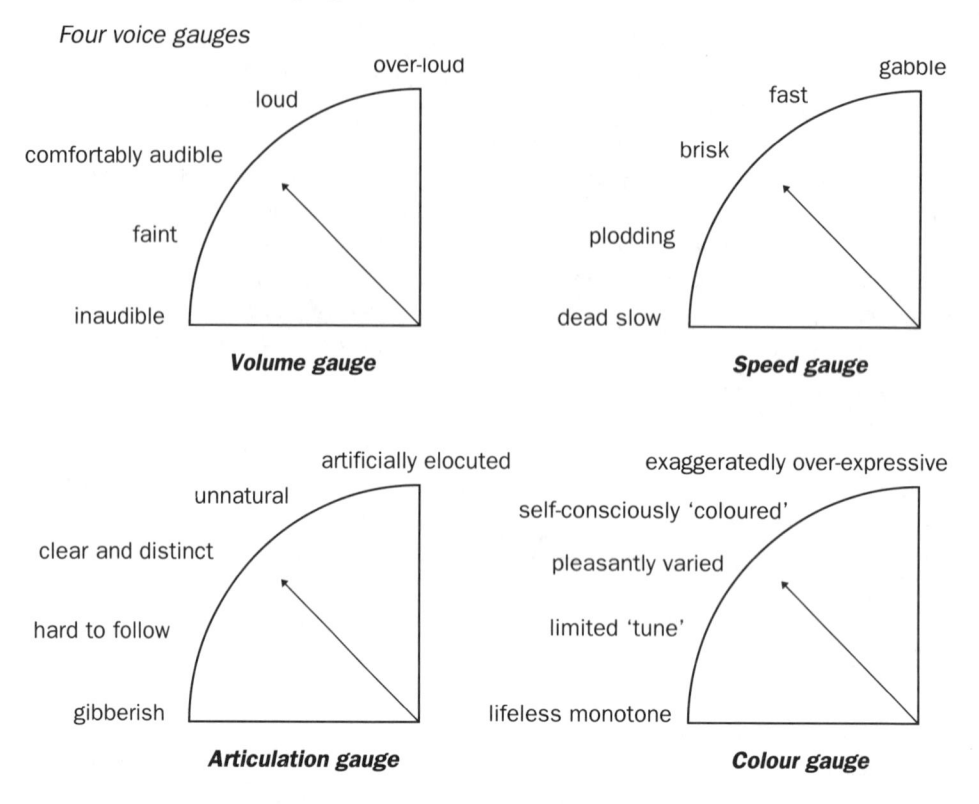

Four voice gauges

Volume gauge
- over-loud
- loud
- comfortably audible
- faint
- inaudible

Speed gauge
- gabble
- fast
- brisk
- plodding
- dead slow

Articulation gauge
- artificially elocuted
- unnatural
- clear and distinct
- hard to follow
- gibberish

Colour gauge
- exaggeratedly over-expressive
- self-consciously 'coloured'
- pleasantly varied
- limited 'tune'
- lifeless monotone

With volume and speed it's easy to see what you're measuring; you may be less sure what is meant by articulation and colour.

Articulation is the process of shaping sound into clear, distinct words by using tongue, lips, and teeth. Poor articulation produces what sounds like gibberish to a listener—words unrecognisable because mispronounced, mumbled, bitten off, swallowed, or slurred.

Colour refers to the variety of *pitch* or *tune* in the voice. A really expressive, colourful voice will use upwards of twenty-five 'notes' in the voice's range. A *monotonous* voice is, literally, one that speaks on just *one* note all the time—like a robot. If you try to imitate the news readers on radio or television you'll find yourself introducing more notes into your voice than you're accustomed to using in everyday conversation.

(1) Aim for variety in each of the four areas:

Volume tips
  (i) Avoid the extremes of softness and loudness: shouting is exhausting to listen to; whispering may be inaudible.
  (ii) Use volume to stress words or phrases and to create drama: at moments of tension a *drop* in volume can be effective.

(iii) Uniform volume will put listeners to sleep.

Speed tips
- (i) Never *gabble*; but *very* slow delivery is almost as bad. Slow speeches lose attention because listeners' minds wander in the pauses and hesitations.
- (ii) Err on the side of fast rather than slow; you can easily check your natural rate (120 words per minute is slow, 190 is fast).
- (iii) Use pauses creatively. A pause before a word highlights that word, gives it emphasis and perhaps feeling.

Articulation tip
Make a conscious effort to overcome lazy habits: *open* your mouth, *move* your lips, make your tongue *work, sound* final consonants (p, d, t, etc.).

Colour tip
Use the *full* range of your voice, particularly the often-neglected lower notes (nervousness tends to make us squeaky).

All these tips can be practised using the solo readings on page 46-7.

(2) Aim for dynamism: This is the quality that above all others can guarantee you an attentive audience. It's hard to pin down exactly what it means, though it's instantly recognisable when present: energy, vitality, controlled force ... Goebbels had, by all accounts, a beautiful voice; his master Hitler's was harsh and rasping, but it was *dynamic*.

Tip
Good delivery posture will help pour out the vital energy. Stand (*always stand for any public delivery*) with feet about 300 mm apart, one foot slightly ahead of the other. Lean forward a little, balancing on the balls of your feet. Straighten your shoulders and hold your chin up.

TASK 4.5 A

Story time

Choose *one* of the following as the basis for a short narrative presentation to the group:
- (i) A story of the supernatural or paranormal
- (ii) I remember the first time I ...
- (iii) A funny thing happened the other day ...
- (iv) I'll tell you a good one about ...
- (v) All's well that ends well.
- (vi) The story of a film you enjoyed.
- (vii) An amazing coincidence.
- (viii) My accident happened like this ...

Don't use notes. Try to introduce dialogue into your narrative, making the voices you bring in different from each other. Don't forget to assess *voice qualities*.

4.6 Stage 3: Questioning, commanding, complaining

The aim of this section is to improve your practice in three very common forms of social interaction. For example, much everyday conversation consists of question and answer. We ask questions for all sorts of reasons: to get information, to show interest in a topic or person, to get permission, to assert ourselves, and to show off our knowledge. In any work-place, orders are given and received, complaints made and dealt with.

The three activities often give rise to misunderstanding, confusion, even conflict. Worse, an unclear order or an order misunderstood could be life-threatening. A thoughtlessly worded command or an abrupt question may give offence. Even reasonable complaints develop into unnecessary confrontations.

When difficulties arise, they can generally be traced back to one or more of the following faults:
- poor choice of words
- poor listening
- failure of empathy (i.e. an inability to understand Another's feelings or point of view).

4.6.1 Questioning

TASK 4.6.1 A

Phone talk

What criticisms might be made of the telephonist's *questions* in this extract? Look particularly at *word choice*:

TELEPHONIST: Yes?
CALLER: Good morning. Is that Oakdon College?
TELEPHONIST: What?
CALLER: Am I through to Oakdon College?
TELEPHONIST: Yes. What do you want?
CALLER: I'd like to speak to the principal, please.
TELEPHONIST: Who is that?
CALLER: My name's O'Reilly, and—
TELEPHONIST: What do you want to speak to her about?
CALLER: It's in connection with evening classes.
TELEPHONIST: Is it urgent?
CALLER: Well, not terribly. I mean—
TELEPHONIST: She's busy. Could you ring back in an hour or two?

TASK 4.6.1 B

Questioning the question

Which of the following questions would you modify, and why? Consider *word choice* ...
  (i)   Nice day, isn't it? (In the street)
  (ii) Is the 10 o'clock flight expected to land on time, please? (In an airport)
  (iii) You wouldn't, I suppose, by any chance happen to have a pound of butter, would you? (In a shop)
  (iv) Are you going out wearing that? (In the home)

(v) What's the lolly like? (Candidate in an interview)
(vi) Were you happy in your last job? I mean, what were the hours like? You know, was there Saturday work? (Questioner at interview)

4.6.2 COMMANDING

In an age that prefers consultation and co-operation to coercion, commanding is a sensitive matter. In which walks of life (careers, leisure pursuits etc.) are direct commands still acceptable everyday practice? Is there any obvious reason *why* commands persist in these areas?

TASK 4.6.2 A

Order form
Discuss the differences between the following, looking particularly at *word choice* and at the *context* in which the words might be said:
(i)   Cut the grass this afternoon.
(ii) I order you to cut the grass this afternoon.
(iii) Will you please cut the grass this afternoon?
(iv) I think the grass could do with a cut, perhaps this afternoon, don't you?
(v)   Would you ever be a dote and give the grass a wee cut this afternoon?

4.6.3 COMPLAINING

We ought to know (*a*) how to *lodge* an effective complaint and (*b*) how to *deal* with a complaint. Advice is often offered on the latter, but being able to complain effectively is also a useful skill to acquire. It's sometimes seen as an Irish failing that we are not assertive enough in making known genuine causes for complaint.

Whether in the role of complainer or receiver, *empathy* is an important asset. If you're coping with a complaint, it's a help to perceive the situation from the complainer's point of view; if you're registering a complaint, some understanding of the receiver's position is also a help.

Making complaints
Tips
(i)   Be calm, polite, reasonable, and forceful.
(ii) Be absolutely sure of your facts.
(iii) Be clear in your own mind what you want to achieve by complaining: moral satisfaction, an apology, a repair, a replacement ...
(iv) Be persistent: it is irrelevant that 'nobody else has ever complained about this before you!'
(v)   Be prepared to listen as well as to talk.
(vi) At all times be in control of your voice (i.e. don't shout!).

Receiving complaints

Tips

(i) If possible, remove the complainant from public view and earshot.
(ii) Stay calm and polite, however abusive the complainer.
(iii) *Look* politely concerned; in this situation, a fixed smile could be misinterpreted.
(iv) Force yourself to listen very carefully.
(v) Get hold of all relevant facts. If these are complicated, take notes.
(vi) Don't waste the complainer's time and aggravate her temper; if she should be talking to someone else in the organisation, make this clear early on.
(vii) Avoid becoming entangled in an argument.
(viii) When you have heard the full story, if you're absolutely satisfied that there is no legitimate foundation for the complaint, politely say that you're sorry the complainer feels dissatisfied but that, in your view, no redress is possible, explaining what has led you to this conclusion.
(ix) At all times, follow company policy in dealing with complaints.

TASK 4.6.3 A

In the complaints department

In pairs, role-play a number of the following situations. At the end of each improvisation, discuss as a group how well both participants handled the situation:

(i) In a crowded train carriage, a passenger has just lit a cigarette. Another passenger leans across to point out that smoking is not permitted on trains.

(ii) A soft drinks firm has provided sponsorship for a youth theatre company. It had been agreed that in return for sponsorship the theatre would feature the firm's name prominently on posters and programmes. Posters advertising forthcoming productions have appeared but they do not mention the firm. The firm's advertising manager phones the theatre company's administrator to complain ...

(iii) A secretary is dealing with an irritated customer who complains that he or she has phoned the secretary's boss a number of times in recent days, to be told that the boss was out of the office and would return the call as soon as possible. The call has not been returned, and the customer has decided to call to complain ...

(iv) A customer has bought an expensive T-shirt in a boutique. After its first wash the T-shirt has shrunk alarmingly and no longer fits. The instructions on the care label were scrupulously obeyed. The customer complains ...

Finally, discuss as a group the sort of complaints that recur in your vocational area—complaints that you know you might be facing in reality during your work placement. Decide which are the three most common forms of complaint. Role-play them. Assess how well participants observed the tips.

4.7 Stage 4: Small talk, conversation, discussion

Good morning!
Hi!
How are you?
Fine, thanks. And yourself?
Grand, great. Nice day.
Isn't it just?
Hope it lasts ...

This kind of interaction is almost meaningless. It's a mechanical formula that keeps the lines of communication open. We'd be taken aback if, instead of 'Fine,' Person described at length his current physical and mental state.

TASK 4.7 A

Chit-chat

Decide in the group which topics traditionally form the basis for small talk (e.g. sporting events). Then role-play in pairs—
  (i) The opening passage of small talk between a driver and hitchhiker.
  (ii) A small talk 'start-up' between two strangers in a public place, such as a park, a queue, or a pub.
  (iii) A typical small-talk interaction that might feature in the work-place for which you are training.

Remember, it is *natural* to pause. At the same time, a 'social' silence lasting more than four seconds is more than most of us can tolerate!

4.7.1 Conversation

We all know how satisfying good conversation can be, to participate in or to listen to. What makes 'good conversation'?

TASK 4.7.1 A

Conversation piece

Have a round using one or more of the following starters:
- A really good conversation is when ...
- I enjoy conversing with people who ...
- To be a good conversationalist you need ...

4.7.2 Discussion

Discussion groups meet to allow participants to share opinions on every conceivable topic. 'Round-table discussions', 'wide-ranging discussions' and 'full and frank discussions' are the stuff of every news bulletin.

There will be further opportunity in chapter 7 to study how groups manage discussion. In this section, review your group's current practice. Are there ways in which you could improve your procedures?

TASK 4.7.2 A

Discussing discussing

Form groups of five or six. Appoint chairpersons and recorders. Study the Problem Page letter below. Your group has the responsibility of replying. There is no need to *write* the response. You should diagnose the exact problem and offer a number of possible solutions, which your recorder should note. Allow ten minutes' discussion. Reconvene the groups and ask recorders to summarise their sub-groups' findings.

Dear Auntie,

We are extremely concerned that our eighteen-year-old daughter seems to have no friends. We knew when she first went to school that she was shy and lacked confidence, but we hoped it was just a stage she'd grow out of. Instead things seem to have got worse, and she has finished secondary school without making any real friends. We think she must be desperately lonely: her brothers and sisters are all long since flown the nest.

We've tried to persuade her to get out and about and meet people, but the only activities she seems to enjoy are the cinema and cycling, and she does them on her own. She won't talk about the problem—just says she's happy and that other people don't want her anyhow.

We'd do anything to help her. What can you suggest?

When all recorders have reported, have a round using one or more of the following starters:

- The most important rule for discussing is ...
- A good discussion is one in which ...
- In every discussion there's somebody who ...

You may wish to rate your group's performance in this discussion or in others elsewhere in the book. Here's a sample evaluation sheet:

Discussion evaluation

Register the extent of your agreement with the following statements by ticking the appropriate box:

1 = strongly disagree
5 = strongly agree

- The group clearly defined its aims at the outset.
- The group stuck to the subject during discussion.
- The chairperson controlled discussion firmly and fairly.
- The group was well aware of time limits.
- Everybody in the group participated.
- The recorder summarised fully and accurately.
- The group obeyed basic rules (not interrupting, etc.).
- The group achieved genuine consensus.
- The group functioned effectively in discussion.

1	2	3	4	5

You now have considerable experience of talking semi-formally to the group. If an oral presentation is a course requirement, you could face the task confidently. Should you feel that further training in the more formal, traditional areas of speech-making is desirable you will find an outline programme of advanced exercises under 'Supplementary tasks' below.

Supplementary tasks
Speech programme
Level 1

'Just-a-minute': Speeches for special occasions. For example, introduce a guest speaker at a society meeting, or thank a speaker on behalf of the group.

Level 2

'Just-a-few-words': Speeches lasting *two* minutes (with or without cue cards) for *family* occasions such as christenings, birthdays, anniversaries etc.

Level 3

'Desperately-accustomed-as-I-am': Formal *three*-minute speeches at weddings, openings, fund-raising occasions, and presentations.

Level 4

A *three-minute* video CV: The student prepares a statement about himself or herself and delivers it to the camera. If no camera is available, use sound.

Level 5

Debating (see also chapter 6, 'Supplementary tasks'): Participating in a formal debate sharpens many speaking skills, and there are always topical issues to provide motions: animal rights, the legalisation of cannabis, the pros and cons of vegetarianism, to smack or not to smack children.

Debates don't have to be formal. You might enjoy holding a 'balloon debate'. The idea here is that a balloon with a gondola suspended below is half way across the Atlantic but rapidly losing altitude. Somebody must be thrown overboard in the general interest. Speakers have a specified time in which to argue their case to remain aboard. Occupants of the gondola might be asked to role-play famous historical personages (Attila the Hun, Florence Nightingale, Oskar Schindler, Elvis Presley), animals (mouse, elephant, snake, etc.), members of selected professions (doctor, teacher, lawyer, etc.), sports people—the range is enormous. Usually, a vote is held to decide who makes the weakest case ...

A variation on the debating theme is a mock trial. This may take some explanation of courtroom roles and a little preparation of agreed facts of the case.

Chapter review
1. Provide clear, simple definitions of: articulation, pitch, vocal colour, fillers.
2. Carry out an audit on your own oral skills. Make a list of (*a*) *improvements* in your practice since starting this course and (*b*) any *further improvements* you'd like to make.
3. Describe the appearance and function of a cue card.
4. Give *three* reasons why eye contact between speaker and listener is important.
5. List *four* important points to remember when *receiving* complaints.

5 STAND AND DELIVER!: MAKING AN ORAL PRESENTATION

THREE PERIODS

5.1 GETTING IT RIGHT

Most communication courses require students to make a formal oral presentation and the task usually carries a good deal of weight in the overall assessment scheme.

An oral presentation tests everything you have learned and practised in carrying out the various assignments in chapter 4. If you have participated conscientiously and listened carefully to advice and criticisms, you have little to fear.

Chapter 4 made the point that the ability to speak well before an audience does not, for most of us, come naturally. It's a *skill*, which anybody can learn. As with most skills, frequent and purposeful practice builds the self-confidence that is the basis of success.

By now you should feel comparatively at ease when addressing the group. You know, both in theory and in practice, how to catch and hold an audience's attention. Experience has taught you that a speech is no more than an *expanded conversation*. You have identified your own strengths and weaknesses. You recognise that speakers have their own characteristic styles and you probably find yourself favouring a particular approach.

In preparing and making your presentation you will not be doing anything *new*. However, you will obviously be taking extra care to ensure that this time you get *everything* right, making use of all the resources at your disposal. You will be doing the same as you've done before—only better.

To help you get it right, this chapter provides advice on
- getting the **message** right (writing and organising the script)
- getting the **medium** right (practising delivery, including the use of visual aids)

- getting it *'right on the night'* (coping with the demands of performance)
- getting the right **answers** (handling questions)
- getting the right **marks** (taking account of assessment criteria).

The only task in this chapter is the preparation of the oral presentation itself. No period allocation is suggested; you may not want to study the chapter *as a group*, preferring to go over the contents (mostly checklists) individually and using them as the basis for student-teacher consultations.

5.1.1 Getting the rules straight

'Oral presentation' is a rather grand name for what amounts to a talk. A typical assignment will ask you to give a talk lasting a minimum of five minutes in the presence of your fellow-students and teacher or assessor. There may be regulations about the subject of the talk and about the inclusion of visual aids. Answering questions at the end of the talk is usually part of the brief.

Be clear about *all* regulations before you start. For instance, are visual aids *mandatory*? If so, they will be written into the marking scheme and therefore should be part of your thinking from the outset. Is there a *maximum duration* for the talk? Must you be *recorded*, either on audio or video tape? What *equipment* for visual aids will speakers have at their disposal? It is advisable to be clear, well in advance, about dates (deadlines), times, venue, physical environment etc.

Regulations check!
- Do you fully understand all the requirements of your oral presentation?
- Do you foresee any problems in complying with any of the requirements?

5.2 Getting the message right

Planning and writing an effective script is an exercise in *matching*. You are making a *match* between

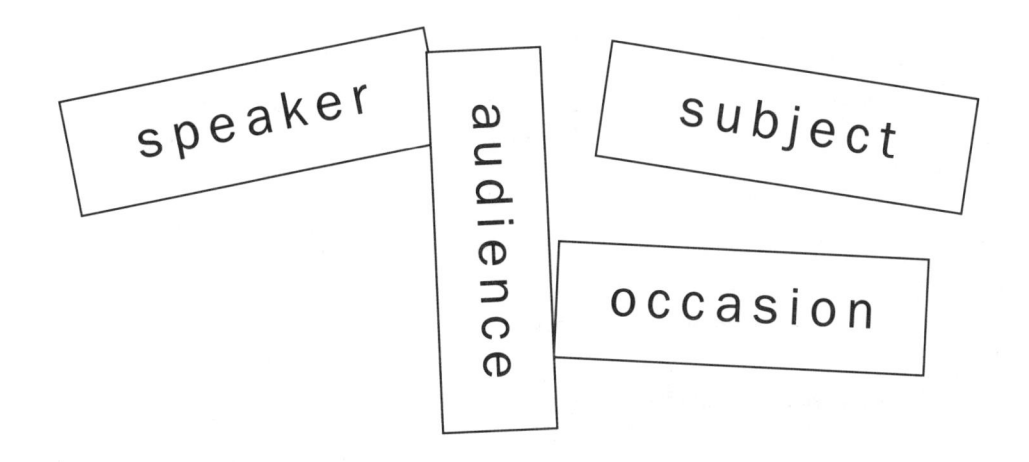

speaker   audience   subject   occasion

As **speaker** you need to find a **subject** that interests you, stands a good chance of holding your **audience**, and suits the **occasion** (e.g. by filling the time slot and allowing the use of visuals).

Remember that, whatever else your talk sets out to do, it should always *entertain* in addition to explaining, informing, describing etc. 'Entertain' doesn't have to mean 'be funny'—though a dash of humour is usually a crowd-pleaser.

Message check!
- Does the subject you've picked genuinely interest you?
- Does the subject lend itself to oral delivery?
- Does the subject suit your oral style?
- Does the subject lend itself to visual illustration?
- Does the subject match your audience's age level, gender balance, interests, tastes, and attitudes?
- Is the subject likely to involve your audience actively, leading to questions?
- Will the subject allow you to entertain your audience?

5.2.1 READING V. RE-DRAFTING

Students sometimes have the option of recycling an existing written assignment (e.g. a project) as an oral presentation. If this is your situation, be aware of the pitfalls.

The natural temptation, where there is an existing written text, is simply to read it aloud word for word. This immediately endangers your relationship with your audience—
- by diminishing vital *eye contact* (a reader-speaker is tied to the page)
- by reducing *audibility* (with head lowered to read, the voice goes 'into the ground' instead of out to the listeners)
- by making you sound stiff and impersonal when you hope to sound natural and relaxed.

The final point above may need clarification. The words we use in *written* communication are usually different from those we *speak*, even when we're speaking fairly formally. You would *say*, 'You'd say.' If you use words written for the *eye* you will be in danger of sounding, to the *ear*, stilted, artificial, even pompous.

'Giving a talk' is the spontaneous, natural, conversational way of describing the activity; 'delivering an oral presentation' is the language of a formal *written* module descriptor. Some formality is desirable when you get up to speak to a group but it is possible to be both formal and conversational.

An important reason for the differences between written and spoken language is that the written word is re-viewable, but the listener is experiencing a unique event. This is why it makes sense to heed the advice to public speakers that is so often repeated:

Tell them what you're going to tell them.
Tell them!
Tell them what you've told them.

Experienced speakers take precautions that writers don't feel necessary. For example:
- They repeat important bits.
- They summarise at regular intervals.
- They give warning when approaching important bits.
- They give examples or helpful explanations.
- They keep their sentences short.

It is unlikely that you will have observed these techniques in your written assignment, but they undoubtedly should be part of your talk.

The very strong recommendation here is that you should *completely re-draft* your existing written assignment to suit the changed context and medium. We'll check in a moment what this involves. However, if you decide to ignore the recommendation and press ahead with the intention of reading off a virtually unchanged script, here are some practical ways to improve your performance:

Reading check!
- Does your existing script fit the allotted time? If not, what can you discard?
- Have you tried reading your script aloud? Could the wording in places be altered to sound more natural?
- Have you taped yourself, listening self-critically for clarity, variety, colour, dynamism etc.?
- Have you tailored a script to suit the demands of oral presentation, considering page and type size, line spacing, and page-turning?
- Have you laid out your script to avoid page-turning in mid-sentence? Are you able to use the ends of paragraphs to coincide with the inevitable pause as you turn the page?
- Have you numbered your pages clearly?
- Are you sufficiently familiar with your script to be able to lift your eyes from the page, knowing you'll be able to find your place again?
- Have you devised a suitable opening that includes an appropriate address ('Good afternoon, Ms Moore and fellow-students …') and clear announcement of your subject ('For the next five minutes I'm going to be speaking to you about …')?

If, on the other hand, you have opted for a completely re-drafted version of an existing script, you will be guided mainly by your own experiences in framing previous talks. To jog your memory:

Re-drafting check!
- Has your re-draft a *title* you can announce confidently?
- Has it an *opening* (e.g. quotation, statistic, anecdote, joke) that will instantly grab your audience's attention?
- Has it a short *introduction* telling them clearly and simply what you're going to be talking about?
- Has it a *body* (middle section) that is logically structured?
- Has it a *close* that tells them what you have said?
- Has the *close* a strong, definite finish? Has the re-draft *links* that smooth the

transition from stage to stage?
- Does it incorporate *visual aids*?
- Is *all* the material *relevant*?
- Are there *signposts* at regular intervals?
- Have you used helpful *examples and repetition*?
- Are there occasional touches of *humour*?
- Are there *dull patches* that need revision?
- Have you built in occasional *highlights* (e.g. topical references, shared understandings) to revive or retain interest?
- Does your re-draft fit the *time slot*?

5.3 GETTING THE MEDIUM RIGHT

What you say in your talk is obviously very important; *how you say it* is at least as important and will probably be recognised as such in the assessment scheme. A good talk may be marred in the delivery; conversely, indifferent material may strike an audience as attractive and interesting when presented in a confident, lively fashion.

Successful presentation involves careful preparation of
- your script
- your visual aids
- your voice
- your body.

5.3.1 SCRIPT

Begin with your re-drafted script. This now needs to be condensed to a series of headings, sub-headings, key words and phrases, links and memory-joggers, and written out boldly and clearly on numbered cue cards. Indicate to yourself where visual aids are introduced.

Toola Heritage Centre   (5)
History
1. Stronghold of <u>O'Driscoll</u> chieftains
2. Early 18-c. hunting lodge for <u>Barrymores</u>
3. Present mansion designed <u>Morrison</u> 1820s
       Slide 3: 'Today's façade'
4. |Anecdote|: Prince Regent and chambermaid

You may wish to notate your cue cards as an actor would a play script, reminding yourself of pauses, pacing, emphasis, gesture etc.

Even veteran speakers learn off their opening and closing passages to ensure a confident start and strong finish—but don't try to memorise your whole talk, however good your memory. Apart from the risk that you might suffer embarrassing memory failure, anything learned off tends to sound artificial and automatic, unless you are a highly skilled actor. The effort of remembering can be surprisingly visible and has a way of erecting a barrier between speaker and audience.

5.3.2 VISUAL AIDS

Visual aids, well selected, well designed, and strategically placed, can greatly enhance a talk. They also have the potential to turn the occasion into a nightmare for even the most practised speakers. On any visual aid should be stamped in large letters, *Handle with care!*

The main advantages of aids are that they
- catch and heighten attention
- clarify difficult information
- illustrate a point or concept
- support a speaker's words
- make material more memorable.

In chapter 11 you will find examples of how graphics (drawings, diagrams, maps etc.) can be used to clarify and illustrate written information. It is an easy matter to transfer graphics from the page to an overhead projector (OHP) transparency or flip-chart, or simply to issue them as photocopied hand-outs. Your choice of aids will to a large degree be determined by the technology at your disposal. Previous experience in handling aids will be another factor in the choice.

These are the commonly used aids:
blackboard or whiteboard
flip-chart (blank or pre-prepared)
overhead projector
slide projector
video
posters and displays
models and specimens
hand-outs (including photographs and samples)

Each of these aids has its own characteristics, advantages and disadvantages. Videos, for example, are standard equipment in educational establishments, may be remotely controlled so that you can watch *with* your audience, and offer a huge range of illustration, *but* may be unsuited to a large audience and can, in ill-prepared, inexpert or nervous hands, prove surprisingly difficult to operate! Hand-outs, to take another example, have the advantage that you can prepare them in advance, but experience teaches that, thoughtlessly distributed, they can fatally divide an audience's attention and in bored hands may even become projectiles.

The best advice is to opt for simplicity and familiarity. In practice, the most effective aids are often the simplest. Whatever you choose, you should be familiar with the techniques involved: if you've never operated an OHP before, the time to learn the tricks of the trade is *not* before an audience! Incidentally, using more than two kinds of visual aid in a talk is usually felt to be unwise.

Some cautions:
- Don't compete with a visual aid for your audience's attention: you'll lose!
- Don't substitute *visual* aids for an *oral* presentation.
- Don't overload aids with *wordy* information.
- Don't address your aid instead of your audience.
- Don't mask your aid with your own body (e.g. write on a flip-chart *from the side*).
- Remove aids you've finished with—OHP transparencies, slides etc. Left on view, they may distract.

Finally, think about the term: 'visual aids'. By definition, the aids must be *visible* to *all* members of your audience. Furthermore, aids are *aids*—servants of your talk, not masters!

5.3.3 VOICE

Work on your voice in rehearsal, bearing in mind all you have learned about clarity, variety, fluency, colour, volume, speed, pause, articulation, and dynamism. Make use of a tape-recorder to learn where improvements are possible. Test yourself on a friend or relative, asking your listener to monitor audibility, variety etc.

5.3.4 BODY

Work also on your body. Chapter 3 showed how our bodies communicate all sorts of messages, consciously and unconsciously. Aim to be in control of the messages your body sends while you talk. This involves thinking about appearance (dress and accessories, hairstyle, grooming), stance (discussed in chapter 4), facial expression, posture, gesture, and the vital eye contact. Rehearse in front of a mirror or, better still, with a video-recorder.

Delivery check!
- Have you devised cue cards and rehearsed with them?
- Have you organised visual aids and rehearsed with them?
- Have you worked out a satisfactory opening and finish? And committed them to memory?
- Are you prepared to wait for your audience to settle before you start?
- Have you made a resolution to start with a smile?
- Do you know what to do with your hands?
- Have you identified and eliminated distracting physical or vocal mannerisms?

- Are you prepared to make eye contact with your audience?
- Are you in the habit of overworking certain words or phrases ('totally', 'like', 'sort of', 'I mean')? Have you cured the habit?
- Is your voice as expressive as it should be?
- Are you positive that all your visual aids are relevant?
- Will you guard against an 'on-the-night' tendency to speed up?

5.4 Getting it 'right on the night'

We are often told that most people put fear of having to speak in public second only to their fear of dying.

Coping with the demands of performance means coming to terms with fear or nervous tension. As chapter 4 stressed,

nerves are natural and normal.

They are also *necessary* if you are to produce your best. Nerves prompt the flow of adrenalin that will heighten your awareness, sharpen your reactions, and allow you to discover and display unexpected reserves. Difficult though it may be to accept, nerves will have a *positive* effect on your performance.

You will have noticed in previous oral assignments how quickly nervousness wears off once you get started. You may also have realised how difficult it is for an audience to spot slips! A theatre audience is rarely conscious of anything amiss, because it doesn't know what *should* have happened. Your audience will only be conscious of error if *you* betray it.

Much of our pre-talk worry is that somehow or other we will break down, lose the thread, and be unable to continue. If you think it through calmly you will realise that, barring something entirely unexpected, it would be very difficult for anything to go seriously wrong, given the thoroughness of your preparations.

Preparations must include familiarising yourself with the environment in which you will speak (classroom? lecture hall? theatre?) and knowing how your audience will be seated (if necessary, adjust the seating arrangement to one you feel more comfortable with). Be sure to research the position from which you will be expected to speak (lectern? podium? desk?).

Pre-performance check!
- Have you checked the venue?
- Can you be there in plenty of time?
- Do you know what the running order will be?
- Have you your cue cards or script?
- Have you checked that any equipment you will be using is set up and ready for action?
- Are your visual aids in place?
- Will you remember as your turn approaches to
    —take several deep breaths
    —pause while your audience settles

—smile
—and begin?

5.5 Getting the right answers

You are bound to feel relieved when you finally wrap up your talk. But the task is not quite complete. You still have to show that you can handle questions professionally, and that means staying on full alert until you've finished your final answer.

You will probably have to chair the question-and-answer session yourself. When you finish speaking you may find you have won a round of applause. Smile in acknowledgment and then, in as friendly a manner as you can manage (keep the smile!), invite questions. Be careful how you *phrase* the invitation. 'Are there any questions?' may sound abrupt and discouraging. 'I'm sure there are lots of questions you're dying to ask' might also silence an audience. Be prepared for a slow start—unless you have taken the trouble to plant an opening question!

Useful techniques for a Q & A session:
- Repeat the question to ensure that the whole audience knows what you are answering (and to give you a little more time to think of your response!).
- Include the *whole* audience in your response, not just the questioner.
- At the end of your answer, ask the questioner if he or she is satisfied.
- Listen carefully right through to the ends of questions: nervous speakers sometimes snatch at a half-heard question.
- Be polite, even if the question is foolish.
- Stick to the point.
- Don't relax!

Remember, it is your job to control the Q & A session right to the point where you hand back to the assessor.

Question check!
- Have you a tactic if you are asked a question to which you don't know the answer?
- Have you worked out how you will invite questions?
- Have you a formula for bringing the Q & A session to a smooth and successful conclusion?

5.6 Getting the right marks

From the start of your preparations you should be aware of the performance criteria by which your talk will eventually be judged.

An assessor's list is likely to feature:
- command of subject and capacity to retain interest
- delivery
- structure

- handling of questions
- visual aids.

Look carefully at the *weighting* of the criteria. You may find that delivery is the most important criterion for marks. Under this heading you will be judged on your ability to establish a rapport with your audience through your handling of your script and through the way you use your body and voice.

It is difficult to separate delivery from command of subject and capacity to retain the interest of your audience. If you deliver your words inaudibly, for example, you will certainly lose your audience's attention! An assessor will reward speakers who evidently know what they are talking about, who manage to communicate their knowledge with enthusiasm and energy, and who respond to their audience's needs.

Assessment check!
- Are you fully aware of the performance criteria by which you will be judged?

The key to success in making an oral presentation is to *prepare thoroughly*. Good public speakers make the activity look effortlessly spontaneous but behind the relaxed flow there is always careful research, hard thinking and hours of practice. In this area, as in so many others,

if you fail to prepare, prepare to fail!

6 GETTING AN EARFUL: LISTENING

FOUR PERIODS

6.1 THE NEGLECTED ART

Making and taking meanings is, we've seen, a *two-way* process. Sender speaks; Receiver *listens*. Generally, Person will talk only if Another is there to listen. If you think about it, Person learned how to talk by listening. From listening came speaking, from speaking came reading, from reading came writing. It's easy to forget that the story of communication begins with listening.

How well do you practise the art of listening?

TASK 6.1 A

Relay story

Remember playing 'Chinese whispers' as a child? This task is similar.

Five volunteers are needed to relay a story. The volunteers number themselves 1 to 5 and leave the room. In their absence the group leader reads aloud to those remaining a very short story that may be found elsewhere in this book.

Volunteer 1 re-enters. The group leader selects at random one of those who *listened* to the story to relay it as fully and accurately as possible to volunteer 1. *No feedback* (e.g. question, confirmation) is allowed. Volunteer 1 now calls in volunteer 2 and relays the story he or she has heard. In this way the story is relayed along the line to volunteer 5, always *without feedback.*

Volunteer 5 tells the whole group the story as he or she has heard it. The group leader now re-reads the original story to the full group. After each version of the story, members of the observing group should record significant changes (e.g. omissions, additions, distortions, modifications) made by the volunteer. If possible, tape-record the volunteer versions. Allow the volunteers and observers to hear the tape before evaluating the exercise.

Feedback discussion:
1. What factors make it difficult to relay a story accurately through five people?
2. Is the responsibility for changes in the original story shared equally among the five volunteers? Is anyone blameless?
3. Does this task tell us anything about listening?

When you have completed this chapter, try repeating this exercise. As a variation, relay a short eye-witness account of an imagined traffic accident.

In task 6.1 A, the final version of the story is often amusingly different from the original. Failure has occurred in the commonest, easiest form of listening: *listening to understand*. The mental processes involved in listening to *evaluate* (e.g. judging the relative merits of two party political broadcasts), in listening to *appreciate* (e.g. poetry or music) or in listening to *empathise* (e.g. lending a sympathetic ear) are all more complicated and demanding.

All day long we listen to understand. As you know, we do far more listening than speaking, with reading and writing coming a very poor third and fourth. Students have to do more listening than most: up to 75 per cent of their day may be spent listening.

Listening is the communication skill we use most and are taught least about. Because there is so little emphasis in schools on learning how to listen, the missing knowledge and expertise must often be sought in adult life through in-service courses and other means. Certain professions require high-level listening skills: think of doctors, nurses, counsellors, priests, and teachers, for instance. Is it surprising that many business management courses feature training in listening?

What can any adult *learn* about listening?

Start by asking yourself about the *barriers* to listening you've experienced personally.

TASK 6.1 B

Listening blocks

In groups of four, spend five minutes brainstorming answers to this question: 'What causes you to switch off listening attention?'

Through group recorders, pool your responses, building up a master list of commonly experienced blocks. Keep individual copies of the master list.

6.2 LEARNING TO LISTEN

Your list of reasons for 'switch-off' or faulty listening will probably put the main responsibility on the listener. But remember that to any listening situation there are *four* contributors:

Speaker
Message

Listener
Environment

In many instances, obstacles are placed in the listener's way by speaker, message, or environment.

Your master list may have identified the following blocks:

Listener

- *Physical* circumstances, such as tiredness, hunger, minor illness (e.g. headache, earache).
- *Psychological* factors, such as feelings of insecurity or anxiety that get in the way of listening.
- *Personality type*, such as the breezy extrovert who is always talking, or the hyperactive child whose attention span is very short.
- Poor *language* skills, in particular limited vocabulary, making comprehension often a struggle.
- *Preconceptions* about speaker or message that hinder listening, such as 'I'm not interested in this subject, so this speaker will bore me.'
- *Prejudice* and *stereotyping*, such as reluctance to give a hearing to an opposing political viewpoint or the refusal to believe that, say, a male wearing earrings could hold serious opinions.
- *Lack of interest* in topic.
- *Preoccupation*, for instance with the very recent past or the immediate future, and hence inattention to the present.
- *Rehearsing mentally* own response.
- *Selective listening*.
- *Thought rate/speech rate differential*—the fact that an average speaker talks at the rate of about 175 words per minute, while the average thought rate (i.e. the speed at which incoming data is mentally processed) is between 400 and 800 words per minute. This is a mixed blessing. The large differential allows us time to take in, evaluate, and digest, but it also tempts us to freewheel, daydream etc., and there's always the possibility that our attention, having wandered, will not return.

Speaker

- *Slow speech rate*, such as anything below 125 words per minute, or speech that is hesitant and full of pauses.
- *Delivery* that is *too* fast, inaudible, monotonous, irritatingly mannered.
- *'Pitch'*, which takes no account of audience's linguistic aptitude (e.g. talking above audience's heads).
- *Status*—perceived high status may overawe listener, while perceived inferiority in speaker often discourages active listening (e.g. parent not listening to child).

Message

- *Information overload*—a particular problem if the information is all new to listeners.

- *Muddled messages* that ramble, are overlong, lack structure.
- *Terminology* unfamiliar to listeners.

Environment

- *Noise* at a level that interferes with listener's attention (e.g. inadequately sound-proofed classrooms into which next door's noise filters).
- *Temperature*, such as extremes of heat or cold.
- *Seat* and *body position* may influence listening capacity.
- *Competing stimuli* in the physical context may distract (e.g. weather or events seen through a window).

It's clear that listening calls for effort, and good listening means mastering skills. To start with, we need to recognise that *hearing* and *listening* are different activities. We don't have to learn how to hear; we do need to learn how to listen. It is possible simultaneously to hear and *not* to listen. Hearing is a physical activity that we carry on during our waking and sleeping hours. You may be reading these words with a background of distant traffic noise or voices speaking in a corridor; you may be *hearing* the traffic or voices and yet not *listening* to them, because, of course, you are concentrating so hard on these words. Your ears pick up the sounds but your brain is 'otherwise engaged'. Hence the line in Paul Simon's 'The Sound of Silence': 'People hearing without listening …'

Unlike hearing, which is *passive*, listening, to be effective, must be *active*. The more obstacles placed in our path by speaker, message or environment, the more actively we need to listen.

Recognising our human limitations is a first step. To know that we can sustain full concentration for no more than approximately 15 to 20 minutes at a spell is to make a useful discovery. We need to understand the rise-fall-rise pattern of our attention. The *middle* sections of anything we're listening to are likely to be the areas where attention will flag; shouldn't this prepare us to make a special effort of concentration at these times?

6.2.1 How to improve listening

We've seen that listening is an *active* process, demanding the listener's *involvement*. How can you involve yourself with speaker and message?

In a formal or semi-formal situation, such as a lecture or interview, the obvious answer is to take notes. (Section 6.3 deals in detail with note-taking techniques.)

Listening will improve if you observe the five Golden Rules:

(1) Make sure you can hear easily.
(2) Focus full attention on the speaker; it usually helps to have an unimpeded view of the speaker's face.
(3) Keep an open mind about both speaker and message.
(4) Discipline yourself in your use of the speech rate/thought rate differential. Instead of daydreaming or composing responses, ask yourself *questions* about the message e.g. 'Why am I being told this?' or 'How does this fit in with what I already know of this subject?'

(5) Provide non-verbal feedback as a social courtesy, as a way of keeping yourself alert, and as an encouragement to the speaker, who will in turn work harder to involve you. Non-verbal feedback includes posture (leaning forward attentively), head movements (nods etc.) and head position, facial expression (including smiles), and encouraging noises such as 'Mm-hm'.

If there are other aids to effective listening that have helped you in the past, share them with the group.

Listening must be one of the easiest skills to practise, because we do so much of it. Over the next few days make a conscious effort to try out the five rules. The quality of your relationships may improve as a result!

As a group you have had an opportunity to test your listening powers in chapter 4 ('Sound circle' and 'Pass the story'). Here are two further, more taxing exercises:

TASK 6.2.1 A

Name-calling

The group sits in a large circle. Person introduces herself, using either a middle name or a fantasy name that she believes is appropriate, and attaching an alliterating adjective to the name – e.g. 'I am Priscilla the prim.' Another, before introducing himself, must repeat Person's name and adjective: 'You are Priscilla the prim and I am Paul the puritanical.' And so on round the circle. Each person should announce him or herself *once* only.

At the end, briefly discuss what participants have learned about listening. Was there any *pattern* to the difficulties people had in remembering?

TASK 6.2.1 B

Lending and bending an ear

Divide the group into threes (A, B, and C)—preferably not on the basis of friendship. Each group of three finds its own space in the room, either sitting or standing. For two minutes, A talks to B about 'how I like to spend my weekend'. B listens, practising all she has learned about good listening technique, and not speaking apart from 'yes', 'no', and paralinguistic noises. C observes the interaction, watching B's listening technique and noting posture, gesture, eye contact, head movements etc. When A is finished, B spends one minute summarising what she has just heard. C should monitor the summary for accuracy.

Change the roles so that B speaks for two minutes to C on 'teachers I will never forget' (or any other topic) while A observes. Finally, repeat the procedure with C talking to A while B observes.

When the three rounds are completed, reassemble as a full group. Feedback discussion:

Listening

1. How did it feel to have to listen without speaking?
2. What helped you to listen well?
3. Did the exercise tell you anything about your listening skills?
4. Are there areas in which you would like

to improve your listening technique?

Observing

5. What did you observe to be well or badly done by those listening?

Speaking

6. What were the clearest signs that your listener was really trying to listen properly?
7. How does it feel to have a listener's full attention?

It is possible to extend this task by asking a volunteer pair (A and B) to carry out the following short exercise in front of the full group:

A talks to B for two minutes on a given subject, e.g. 'Favourite outfits'. B may either genuinely listen or not, as he wishes, but if not, he must *fake* all the appearances of listening. A repeats the talk and again B listens—or not, as the case may be. The full group observing must decide to which of the two versions B *genuinely* listened. How was it obvious, if at all? B should genuinely listen to *one* of the two versions and be able to prove it by summarising at the end of the exercise. (When faking, B should mentally repeat the alphabet backwards.)

Repeat this task at intervals over the course by periodically asking people to summarise the contents of a discussion or of a class. In discussion itself, occasionally rule that student A must *summarise* the previous speaker's point—to student B's satisfaction—before proceeding to make her own point. The effect of this ruling can be highly instructive.

6.3 Note-taking

Listening and *memory* are closely related. When we listen attentively, what we take in is deposited in our **short-term memory**, where it remains for a frighteningly short span. Our short-term memories have a limited capacity and the contents are constantly being 'dumped' to make way for fresh material.

Say you attend closely to a speaker who spends ten minutes explaining a moderately complex operation or concept. When the speaker finishes, your short-term memory will retain about 50 per cent of the explanation. A fortnight later you will recall 25 per cent. In a relay story task (task 6.1 A) there is always a striking difference between the *lengths* of the original and final versions.

Note-taking is a way of overcoming the limitations of short-term memory. If we take notes, the original information will always be available to us, reduced to its essentials, in written form: who knows how many years hence you will wish to consult notes taken today? The process of note-taking helps us, as we shall see, to transfer information to our **long-term memory**. For students faced with end-of-year exams, notes have to become *routine*. If you are fortunate to possess excellent short-term memory, the material you will want to load in during those frantic final days will be *notes*, not the contents of entire books.

Good note-taking does not come naturally. The skill ought to be introduced at second level; regrettably, students often find themselves having to acquire it by trial and error at third level.

There are, ideally, *three* stages in the process:

6.3.1 STAGE 1: CRUDE NOTES

These are taken, usually at speed, from a speaker talking at normal pace. The obvious problem, particularly if the speaker is giving out unfamiliar information, is that you seem to have to *listen, understand and write* almost simultaneously. While you are busily recording one piece of information, the speaker moves on to the next.

You may, of course, be taking notes from a reference book, textbook, or critical work—the process known as 'gutting', where you quickly extract the relevant passages.

Tips

- Notes are, almost by definition, *short:* never attempt verbatim reporting unless there's a very specific reason (e.g. need for a journalistic quotation).
- Try to see the shape or structure underlying the speaker's words; your own experience in devising speeches will heighten your awareness of structure.
- Try to find *keywords* or *key phrases*, which will usually be related to structure.
- Try allowing the speaker to talk for two or three minutes while you listen and understand. Then put down a summary of what he or she has said, preferably using your own words. If you get the *main* points, you may be able to fill in the details later.
- Devise your personal 'shorthand' (yr, tho, 2 B R not 2 B) as well as using all recognised abbreviations (this is one reason why crude notes are usually non-transferable).
- Restrict notes to *important* points or facts. Omit anecdotes, digressions, multiple examples etc.
- Don't be afraid to use up paper. Even at the crude notes stage, wise use of space on the page can indicate structure, show relationships between ideas or topics, and avoid clutter.

6.3.2 STAGE 2: REFINED NOTES

The 'crude' material gathered at a lecture, talk, meeting or library session needs to be 'refined'. The best time for doing this is later the same day: then you can be reasonably sure of some help from your short-term memory. Refining means re-reading and eventually rewriting, perhaps on a word-processor, to produce a text you can confidently revise.

Tips

- Re-read critically your crude notes, looking for shape and structure, reappraising what is important, what is not.
- Reorganise if necessary to emphasise structure, always alert to the possibilities of helpful *layout*. Blocks of unbroken writing are usually unhelpful. Where practicable, use diagrams, flow charts etc.
- *Reduce* and *replace*. Overall, your aim should be to pare down further, by omitting material you now judge inessential. On the other hand, you may wish to replace what is excised with material from your short-term memory that you now perceive to be valuable.

- Translate wherever possible into your own words. By doing so you will increase understanding, make it your own property and become more familiar with the material.
- Headings, titles and sub-titles may later be very helpful in finding your way round your own notes.

6.3.3 Stage 3: Review notes

If you are note-making for exam purposes, the refined version needs to be committed to your long-term memory. The repetition involved in carrying out the first two stages will help to load the material in. Now you need to *review* (which means just that: view again) your notes at regular intervals, always becoming more familiar with their contents.

Tips
- Over time, it may be possible to pare down even further. You will certainly want to *underline* and use colour highlighting.
- If preparing for an exam, use **mnemonics** (i.e. rhymes, acronyms etc.) to recall the substance of your notes.

Warning!
There is nothing worse than learning inaccurate information. Do all in your power to ensure that your notes are factually accurate.

If you know of other aids to good note-taking, share them with the group. Remember, it is vital to establish a technique that suits you and then to practise it.

TASK 6.3.3 A

Practise note-taking

Your teacher will read the following passage aloud, padding it out to sound like a lecture. (Resist any temptation to skim the passage!) Make crude notes during the delivery and refine them overnight. In class, compare and contrast your refined versions, paying particular attention to layout, diagrams etc.

Repeat the exercise at regular intervals, using short or abridged articles from magazines or newspapers.

'Much of what we know, or think we know, about the roots of language comes from watching children learn to speak. For a long time it was believed that language was simply learned. Just as we learn, say, the names and locations of the capitals of Europe or our multiplication tables, so we must learn the "rules" of speech—that we don't say "house white is the" but rather "the house is white." The presumption was that our minds at birth were blank slates onto which the rules and quirks of our native languages were written. But then other authorities, notably Noam Chomsky of the Massachusetts Institute of Technology, began to challenge this view, arguing that some structural facets of language—the *ground rules* of speech, if you like—must be innate. That isn't to suggest that you would have learned English spontaneously had you been brought up among wolves. But perhaps you are born with an instinctive sense of how language works, as a general thing. There are a number of reasons to suppose so. For one thing, we appear to have an innate appreciation of language. By the end of the first months of life infants show a clear preference for speechlike sounds over all others. It doesn't matter what language it is. To a baby no language is easier or more difficult than any other. They are all mastered at about the same pace, however irregular and wildly inflected they may be. In short, children seem to be programmed to learn language, just as they seem to be programmed to learn to walk. The process has been called basic child grammar. Indeed, children in the first five years of life have such a remarkable facility for language that they can effortlessly learn two structurally quite different languages simultaneously—if, for instance, their mother is Chinese and their father American—without evincing the slightest signs of stress or confusion.'—Bill Bryson, *Mother Tongue*, p. 16 (322 words).

6.4 USING THE PHONE

Why should a chapter on listening contain advice on use of the phone? Because good phone technique depends on good listening; because the phone is an oral-aural medium that is in constant use in any work-place and also (some parents would complain) in the home; because this form of medio-communication is becoming ever more dominant with the rapid increase in the number of mobile phones. (In 1995 there were 100,000 mobile phone users in the Republic; by 2000 it's expected that there will be 500,000, and by 2005, a million.)

The phone that will allow us to see the person we're talking to 'televisually' is in the offing. However, until it becomes widely available we're dependent on our ears and voices to take and make meanings via the technology. We need to train our ears to pick up information that in a face-to-face interaction is readily available to the eye. It is possible to develop a 'good ear' for the phone and to become sensitive to vocal clues that tell us how the other person is thinking and reacting and feeling. It is, for example, possible to *hear* a smile in the voice. You'll have noticed, too, how the accents even of those you know best seem much stronger down the phone. Their voices haven't changed; the difference is that you are listening more keenly: your ears are trained on the *sounds* with unusual intentness.

Your vocational specialisation may take you into areas where mastery of telephone techniques is an essential and where you require detailed knowledge of the latest improvements in phone systems. If so, you will need to go beyond the steps set out here. What follows is a primer of good phone use for the *average* user.

For most of us, phone use might be considered under four headings:
- Good phone conduct
- Making calls
- Taking calls
- Passing on messages

6.4.1 CODE OF GOOD PHONE CONDUCT

Much of what is generally considered good phone technique is actually common (would that it were!) courtesy. Aren't most of the items in the following check-list ways of showing consideration for others?

Top ten check-list

(1) Show normal good manners—where possible, recognising voices and using names, being polite, tactful, helpful etc.

(2) Clearly introduce yourself and your background (organisation, society etc.) when making or taking calls.

(3) Concentrate *full* attention on the phone conversation: it is rude to overlap a phone conversation and another one with the person beside you.

(4) Speak audibly and distinctly into the mouthpiece.

(5) Use language appropriate to the nature of the phone call: in formal circumstances, phrases such as 'Hang on a mo' or 'Okay, just a tick' may be out of place.

(6) To compensate for the lack of gesture, facial expression etc., take care to emphasise key words and key phrases by vocal means such as volume and pitch.

(7) To avoid uncertainty, whether giving or requiring feedback, repeat important bits, if necessary spelling out words and numbers.

(8) Have to hand at all times a notebook and ballpoint pen.

(9) Have to hand the phone directory, phone index book or list of regularly used numbers.

(10) Find a formula that enables you to say goodbye clearly and politely—e.g. 'Is there anything else you wish to know?'

6.4.2 MAKING CALLS

In making a call, you, the caller, start with the initiative. The caller sets the agenda ('I'm phoning to …') and tone for the interaction. It is surprising how many callers are still nonplussed by an answering machine, surrendering the initiative to the machine.

Tips

- Know exactly for what *purpose* you're phoning.
- Know to whom you wish to speak—one reason for keeping a personal phone directory with names, extension numbers etc.
- Note down beforehand the points you wish to raise in logical sequence, and tick them off as they are dealt with.
- Make sure you have the right area code and phone number.
- State your reason for calling at the outset, being careful not to waste a receptionist's time with unnecessary detail.
- Be direct and to the point.
- Be aware of time and of the cost of phoning.

- Have by you any documents you may need.
- Re-connect immediately if accidentally disconnected: this is the *caller's* obligation.
- End smoothly and courteously. Often, thanks are appropriate—for help, time, interest, or patience.

TASK 6.4.2 A

Taking calls

Imagine that a check-list of 'Top ten tips for taking a call' were to be posted beside the desk of the secretary or receptionist in your college or school. What suggestions should it contain? Is it, for example, a good idea to pick up a phone *immediately* it rings?

In compiling your 'Top ten tips', think of identification, message-taking, holding on, coping with awkward calls etc.

6.4.3 PASSING ON MESSAGES

Phone use, whether domestic or professional, often involves the chore of taking a message and passing it on. Most work-places will have customised telephone message pads or use a standard issue such as this:

IMPORTANT MESSAGE

FOR: Barry Kelly
FROM: William Kletner
OF: Spray Chemicals   PHONE: 01 6238 952

| TELEPHONED | ✓ | WILL CALL AGAIN | | PLEASE PHONE | ✓ | URGENT | ✓ |
| VISITED YOU | | WANTS TO SEE YOU | | RETURNED CALL | | CHECK WITH ME | ✓ |

MESSAGE: Delayed in Dublin! Will be late for this afternoon's 4pm appointment. Please call 088 NO! ASAP

TAKEN BY: DOD   DATE: 31:10:95   TIME: 10.50am

The use of a message pad in the home can avoid much unnecessary irritation, not to mention confusion. If no message pad is available, remember to provide the following information:

(1) date and time of taking message
(2) person for whom message is intended
(3) caller's name, organisation (if relevant), and phone number (including area code and extension)
(4) message
(5) follow-up required (whether caller will phone again or wishes call to be returned etc.)
(6) name of message-taker

TASK 6.4.3 A

Get on the blower ...

Time to translate theory into practice! Easily the best way to test your technique is by making *real* phone calls, taping your side of the conversation and analysing it afterwards with the group in the light of the recommendations in this chapter.

Here are some suggestions about *types* of call:

- Make an *enquiry* (e.g. about bus, train or plane times and costs).
- Make an *appointment* (e.g. with doctor, dentist, or hairdresser).
- Make a *reservation or cancellation* (e.g. restaurant or cinema).
- Make a *complaint or apology* (e.g. for failure to meet a deadline or to keep an appointment).
- Report a *fault* (e.g. in a neighbour's phone).
- Make a *date*.
- Offer *congratulations or sympathy* (e.g. to someone who has just passed or failed an exam or test).
- Seek a *service* (e.g. someone to clean a chimney or clear blocked drains).
- Issue an *invitation or convey thanks* (e.g. for a party).
- Leave a *message on the answering machine* of a fuel merchant about the delivery of a consignment of fuel to your home in your absence.

If access to a phone is difficult, an alternative is to role-play in groups of three, so that the caller–receiver exchange will be observed by a fellow-student prepared to be constructively critical of technique. Keep switching roles so that each of the three has a turn at observing. Those 'on the phone' should sit back-to-back. As a group, discuss what members observed.

Here are some situations to role-play:

(1) A school secretary has been warned by the principal that she is attending an important board of management meeting and is on no account to be disturbed. A parent rings to say he wishes to speak to the principal urgently on a matter that is confidential. The secretary explains, but the parent insists ...

(2) 'Telebusiness' is a growing feature of business life. Phones are increasingly used to sell products and services. Every morning teams of salespersons working from lists of potential customers or using the computer to dial random numbers begin a schedule of 'cold calls'.

Make a series of cold calls to sell double glazing. Remember, your job is to sell this product to an unsuspecting member of the public who may never have considered the possibility of double glazing.

You may be able to adapt this exercise to suit your vocational area.

(3) You are eighteen and wish to buy a second-hand moped. You spot an ad in an evening newspaper:

FOR SALE 50 c.c. moped. Excellent condition. £150 o.n.o. Phone 5337981 after 6 p.m.

(i) Ring the number and get more detailed information about the machine. Remember to make notes of the queries you want to make.

(ii) You are tempted to buy the moped, which is indeed in excellent condition, even if thirteen years old. However, you are worried that the cost of insurance may be beyond your resources. Phone an insurance company to enquire about premium costs (somebody in the group may be knowledgeable in this area). Work out your questions in advance—for example, you are only a month away from your nineteenth birthday ...

(iii) The insurance costs, though high, are within your means. However, the insurance company requires a certificate of roadworthiness (given your bike's age). Phone a local motorcycle and scooter centre and arrange to have the moped tested, remembering to ask about cost, the nature of the tests etc. Mention that the speedometer is faulty, and ask about the cost of a replacement.

(iv) You have a taxed and insured moped but not yet a driving licence. Phone the motor licensing department of the county council to ask for an application form for a provisional licence to be sent to you. Ask about costs etc.

(v) In your haste to become mobile you almost overlooked the fact that a helmet is compulsory. You have also been told that gloves are vital. Phone a motor factor to ask about products, prices etc.

4. Finally, use your school or college public address system to make an announcement about an important charity event (e.g. bed-push) for which support is needed.

Supplementary tasks

1. 'Most people are perfectly well aware that they do not listen well.' Do you agree?
2. 'In the world at large, listening is often replaced by waiting to speak.' Is this your experience?
3. What is the most important discovery you have made about listening in working through this chapter?
4. On what occasions do humans talk aloud without another human listener present?
5. One of the best ways of forcing ourselves to listen carefully is by participating in a debate. Organise a debate on one of these motions:
   (i) This house believes that the family is finished.
   (ii) This house believes in UFOs.
   (iii) This house would rather be anywhere than here.

6. A student produced the following notes in response to task 6.3.3 A:

Stage 1 (crude notes):

ORIGIN OF LANG.

1. Routes of lang. from kids
2. Learn rules of speech (word order etc.)
3. Presumed blank mind at birth
4. Noam Chomsky challenged - structures inborn
5. Not necessary mother tongue - maybe instinctive
6. Seem 2 have inborn appreciation - 1 month babies prefer speechy sounds
7. Kids - as if they're programmed to learn lang.
8. BASIC CHILD GRAMMAR 0-5 capacity is huge - learn 2 lang. - not confused

Stage 2 (refined notes):

BASIC CHILD GRAMMAR?

1. Most information on the roots of language comes from children. It was believed that our minds were blank at birth and language was simply learned.

2. Noam Chomsky - challenged these views and said that some structural facts must be innate. This suggests that you are born with an instinct as to how language works.

3. Babies seem to respond much more to speech-like sounds than to anything else they hear. This again stresses the possibility of inborn appreciation.

4. 0-5 years children can effortlessly learn two structurally different languages simultaneously eg. from a Chinese mum and U.S. Dad.

(a) Has this student fully understood the passage read?
(b) Is any important information missing from the refined version?
(c) Are significant improvements made between crude and refined stages?
(d) Do you spot opportunities for further paring down or improvement?

Chapter review

1. List *four* common reasons for not listening.
2. Explain the concept of thought rate/speech rate differential.
3. What is the difference between hearing and listening?
4. List five Golden Rules for good listening.
5. List no fewer than six features of good phone technique.
6. Offer four pieces of advice on how to make a phone call.
7. What essential information should any phone message contain?

7 BETWEEN OURSELVES: INTERACTIVE SKILLS

SIX PERIODS

7.1 INTERACTIVE SKILLS

Most of our waking hours are spent interacting with other people through speaking and listening, and earlier chapters have investigated some of our habits when we make small talk, converse, discuss and listen in formal and informal contexts.

This chapter seeks to determine what is good practice in speaking and listening when we are interacting socially. Chapter 4 encouraged you to aim for clarity when making a formal address. But there are social situations when to be clear might seem brutally insensitive: if breaking bad news, for instance. Interacting skilfully means empathising, understanding an opposing viewpoint, exercising tact, displaying tolerance, withholding judgment, and being assertive when necessary.

Employers value these skills more than cleverness, energy, or initiative. Heading their list of desirable characteristics is usually 'ability to work as part of a group or team'. Will the candidate fit easily into the work force, co-operate good-humouredly, respect the roles and needs of others—in short, *interact* satisfactorily?

Our interactive skills come into play in group situations. We live our lives in groups. We are born into families, form circles of friends, become parishioners, join youth clubs, play for and support teams, associate with those who enjoy the same kinds of music, and form ourselves into unions, residents' associations, conservation societies, support groups, and political parties.

In seeking to improve our interactive skills we must start with the *group*. What is a group? How does one function? What is my customary role in groups to which I belong?

What are my strengths and weaknesses as a group member?

We begin by looking at group interaction (section 7.1.1). Our everyday lives are heavily influenced by group decisions, ranging from those made by the Government to the very informal ones taken by the crowd we knock around with. We should know how groups arrive at decisions. Generally they are taken at *meetings* (section 7.3), whether formal or informal. If you intend to take your social role seriously, you cannot avoid meetings. Once there, you will need to know the rules, because otherwise you will feel at the mercy of those who do.

A formal meeting that most of us find intimidating is the job interview (section 7.4). We will probably face a number of these over a working life; within an organisation, the path to promotion usually lies through further interviews. It pays (literally) to think hard about the interview process, to prepare carefully, and to assess hard-headedly your own strengths and limitations.

7.1.1 INTERACTING IN GROUPS

Experts disagree on what constitutes a group. They differ on basic questions such as
- How many are needed to form a group?
- For what reasons do people form groups?
- How do you recognise a group?
- Have all groups got leaders?
- How do groups organise themselves?

TASK 7.1.1 A

What is a group?

Spend five minute brainstorming answers to the title question. Keep in mind the five questions listed above. Can you arrive at a definition that will satisfy the majority?

Here is what the experts say:
(1) Groups come in two sizes: small or 'primary' (2–20 people) and large or 'secondary' (more than 20).
(2) Groups happen naturally (e.g. the family) or are created (e.g. a committee).
(3) Primary groups usually feature
 - direct face-to-face interaction
 - a strong personal involvement
 - knowledge of other people in the group
 - regular contact or meetings
 - the possibility of influencing or being influenced by other members of the group.
(4) Groups (primary and secondary) usually offer a shared identity or purpose.
(5) Groups' participants perceive themselves as *members* and may stress membership by dress (e.g. tie or scarf) or language (e.g. specialist jargon or private words or names).

(6) Groups may be categorised in various ways, such as
- those based on family, friendship, or work
- those formed to benefit members (e.g. support groups) and those formed for the benefit of non-members (e.g. charities)
- those that favour a *formal* as opposed to an *informal* way of conducting group business.

TASK 7.1.1 B

Groupies!

Individually, spend five minutes listing the various groups to which you belong. Then, using the group analysis grid below as a guideline, see how the groups of which you are a member might be classified. Follow the example given.

Group analysis grid

Group	Primary/ secondary	Naturally occurring/ created	Formal/ informal	Dress or language conventions	Frequency of meetings	Approx. time spent weekly as member
Youth theatre	Secondary (80 members)	Created	Mostly informal but occasionally formal (e.g. AGM)	Company T-shirt?	Twice weekly	Normally 4 hours, but 'day and night' during productions!

Circulate the completed grids. How many included membership of this communication group? Would it have been easier to list those parts of your week you do *not* spend in a group setting?

Reasons regularly given for the formation of groups include
- to provide access to information (e.g. guest lecturer at society)
- to satisfy a shared interest (e.g. bird-watching)
- to enhance social status (e.g. an 'exclusive' club)
- to facilitate social contact and communication (e.g. friendship clubs)
- to ensure material benefit for members (e.g. trade union)
- to promote solidarity and a sense of belonging (e.g. works social club)

TASK 7.1.1 C

Why a group?

Pick any *three* of the created or formal groups you listed in the previous task and, using a couple of sentences for each, explain what seem to you to be the principal reasons for the groups' formation and continuing existence. Share a selection of the responses.

The groups to which we belong help to shape our perceptions, personalities, tastes, attitudes, values, and behaviour. If the family unit and school peer group are formative influences on the growing child, the groups we *voluntarily* join in adult life also exert powerful influences. They encourage us to conform to written or unwritten rules of behaviour and to accept the group's definition of what is 'normal' conduct. 'Groupthink' and 'mindset' are terms we use to describe a manner of thinking that characterises a group; another word for the phenomenon is ***ideology*** (see section 15.7).

7.2 THE GROUP AT WORK

The best way to learn about group dynamics is to experience them at first hand as one of a group solving a problem.

TASK 7.2 A

Wanted: manager ...

Divide into groups of four or five. Solve the following problem:

A promising young band needs a manager to improve its prospects of success. The band members have narrowed the choice to five candidates. As members, you must pick one of the following, having carefully considered the full range of options.

You have fifteen minutes in which to reach a decision. Your choice, together with your reasons for arriving at it, will be revealed to the full group.

The candidates

(i) *Mick*. Early twenties. Mediocre Leaving Cert results. Great charm and very popular. Could talk his way out of anything. Bit of a chancer. No musical talent of his own. Daytime job as salesperson. Never lets things get on top of him. Close friend of band since schooldays together.

(ii) *Alan*. Late twenties. Boy-friend of band's lead singer. Accountant. Rather reserved—perhaps shy. Extremely efficient and clear-headed. Dresses conservatively. A perfectionist, he's interested in the business possibilities.

(iii) *Síle*. Mid-twenties. Degree in theatre studies. Some experience working in an arts centre. Vivacious, with a sympathetic personality. Level-headed and sensible, she relates easily to others. No particular knowledge of music scene but she knows what she likes.

(iv) *Don*. Mid-thirties. Has extensive experience of DJ work and local radio. Encyclopaedic knowledge of music world. Thinks that at last he has spotted a winner. Tends to boss, and keen on doing things his way. Superficial jollity but quite a cold personality. Ambitious to make it, but time is running out.

(v) *Lucilla*. Has done a PLC course in journalism and, at twenty, is looking for openings in the media. Very energetic and bright. Good organiser but makes no secret of the fact that she doesn't suffer fools gladly. Sarcastic and funny. Quick to learn. Comes from a wealthy background.

Solutions to the problem may be *briefly*

shared in the full group.

With the experience of interacting as members of a group still fresh in your minds, assess your own performance and that of your group, using the evaluation sheet below. When you have completed your individual evaluation sheets, see if your answers match those of other members of your group.

Register the extent of your agreement with the following statements by ticking the appropriate box in the evaluation form:

1 = strongly disagree
5 = strongly agree

The group

	1	2	3	4	5

- All members had a clear idea of what was to be achieved.
- The group approached the problem methodically.
- All members of the group co-operated fully.
- The group had a leader.
- There were no conflicts.
- The group arrived at genuine consensus.
- The group performed to its full potential.
- Members listened thoughtfully to one another.
- The group achieved its aim.
- The group would alter its approach the next time round.

Self

	1	2	3	4	5

- I was fully committed to the task.
- I made a positive contribution towards the solution.
- I could have solved the problem better on my own.
- The task has taught me something useful about groups.
- I expressed my opinions clearly and firmly.
- I listened carefully to the views of others.
- I tend to play the same role in any group I join.
- I would like to improve my interactive skills.

7.2.1 ROLES, LEADERSHIP, AND CONFLICT

Individuals in small groups fill *roles*. The word may be taken to refer to formal roles such as those of secretary and treasurer but more importantly it applies to those *patterns of behaviour* (see section 2.2.1) that we come to expect of people we meet regularly.

Within groups, certain roles need to be filled. A class is just another group and will offer parts for joker, bully, scapegoat etc. Ask yourself which of these familiar group roles you find yourself playing:

- the information giver
- the opinion giver
- the asker of hard questions
- the morale booster
- the peacemaker
- the compromiser
- the aggressor
- the blocker
- the dominator
- the isolate (i.e. one who stands apart)

The plum role in any group might seem to be that of leader. Groups, whether formal or informal, tend to organise themselves as **hierarchies**, that is, according to **status**, with the leader at the top of the pyramid and those of inferior status forming the base; for example, the civil service, some churches and the army organise themselves in hierarchies.

Leadership brings responsibilities as well as power, status, or privilege. Its pressures include the constant threat of conflict. This may emerge in the form of a challenge to the leader, or it may be a continuing clash of personalities or attitudes among those lower down the scale that threatens the harmony, productivity and even continued existence of the group. Whatever the cause, it is ultimately the responsibility of the leader to resolve the conflict.

It's hard to believe that any leader, however humble the group, could maintain her position for long without possessing uncommon interactive skills.

7.3 Formal meetings

From group problem-solving to a formal meeting is a very short step. Many formal meetings consist of small groups (some say seven is the ideal number) solving problems, often in a fairly informal way. The larger the attendance at a meeting, the more formal it needs to become; rules and procedures are necessary to control a gathering of individuals whose differing aims, demands and interests might otherwise conflict and produce chaos.

This section aims to acquaint you with the basic rules that govern all formal meetings and with the personnel who operate them by setting you the task of holding your own meeting.

Begin by establishing clearly the requirements of task 7.3. Then spend about twenty minutes reading sections 7.3.1–7.3.7, which explain how formal meetings are conducted. Armed with this information, take fifteen minutes to organise the meeting that you will hold in your next session together. (A little time needs to elapse to allow the elected officers to make their preparations.)

TASK 7.3 A

Notice of meeting ...

Organise and hold an **ordinary general meeting** for the full communication group, basing the meeting on an *agenda* related to the genuine concerns of the group. The principal item on the agenda should be the organisation of a social function to mark the end of term *or* Christmas *or* the completion of the course. Other items on the agenda, which should include *any other business*, are at the group's discretion. Time may not permit more than two further items. They may be informally agreed in advance of *the election of officers*. The group, to satisfy the requirements of a formal meeting, should elect a *chairperson, secretary*, and (optional) *treasurer*.

Formal *notice* of the meeting should be issued, a *venue* should be organised and *laid out* by the officers, and the agenda should be distributed before the meeting.

The meeting itself should be conducted on formal lines, with *minutes* kept and *decisions* taken and recorded.

If time and the group leader permit and business is incomplete, a short series of further meetings (say, ten minutes at the start of a session) might be held. You might wish to elect new officers.

Note

While the purpose of this task is served if the group simulates a meeting, in practice the exercise becomes more interesting and meaningful if the meeting can be geared to the real concerns of the group. For example, you might wish to act as a pressure group on a local issue or to air grievances, to solve a perceived problem, or to negotiate a change in conditions or practices.

7.3.1 TYPES OF MEETING

One way of classifying meetings is according to the purposes for which they are called, the type of people who attend, and the frequency with which they are held. Here are five common types:

Type	Frequency	Purpose	Attendance
Annual general meeting (AGM)	Once yearly	To review past year and elect officers	All members or shareholders may attend
Ordinary general meeting	Weekly/monthly/quarterly	To transact routine business of organisation	As above
Extraordinary meeting	When required	To deal with one specific topic or issue	May be all members or a selection (e.g. committee)
Committee	Regularly (e.g. weekly/monthly)	To act, as authorised, on behalf of parent body, including making decisions	Only committee members may attend

| Mass/public | When required | To mobilise support for a particular campaign | Any member of the public |

A student council is like a committee in that it is usually a small group, elected by the full student body, that meets regularly to discuss matters relating to the welfare of all students. However, it is not generally a true committee, because it does not have the power to reach and implement decisions that may affect all members of the educational institution. In effect it is an *advisory* or *consultative* body—that is, it may make recommendations to those with genuine executive power or it may be consulted by them before decision-taking.

7.3.2 WHY HOLD A MEETING?

'Why indeed?' you might wonder, emerging from yet another frustrating, bad-tempered or inconclusive session. It's easy to be cynical: 'Meetings are composed of people who individually can do nothing and who collectively decide that nothing can be done.'

Meetings are held—
- to communicate information—e.g. releasing information at a news conference or receiving information at a briefing session
- to generate ideas on solving problems—e.g. 'think tanks', the Forum for Peace and Reconciliation
- to promote a sense of corporate or co-operative identity—e.g. party conferences
- to negotiate—e.g. management meeting unions to negotiate settlement of pay claims; and, yes, *sometimes*,
- to make decisions!

A well-conducted meeting will probably realise a number of these aims, promoting good communications, heightening job satisfaction, defusing potential conflict etc.

On the other hand, meetings may
- delay (deliberately?) decision-taking
- be costly
- waste time
- cause disagreement and frustration.

Very basic factors, such as venue and time, can make or break a meeting. A study group that had been lively and responsive in the morning session might be sluggish and sleepy after lunch. A small group might feel lost and cold in a huge, draughty, badly lit hall and as a consequence participate listlessly, taking hasty, ill-considered decisions in its eagerness to escape.

In arranging your meeting, carefully consider the layout of the room. The way furniture is arranged can stimulate or inhibit interaction, can create atmosphere, and set tone.

There are said to be at least thirty possible arrangements for a meeting, including 'freestyle' (seats scattered randomly) and 'classroom' (chairperson in teacher's place, facing rows of seats). You might like to consider the pros and cons of these four alternatives:

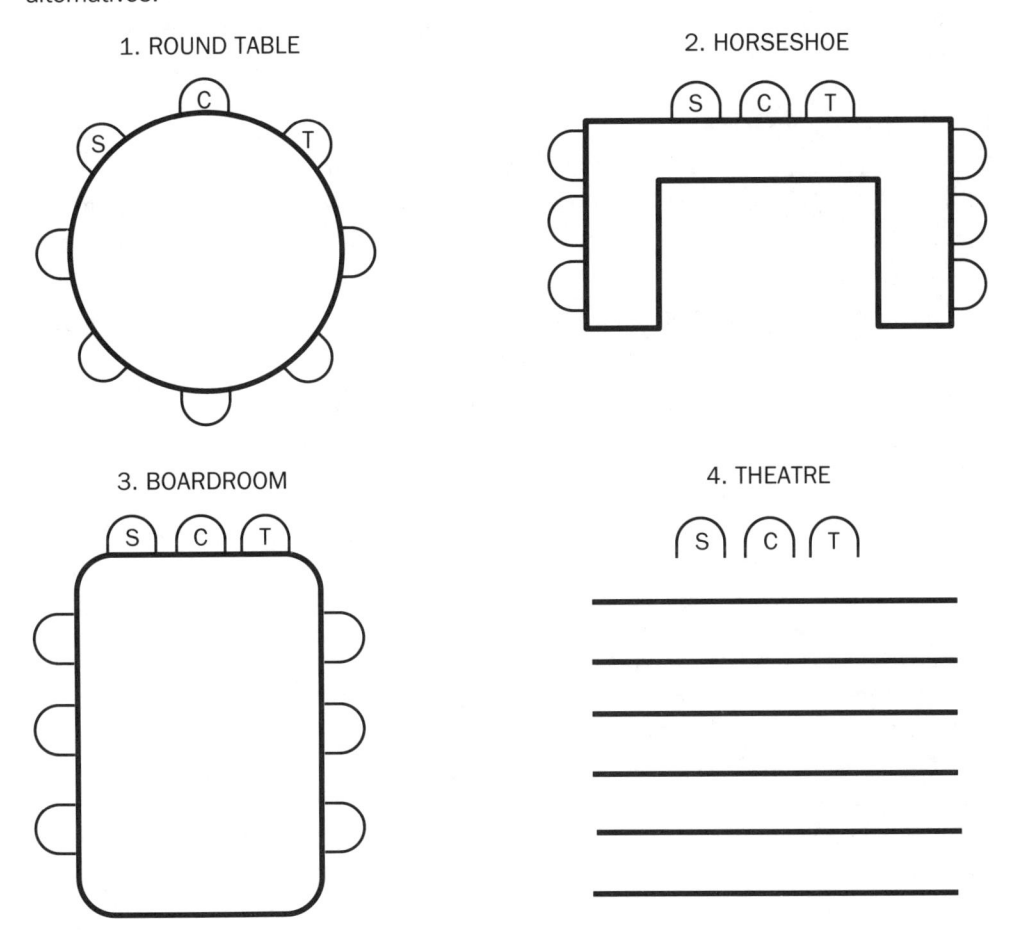

1. ROUND TABLE

2. HORSESHOE

3. BOARDROOM

4. THEATRE

C: chairperson
S: secretary
T: treasurer

Note that the secretary usually sits on the right of the chairperson, with the treasurer on the left.

7.3.3 DISCIPLINE

An effective meeting, formal or informal, is virtually impossible unless all present agree to abide by *four* simple rules:
(1) to obey the chair at all times
(2) to seek the chair's permission to speak

(3) to refrain from interrupting
(4) to address all remarks to the chair.

Speaking 'through the chair' may at first feel artificial but it is a *practical* measure, ensuring audibility for all present, depersonalising disagreement, and enhancing the chair's status.

7.3.4 NOTICE AND AGENDA

It is the secretary's responsibility to issue adequate notice of a forthcoming meeting to all who are entitled to attend. This is normally done by a brief letter that incorporates an agenda:

Dear member,

The next meeting of the Student Council will be held at 3 p.m. on Tuesday 25 October 1996 in the College Library. The agenda is given below.

Yours faithfully,

Deirdre McEvoy

Secretary

St Ann's College of Commerce
Student Council
Agenda

1. Apologies for absence
2. Minutes of previous meeting
3. Matters arising from the minutes
4. Correspondence
5. Treasurer's report
6. Canteen overcrowding
7. Any other business
8. Date of next meeting

The agenda is a list of topics to be discussed at the meeting. It is usually drawn up by the secretary and chairperson (which may give them considerable power). If issued, as above, with the notice of the meeting it will allow members to prepare opinions and 'do their homework'.

The specimen agenda above follows a time-honoured pattern. You might note that even if the minutes of the previous meeting have been circulated in advance (they are often sent out with the notice and agenda) it may be desirable to have them read aloud by the secretary, since there will always be those who neglect homework. After the reading aloud a common formula is:

CHAIRPERSON: May I sign these minutes as a true and accurate record of our last meeting?
ALL: Yes.
CHAIRPERSON: Those against? [*Silence*] In that case ... [*chairperson signs and dates*]

Under item 3 of the sample agenda, members have the opportunity to question or report progress, comment on inaccuracy, etc.

'Any other business' gives an opportunity for any member to raise any issue relevant to the meeting.

7.3.5 ROLE OF THE CHAIRPERSON

The chairperson's role is easily the most important at any meeting. Ideally the chairperson is 'invisible' yet fully in control. An inexperienced chairperson may feel the need to dominate but the role is that of servant rather than master. A bad meeting is one at which a dictatorial chairperson's voice and opinions monopolise; almost as bad is an anonymous chairperson who allows the proceedings to drift aimlessly and endlessly towards chaos.

Ten basic tips for the novice chairperson
(1) Ensure that all agenda items are dealt with in the allotted time.
(2) Decide *in advance* roughly what time should be spent on each item, and stick to it!
(3) Actively encourage participation, drawing out the faint-hearted.
(4) Ensure that discussion is *relevant*.
(5) Maintain order: no interruptions, no private conversations, all contributions 'through the chair'.
(6) Ensure decision-making, preferably through consensus but by vote if necessary.
(7) Remain at all times impartial, and avoid speechifying.
(8) Be firm but friendly.
(9) Assist the secretary's note-taking by controlling the pace and summarising at intervals.
(10) Stay on 'red alert' throughout the proceedings!

The chairperson should give some thought to the manner in which he or she opens and closes the meeting. The chairperson can set the tone of what follows by a brisk, business-like yet warm and welcoming introduction, with humorous touches, while a closure that includes a thank-you for the group's co-operation, time and effort will end the meeting on a positive note.

7.3.6 ROLES OF THE SECRETARY AND TREASURER

If the chairperson is the meeting's principal servant, the secretary is the servant's servant. The pair must work closely together from the compilation of the agenda to the end of the meeting.

The secretary works before, during and after the meeting. **Beforehand** the secretary should
- issue the notice, agenda, and minutes of the previous meeting
- prepare relevant documents—e.g. correspondence
- check the suitability of the venue and room layout.

During the meeting the secretary should

- circulate an attendance sheet, together with any necessary documents
- read the minutes
- read any correspondence
- make notes for the minutes
- support, advise and guide the chairperson.

Afterwards the secretary should
- write a new set of minutes, using notes
- deal with correspondence
- carry out the instructions of the meeting.

You may decide that your needs do not include a treasurer, though social functions usually involve a financial outlay! A treasurer's brief will include
- management of funds (including collection of subscriptions etc.)
- keeping accounts
- reporting on current financial status
- advising on financial matters.

7.3.7 MINUTES

Minutes should be a brief, accurate, unbiased, factual record of what was said and decided at a meeting. They are essential to the smooth and efficient administration of meetings and organisations; they encourage accountability and transparency by clearly recording who said what and whose responsibility it is to undertake further action.

Narrative (or summary) minutes, which provide a very brief account of the discussion leading to a decision followed by a record of the decision itself, may best suit your needs. Use the following sample as a model:

MINUTES
of the meeting of
ST ANN'S COLLEGE OF COMMERCE
STUDENT COUNCIL
held on 11 October 1996 at 3 p.m. in the Library

Present: Eddie Molloy (chairperson), Deirdre McEvoy (secretary), Ruairí McCarthy (staff), Wes Hutchinson (staff), Declan O'Donovan, Oliver Fox, Eileen Horgan, Clíona French, Geoff Emerson.

Apologies: Kevin O'Sullivan, Teresa Loane.

1. MINUTES OF THE PREVIOUS MEETING

Minutes of the meeting held on 28 September 1996 were read and signed.

2. MATTERS ARISING

Mr Hutchinson stated that the staff had accepted the recommendation of the Student Council that a card phone be installed in the Blue Corridor. An order had been placed with Telecom Éireann.

3. CORRESPONDENCE

The secretary read three letters from charitable bodies seeking assistance from students as flag day collectors. After a brief discussion of potential disruption of studies it was suggested that the secretary reply to the charities, pointing out that the college annually undertakes an intensive week of fund-raising. The council regretted its inability to assist and wished the charities well.

4. STUDENT SMOKING AREA

Declan O'Donovan requested that a smoking area be provided for students. A number of conflicting views was expressed. Those supporting the proposal argued

(a) that such a facility was available in other local educational establishments (Oliver Fox);
(b) that students had a legal right to indulge this habit (Oliver Fox);
(c) that in practice 'smoking areas' already existed and would merely be legitimised (Eileen Horgan);
(d) that the 'decriminalisation' of smoking would remove some of the practice's attraction (Eileen Horgan).

Those opposing argued

(a) that such a facility would run counter to all current trends (Mr McCarthy);
(b) that it would send confusing signals to the student body, given the existence of health education courses (Mr McCarthy);
(c) that it would lead students to start smoking (Deirdre McEvoy);
(d) that it would damage the college's reputation in the community (Mr Hutchinson).

It was agreed that a sub-committee (Declan O'Donovan, Clíona French, Oliver Fox) should ascertain the degree of support among students for the proposal and report back to the next meeting.

5. COLLEGE HEATING

Under AOB, Eileen Horgan suggested that a recommendation be made to the staff that the college central heating be turned on forthwith. A clear majority supporting Ms Horgan, Mr McCarthy agreed to convey the recommendation.

6. DATE OF NEXT MEETING

There being no further business, the meeting closed at 3:50 p.m., and the next meeting was set for 25 October 1996.

7.3.8 DECISION-MAKING

Getting a decision may be a real problem at a meeting. Every chairperson dreams of decisions magically emerging by consensus but it doesn't always happen. What are the alternatives?

- Setting up a sub-committee—often cynically seen as a means of permanently shelving a decision.
- Adjournment—in effect, postponing a decision to allow further discussion, consideration, or consultation; sometimes a useful solution to heated disagreement.

- Voting—used sparingly, since it can prove divisive. If a vote is taken, it is *essential* that all present be clear on the motion. Abstention is always possible.

The chairperson doesn't normally vote, unless there's a tie, in which case the chairperson should vote to break the deadlock *or* rule that the status quo be maintained, i.e. that the proposal be defeated. In your meeting, aim for consensus. It may take longer to achieve but the advantage is that ordinary members will be more supportive of the decision.

A successful meeting requires the active participation of *all* present. This doesn't mean members speaking just for the sake of speaking. It does mean listening intently, judging the moment to intervene, sticking to the subject, explaining fully and clearly your opinion (a single, tentative, incomplete sentence contributes little), making a mini-speech containing a cluster of perhaps two or three related points—in short, practising many of the skills encountered in chapters 4 and 5.

Have a good meeting; and remember, once it is over, to hold an *immediate* post-mortem, evaluating what worked and what didn't.

7.4 BEING INTERVIEWED

From our tenderest years we are subjected to interviews. We are interviewed (along with parents) for admission to schools; once there we are interviewed about academic performance, misbehaviour, posts of responsibility, career intentions etc. Interviews are set up to exchange information, to counsel, to select, to solve problems, and to entertain a mass audience. We are hired (and sometimes fired) through interview.

This section concentrates on the hiring (or employment) interview. Most of us find any formal interview process stressful. When the prize is a highly desirable job, the tensions may be considerable; thoughtful preparation will remove some of the stress and improve your prospects of success. The best preparation is to undergo a mock interview (task 7.4.2 A).

7.4.1 THE EMPLOYER'S AIMS

The employer has, on paper, a wealth of information about the applicant—typically, a completed application form, together with the candidate's CV and covering letter, backed up by references from school or college and a previous employer (chapter 9 deals with the documents). If you have been called to interview you have probably made it to a short-list. What further information does the employer want?

In the limited time available, the employer wants to put a face and personality to the paper credentials. What clues can she find to help her make an intelligent 'guesstimate' of your strength of character, warmth, motivation, ambition, interest in the job—all those aspects that simply can't be got from an impersonal CV? The employer will have in mind the profile of an ideal candidate; how do *you* match that profile when viewed alongside the other short-listed applicants?

Hiring is a guessing game. For the employer, meeting the candidate may remove some of the unknowns and permit a better-informed guess. As with all human interaction, information communicated non-verbally (through dress, posture, facial expression, gesture etc.) vitally affects judgment.

7.4.2 COPING WITH INTERVIEWS

The applicant may see the interview as the final hurdle; but it is also a chance to find out more about the job. Even if no offer of a job is made, more will have been learned about the interview process.

That process, for the applicant, breaks down into three stages:

Before
- Find out as much as you can about the organisation and the job: you may be asked about both. If possible, pump a current employee for information.
- Know your own CV inside out. Seek out areas you feel would be worth highlighting.
- Find out how to get to the place of the interview and plan to be there with at least fifteen minutes to spare.
- Plan how to present yourself: dress, hairstyle etc. The standard advice is that you should dress more or less as you expect to find your interviewer dressed.
- Prepare any documents you need: portfolio, project, reports, references etc. Package documents to their best advantage.
- You will almost certainly be invited to ask your own questions, so be sure to have some ready—preferably ones you'd really like answered. Ask job-centred rather than self-centred questions. You may wish to discover more about working conditions, the people you'd be working with, hours, overtime, training, responsibilities, salary, promotion, what happens next ...
- Think about how you would answer such old interview favourites as
—'Why have you applied for this job?'
—'What have you to offer our firm?'
—'What are your ambitions?'
—'Is there anything else you'd like us to take into account?'
- Think about how you will cope with all the non-verbal aspects, from the seating arrangements and the introductions to the final handshake and exit. What impression do you want to give of your personality?
- Arrange a dry run with a competent interviewer.

During
- 'Best behaviour' manners are advisable, including being prepared to return a handshake at the start and finish, not sitting until invited to, etc. Being formal need *not* stop you smiling!
- The first three minutes are crucial: during them the interviewer can't help making judgments that will be hard to dislodge later. If you seem polite, warm, friendly and sincere at first, the impression may stick. Everything you studied in chapter 3 is relevant; take particular care—

(*a*) to sit in a way that suggests alertness, attentiveness, and enthusiasm;

(*b*) to make eye contact with your interviewers;

(*c*) to control nervous mannerisms (with feet, hands etc.).

- Interviews are conducted through *the spoken word*. All your training from chapter 4 should be of value. Remember

(*a*) if you're nervous, take deep breaths before entering;

(*b*) speak audibly and clearly: at no time should your interviewer have to ask you to repeat;

(*c*) aim for fluency, avoiding fillers.

- Avoid monosyllabic replies. Interviewers use 'open' questions to get you to talk: e.g.

Closed: 'Did you find your communications course useful?' (Answer could be simply 'Yes' or 'No.')

Open: 'Talk to me about your communications course.' (Answer: 'I found it very helpful because ...')

- While giving *full* answers, stick to the point. In an effort to please, interviewees sometimes waffle on ... and on ...
- Be honest and open. If you don't know an answer, say, 'I'm sorry, I don't know the answer to that question.' If you don't understand a question, ask to have it explained more fully.
- Listen intently. When nervous, we sometimes 'snatch' at the question and hear selectively. Don't be afraid to pause for a moment before answering: give yourself time to think.
- Aim to speak fairly formally, avoiding slang. As with dress, match the tone set by the interviewer.
- Use your own prepared questions, listen to the answers, and don't be afraid to ask supplementary questions. Remember, you will be judged partly by the intelligence of your questions.
- Don't fully relax until you're out of *sight and earshot!*

After

- Analyse and evaluate. Remember, it's a human tendency to replay reality in a more flattering light. Keep a *written* record of your performance. Assess yourself honestly under such headings as:
- My appearance
- My entrance
- My non-verbal communication
- My good answers
- My problem answers
- My listening
- My questioning
- Tricky questions
- My exit
- Memo to myself: In future ...

Store your written self-assessment in your job-search file (see section 9.1.1), together with all other documents relating to this particular application.

TASK 7.4.2 A

Mock interviewing

Find a genuine job advertisement for a post that is directly related to your vocational area. Persuade three volunteers to apply for the post, submitting CVs and covering letters. Appoint from the group a panel of five interviewers, of whom one should be the group leader or chairperson. The panel should meet briefly to arrange an interviewing strategy—e.g. interviewer 1 might 'break the ice' and lead questioning on the applicant's school career, interviewer 2 on PLC career, interviewer 3 on experience of the world of work, interviewer 4 on personal circumstances and interests, interviewer 5 on general matters—e.g. aims, ambitions, motivation. The panel should aim to ask 'open' questions (those beginning 'Tell us about', 'How', 'Why') and be prepared to answer candidates' questions.

Non-participating group members should take notes throughout and provide the applicants with constructive evaluative comments at the end.

You might wish to record the interviews on audio or videotape.

We continue to think of the job selection interview as the traditional one-to-one meeting in an employer's office, despite increasing evidence that employers are seeking new ways of assessing candidates. Interview by panel has long been commonplace; in an industry that contains far fewer jobs than job-seekers, the group interview (where groups of candidates are assessed simultaneously) is sometimes used as a preliminary screening device. From the applicant's point of view it makes sense to find out, as soon as possible, as much as possible about the kind of interview he or she will be given.

Supplementary tasks

1. Research the meaning of the following terms often used in connection with meetings: quorum, motion, proxy, ex officio, co-opt, ad hoc committee, chairperson's agenda, point of order, point of information.
2. 'The rules and regulations governing meetings sometimes seem tiresome and petty, but the truth is that without them meetings would achieve very little.' Write a short essay discussing this statement.
3. The following items appear on the agenda of a student council meeting at which you act as secretary:
    (a) Shortage of locker provision
    (b) Rag Day
    (c) Request for student recreation facilities.
    Write the section of the minutes dealing with these items. You will have to use your imagination!

4. Prepare an oral response to the following interview question: 'How do you see the role you typically play in any group situation?'

Chapter review
1. List some common reasons for forming groups.
2. Describe a selection (say, five) of the stereotypical roles played in groups.
3. What are the commonest causes of conflict in a group?
4. Explain each of the following: primary group, extraordinary meeting, notice, agenda, minutes, open question.
5. List five practical steps to take in preparing for a job interview.

PART 3

WORDS WE WRITE

8 IN MY OWN WRITE: PERSONAL WRITING

SIX PERIODS (MINIMUM)

8.1 THE WRITTEN WORD

Of the four language arts, writing is the one we practise least. According to some estimates, in the lives of up to half the world's population, writing figures not at all, because they are illiterate; some of the world's 6,000 languages simply don't exist in written form. In Britain, a study in 1992 suggested that about 6 million British adults were 'functionally illiterate'—able to sign their names or write a simple message but incapable of, for instance, following up a job ad in writing. UNESCO has designated the year 2000 as the date by which illiteracy will be abolished throughout the world; there seems little likelihood of this target being achieved.

Broadly, we use writing in two distinct ways:

- to make meanings, to ourselves and others, about *personal experience* (**personal writing**)
- to make and take meanings as individuals functioning in a variety of *social contexts that include the world of work* (**functional writing**).

We ought to be able to communicate effectively in writing, whether confiding our innermost feelings to a private diary or publicising an event or product to a mass audience. A communications course should provide opportunities for trying out a range of forms and styles that best conduct meanings about ourselves. Equally, it should make clear the conventions that govern the written word when it is used in a formal context, such as a business letter or an agenda (chapters 9 and 10).

A *written project* and an *oral presentation* are often the twin peaks of communications courses. You, the student, may be asked to write a project consisting of a couple of thousand words, and wonder where on earth to begin. Chapter 11 contains practical guidelines.

Between the sender and receiver of a written message there is sometimes confusion. Generally this is caused by the sender's uncertainty in spelling or punctuation—though handwriting, too, may create noise in the channel. Misunderstandings arise when sender and receiver write and read different meanings into the same word—when, in effect, the language code breaks down. If you wish to brush up basic skills, you will find chapter 12 helpful.

The virtues of good *speech* are also those of good *writing*. You might test this by occasionally reading aloud specimens of your written work to the group or by devoting a whole session to the oral delivery of selected written pieces. A piece of writing needs *structure* as much as any speech. A speech needs a *tone* suited to the occasion and audience; so does a letter. Above all, in writing as in speech, if you fail to prepare, you should prepare to fail!

8.1.1 Defining personal writing

Does personal writing *belong* on a communications course? Surely 'personal' means 'written for self', and isn't communication all about *sharing* meanings?

Personal writing may certainly be likened to having a conversation with yourself on paper—a *written* form of *intra*personal communication. Many people find that such writing (e.g. keeping a diary) fulfils a need to express feelings, to define ideas, to record experience, to get something out of their system; some take pleasure in using words well—as in writing a poem. Personal writing may even serve as a kind of therapy.

Personal writing is *based* on Person's experience, but there's no rule that it must be produced solely for Person's consumption. Poetry sometimes lets us see the poet's deepest feelings on matters that most of us would regard as very private, and yet it was evidently intended for *public* consumption—a 'letter to the world', as Emily Dickinson called her own intensely private work.

Personal writing could be defined as writing about Person's own experience that he or she is willing to share with Other(s). It may take many forms:

diary	letter
memoir	review
autobiography	poetry
biography	prose poem
anecdote	monologue
short story	dialogue
reportage	play script
travelogue	personal essay
sermon	song lyric

Options include combinations of these (e.g. diary incorporating song lyric). Experiment. Be adventurous!

8.1.2 Writing as communicated personality

By its very nature, personal writing reveals quite a lot of your personality. In effect, you are meeting and interacting with another person on *paper*. When you pick up a novel by an unfamiliar author you are *meeting* that writer for the first time.

Picture somebody opening a letter from a stranger. That quick first glance at the sheet is like the 'first impression' the interviewer takes of an applicant entering the room. The sheet may give an impression of organisation, orderliness, and neatness. You don't have to be a graphologist to receive some impression of personality traits from handwriting. The way you present your script is almost as important as the way you present yourself.

What you write (the *matter*) and *how* you write it (the *manner*) tell your reader a great deal about you. You might come across as an opinionated, well-informed person with a sly sense of humour and a clear mind, or you might be perceived as honest, open, sincere, not terribly bright but very earnest and likeable. As *readers* we can't help making judgments, because writing, particularly personal writing, is *communicated personality*.

We like to create a favourable impression face-to-face; to do the same on paper you will have to go through the sequence that underlies all effective written communication:

(1) Think and observe.
(2) Make notes.
(3) Draft a rough version.
(4) Compose a polished version.
(5) Proof-read and present.

What is entailed in these stages is best discovered by doing. You may feel that you've done it all before throughout your school career. Console yourself that the greatest writers spend their lives doing it, because they know it's the way to get good results.

It isn't possible to illustrate the full range of personal writing in one chapter. Instead, you will find a practical *method* that may be used whatever your choice of form. You will have the opportunity to test this method in one or more of five common forms.

Personal writing consists of a series of *choices*:

- Choice of **subject** (*what* will I write about?)
- Choice of **form** (*how* should I write—in prose or verse, in narrative or dialogue?)
- Choice of **words** (*which* words best convey what I want to say?)
- Choice of **punctuation, layout, script** (e.g. manuscript or typescript?)

The sum of these choices communicates much about your personality.

8.1.3 Assembling the raw material

Here's a simple way to try out the first two stages of the sequence outlined above:

> **TASK 8.1.3 A**

Thought cascade

Write down *as fast as possible* whatever thoughts come into your head over the next fifteen minutes. Thoughts will flash through your mind and you won't be able to capture them all, however fast you write. Don't waste time worrying about spelling, punctuation, handwriting, continuity, or correctness: the aim is to spill the contents of your mind onto paper. Nobody else will ever read what you write.

Don't worry if your thoughts at first seem to trickle. Relax and the trickle will become a cascade. Enjoy it!

You now have to hand stage 2 notes, the *raw material* for a piece of polished writing entitled, say, 'Thoughts in a classroom' or 'The inside of my head'. The purpose of the exercise was to demonstrate the *method* of note-making.

Spend a few minutes discussing what it felt like to write *spontaneously*. Students often say they found it exhilarating but exhausting—and surprisingly easy to cover paper. Note that the technique can be applied to virtually any topic. You could have a 'memory cascade' or 'fears cascade', or you could narrow the focus to specific memories or fears.

8.2 USING THE SENSES

This section is centred on one task, which should, if worked through, result in a finished piece of personal writing.

> **TASK 8.2 A**

The doors

Most of us spend most of our time with the doors of perception barely ajar. This task requires you to throw them wide open.

Following this briefing, each member of the group, armed with pen and writing pad, should go to a specified place somewhere in the school or college. (Some prior arranging may be necessary.) Possible locations might be a classroom where a practical class is taking place, a library, a canteen, a science lab or workshop, a kitchen, a corridor, or an office. Spend fifteen minutes 'on location', observing and recording (in writing) as fully as possible the evidence of the senses: sights, sounds, smells, tastes, touch. Aim to be an extraordinarily sensitive 'sense recorder' that misses *nothing*.

As in the previous task, speed, fullness and spontaneity are much more important than handwriting, spelling, punctuation etc. Only you, the recorder, will see the resulting notes.

This time you have to hand a cascade of *sense* impressions, raw material that you will spend the rest of the session processing into a rough version.

Your notes at present are an incoherent jumble, possibly illegible to anybody else; they would communicate little to a reader. The next stage of the sequence is to begin composing your private, personal impressions into a form in which they will make meanings to others. Your notes, when composed, could powerfully evoke a particular place at a particular time.

First, read your notes *with the eyes of another person*. What help might that person need to make sense of what you've written? For example, *where* is all this happening? Would a title help?

Next, be ruthlessly self-critical. Which of your jottings capture accurately the evidence of your senses? Is there *repetition*? Which bits need *improvement*? Is there any *pattern* in your observations? Any *shape*, however faint?

Composing your notes is like arranging a basket of flowers to make a floral display. Stuck haphazardly into a vase, the flowers, however beautiful in themselves, would probably not earn a second glance. They need to be sorted, trimmed, and artfully shaped according to some design the arranger hopes to achieve.

TASK 8.2 B

Rough drafting

Having studied your notes, draft a rough attempt at a composition. Keep in mind an average reader whose interest you must attract and hold. You have complete freedom to add, subtract, rewrite, alter, and rearrange. Keep in mind your aim: *to re-create in writing your experience of a particular place at a specific time.*

Spend fifteen minutes making your rough version.

During this session you have observed, noted, and made a rough version. You now need to distance yourself from the experience and your records of it. It might also help to get the a reader's quick reaction to your rough version: another member of the group or the group leader might oblige. In any case, allow a day or two to pass before moving on to stage 4—the fully composed, polished version.

TASK 8.2 C

Kilroy was here

Assuming time has passed since the rough draft, complete the fourth stage of the sequence. Critically re-read your rough version. Once again you have complete freedom to add, subtract, rearrange, rewrite. As you re-read, be particularly alert to improvements you might make in *layout*. For example, does your paragraphing help to make meaning? Are there ways in which you can *lay out* your writing creatively? Don't be easily satisfied. Generally, it's a *bad* sign if your polished version is pretty much the same as your notes or rough draft. Given time, a more expressive word may occur, or a more elegant shape to a sentence may suggest itself.

When you are satisfied, make a fair copy of your polished version. 'Fair' means neatly presented, imaginatively laid out, and clearly handwritten or faultlessly typed or word-processed. Make sure to supply a title and author's name.

Now carry out the final stage: *proof-reading*. This means checking for accuracy, not tinkering further with content. You need to check that words aren't omitted, that punctuation is present and correct, that spelling is accurate. One way to proof-read is to read aloud, slowly and expressively, what you have written. At the same time run your pen like a finger along the line, pointing at each word as you speak it. Listen to your own voice rising, falling, pausing, stopping; it may be very revealing about the placing of full stops and commas. You are now ready to present!

8.3 Using memory

This section suggests ways in which you might mine your *memories* as a source of personal writing.

An obvious possibility is to repeat, with minor modifications, the technique you used with your senses.

TASK 8.3 A

I remember, I remember ...

1. (*a*) Start with a fifteen-minute cascade, jotting down as fast as possible *any* memories that come into your mind. One thing will lead to another ...

    (*b*) Pause and re-read what you have written. Choose *one* memory in your list that really interests you and that might interest others. Spend fifteen minutes jotting down *everything* you can recall about your selected memory. Draw on your sense memories. Put the work aside for a time.

2. Draft a rough version, always keeping in mind the need to make what is *private* into *public* property. Remember that *details* make work 'live' for the reader. Remember, too, all the usual tips for successful composition, such as having an attention-grabbing opening and *varying* the form wherever possible (e.g. incorporating snatches of dialogue). Would *verse* be a better medium than *prose*?

3. Polish up the rough draft, giving the piece an appropriate title.

4. Proof-read and present.

Another method might involve keeping a diary. Each night for a week have a memory cascade on the day's events. (Alternatively, use ten minutes at the start of five successive classes to jot down memories of the previous day.) Events include thoughts, feelings, and changes in relationships.

At the end of the week, study your entries. This is the raw material, which you might process in a variety of ways. For example, you could compose it under the title 'A life in the week of ...' This would involve selecting the typical weekly activities from the entries and arranging them to serve as a window through which the reader could look into your 'life and times'.

Or you might select a day that, looking back, was representative of all the other days in the week. By adding new material and subtracting from what is there you might arrive at 'A life in the day of ...' The *ordinary* doings of *ordinary* people can be riveting!

Or you might pick just *one* event or episode from the week that seems to you to sum up your whole life at the moment. Explore the reasons why it seems so typical. Could it be worked up into a piece entitled 'Story of my life'?

From autobiography you might like to move on to biography—providing a window through which to look into somebody else's world. Pick somebody you know really well. Don't attempt to tell the *full* life history: focus on a period or phase of your subject's life with which you are very familiar and show what led up to it and what resulted from it (if that is known). Beware of allowing the spotlight to fall on yourself.

8.4 USING DIALOGUE

Dialogue may be the medium through which you wish to express yourself—pure dialogue as in a play script, or dialogue mixed with another form, such as narrative or verse.

Before dialogue comes **monologue**, in which we hear the voice of a *single* speaker. A monologue that may happen *inside* the head is the stream of *unspoken* thoughts that flow endlessly through our minds—'mentalese', as Steven Pinker calls them (*The Language Instinct*, p. 55–82). The finished product of task 8.2 C could have been called an interior monologue or stream-of-consciousness writing.

A first step to writing dialogue might be to invent a monologue spoken by a real person of your acquaintance or an invented character based on a real person.

TASK 8.4 A

Monologue

Choose a person you know really well. Spend a couple of minutes trying to hear your subject's voice inside your own head. Close your eyes if that helps. What topics do you regularly hear that voice speaking about—complaining, scolding, planning, gossiping?

Listen to the voice making one of its typical statements, and then start recording on paper what you hear. Be sure to catch your subject's speech habits and mannerisms.

When you make your polished version you may need to write in extra lines to help your reader understand *where* the monologue is delivered and at what time. Your speaker may be engaged in an activity. All this information should emerge *naturally* from the lines. It is also possible to suggest the presence and reactions or responses of a listener. Remember how, when listening to *one* side of a phone conversation, we can supply the unheard voice.

When writing dialogue, it helps to have a 'good ear'. There's not much difference between oral mimicry and the task you've just completed. It's like writing down a well-rehearsed and often-performed take-off of a former teacher.

In starting to write dialogue it would be wise to restrict yourself to *two* characters, perhaps choosing people well known to you (e.g. two neighbours). A period of work experience might have featured conversations that have stuck in your mind. For many students, work experience is a time of heightened awareness—of self, of others, of environment—and recollections of people and incidents may be a fertile source of personal writing.

TASK 8.4 B

Dialogue

Invent or reproduce a slice of realistic conversation between *two* people. Try to bring out, in the words spoken, the characters of your individuals and the nature of the relationship between them. A situation containing *conflict* usually leads to lively dialogue. Avoid the temptation to overload your script with *stage directions*: make the spoken words do the work. Follow the layout of a drama text:

TITLE
Author's name
Names of characters (and short description)
Setting and time

FIRST SPEAKER'S NAME: Opening line of dialogue.
SECOND SPEAKER'S NAME: Note the absence of quotation marks. [*Stage directions are usually enclosed in brackets, as here.*]

Students sometimes seem to feel that punctuation is optional when it comes to writing dialogue. The reverse is true: the reader or actor *must* be told whether the line is a statement, question, or exclamation.

It is, of course, possible to write a poem that consists of dialogue:

'Ah, he was a grand man.'
'He was: he fell out of the train going to Sligo.'
'He did: he thought he was going to the lavatory.'
'He did: in fact he stepped out the rear door of the train.'
'He did: God, he must have got an awful fright.'
'He did: he saw it wasn't the lavatory at all.'
'He did: he saw that it was the railway tracks going away from him.'
'He did: I wonder if … but he was a grand man …'

Paul Durcan ('Tullynoe: Tête-à-tête in the Parish Priest's Parlour')

You might enjoy trying your hand at something similar, starting (as this poet does) from a stereotypical situation and characters.

If you're feeling ambitious, have a go at a sketch or a one-act play. To start, you need two or three characters, a setting, and some disagreement—e.g. an employer in an office interviewing an employee about persistent unpunctuality. A tantalising snippet of conversation overheard at a supermarket check-out or on a bus or train might be enough to get you going.

8.5 USING REPORTAGE

Reportage involves passing on information. We associate the activity primarily with newspapers but many forms of personal writing—letters, biography, travelogue etc.—engage in it. We don't expect newspapers to confine themselves to objective, factual reporting. A review of a new television programme may state objectively its format and contents, but we would be surprised and probably disappointed not to find the reviewer's personal opinion of the programme. A newspaper's editorial is unashamedly opinionated.

The dividing line between descriptive writing and reporting is, in places, extremely thin, so if you have a flair for describing, you'll be able to exercise it in this section.

Personal reporting, which is the kind we're concerned with here, means reporting on your personal experiences and observation. It is to be expected that your report will be coloured by your personal beliefs, opinions, and attitudes. Naturally it will contain information; it will also show how you view this information.

The ABC of good *formal* reporting applies equally to personal reporting:

- **Accuracy** is *essential*—the information must be correct and opinions should be honest.
- **Brevity** is *desirable*.
- **Clarity** is *essential*.

The clarity of your reporting is largely a matter of showing consideration for your audience. You have a written message to send—to whom? When framing the message, take into account your receiver's level of maturity, existing knowledge of the topic, likely level of interest etc.

Over and above these virtues your report should be as interesting, stimulating and readable as you can make it. As always, look for a strong start and finish, for the surprising detail, and for the unusual angle.

TASK 8.5 A

The world at work

The basis for this task is the personal observation of the eye-witness (you). Ideally your report should stem from your work experience placement but if this proves difficult an alternative approach is suggested.

(*a*) Write an accurate, clear and lively report of about ten paragraphs on your place of work for a magazine aimed at the 18–24 age bracket. You should draw heavily on your first-hand knowledge. You may need to introduce your readers to the nature of the work carried on. Give information about the working environment, its sights, sounds, and smells, the working personnel, the relationships, the rhythm of the working week or day, and the stresses and satisfactions.

(*b*) Pick a person who made a strong impression on you during your work placement. Under a title such as 'Unforgettable!' write a pen-portrait of your subject that will bring him or her clearly before the reader. Place your subject in the work context, including in your 'report' physical appearance, characteristic activities, habits, mannerisms, overall impression of personality, favourite topics of conversation, and repeated sayings.

(c) Make a 'field trip' to a local workplace, such as a factory, supermarket, courthouse, fire station, newspaper office, or farm. Take notes on the activities and operations carried on in the chosen place. If possible, take photographs and record interviews.

From your eye-witness records compile a report on the visit that will accurately inform the reader and also convey atmosphere and the effect the place had on you.

8.6 Using narrative

Story-telling must be as old as language itself. Despite its long pedigree, it doesn't get any easier to do well.

The first stories were orally transmitted, and the tradition of oral story-telling is still alive and well in societies the world over. You've had the chance to try out your own skills in chapter 4. Television is the dominant mass medium of our age, and most television is really story-telling, whether in the form of a cookery demonstration (always ending happily in a simply delicious dish) or an antiques programme (ending with the few pieces of wormy wood 'magically' transformed into a shining, precious antique).

It is not easy to write a good short story. The main recommendation here is that you begin by basing your narratives very firmly on true *personal* experiences. Choose settings with which you are familiar, construct characters based on people you know, reproduce the kind of speech you're used to hearing from those people, and keep everything as simple as possible—and Roddy Doyle, watch out!

Remember that poems may also tell stories. Indeed, there is much to be learned from ballads hundreds of years old, not least their sparing use of description, concentration on a limited cast of characters, and simplicity of story line. The parables in the New Testament are miracles of economy: the parable of the Good Samaritan in the New English Bible is told in 158 words.

Don't be afraid to model your narratives on the work of writers you admire. Any craft has to be learned and it would be foolish or even arrogant to ignore master-craftspeople, past or present.

In carrying out the task that follows, aim to
- create **characters** who behave and talk like real people of your acquaintance
- devise a **story line** that results from the characters acting characteristically

- ensure that the story has a **structure** (beginning, middle, and end—though they don't have to be in that order!)
- keep the reader in **suspense**, wondering what will happen next
- include at the heart of the story **conflict** (which is as vital to narrative as to drama)
- **vary the form**, bearing in mind that dialogue, for example, may be a very natural and economical way of informing the reader about characters, motivation, atmosphere etc.

TASK 8.6 A

Story time

The central character of your narrative will be the person whose portrait you painted in task 8.5 A (*b*). Put that person in an *imaginary* situation, without placing too much strain on the reader's belief: people win the National Lottery, are suddenly made redundant or are promoted, face crises, are wrongly accused ... If you have difficulty in imagining a situation, re-create a real situation that you know the character has been involved in, even though you didn't witness it. Make sure the situation contains the seeds of conflict, either interpersonal or intrapersonal.

Develop the story in whatever direction it seems probable it might have taken had it happened in reality. Don't overload your story with events or characters.

When you re-read your rough version, see what would happen if you threw away the first third. Is it possible that what you have left, with minor modifications, would be a perfectly adequate story? Throughout your revising, be alert to what might be omitted without loss to the story.

This chapter can do no more than alert you to some varieties of personal writing that you might be tempted to experiment with. The accent has been on personal experience as a promising source of good writing and on a process that involves self-criticism, second thoughts, composing, and revision. Little has been said about poetry as a form, or imagination as a source. And there will always be those who have something they are bursting to communicate, who break all 'rules', ignore all advice, and succeed brilliantly.

Supplementary tasks

(In this chapter an expanded 'Supplementary tasks' section replaces the customary chapter review.)

Here are four passages by well-known authors. They are linked in various ways with the forms of personal writing you've been practising in this chapter. You may wish to discuss their approaches to the problems you're facing; you may want to use them as models; or you may react strongly against them and want to do better yourself.

(1) Trouble in the Works

Harold Pinter

An office in a factory. Mr Fibbs at the desk. A knock at the door. Enter Mr Wills.

FIBBS: Ah, Wills. Good. Come in. Sit down, will you?
WILLS: Thanks, Mr Fibbs.
FIBBS: You got my message?
WILLS: I just got it.
FIBBS: Good. Good. [*Pause.*] Good. Well now … Have a cigar?
WILLS: No, thanks, not for me, Mr Fibbs.
FIBBS: Well, now, Wills, I hear there's been a little trouble in the factory.
WILLS: Yes, I—I suppose you could call it that, Mr Fibbs.
FIBBS: Well, what in heaven's name is it all about?
WILLS: Well, I don't exactly know how to put it, Mr Fibbs.
FIBBS: Now come on, Wills, I've got to know what it is, before I can do anything about it.
WILLS: Well, Mr Fibbs, it's simply a matter that the men have … well, they seem to have taken a turn against some of the products.
FIBBS: Taken a turn?
WILLS: They just don't seem to like them much any more.
FIBBS: Don't like them? But we've got the reputation of having the finest machine part turnover in the country. They're the best-paid men in the industry. We've got the cheapest canteen in Yorkshire. No two menus are alike. We've got a billiard hall, haven't we, on the premises, we've got a swimming pool for use of staff. And what about the long-playing record room? And you tell me they're dissatisfied?
Wills: Oh, the men are very grateful for all the amenities, sir. They just don't like the products.
FIBBS: But they're beautiful products. I've been in the business a lifetime. I've never seen such beautiful products.
WILLS: There it is, sir.
FIBBS: Which ones don't they like?
WILLS: Well, there's the brass petcock, for instance.
FIBBS: The brass petcock? What's the matter with the brass petcock?
WILLS: They just don't seem to like it any more.
FIBBS: But what exactly don't they like about it?
WILLS: Perhaps it's just the look of it.
FIBBS: That brass petcock? But I tell you it's perfection. Nothing short of perfection.
WILLS: They've just gone right off it.
FIBBS: Well, I'm flabbergasted.
WILLS: It's not only the brass petcock, Mr Fibbs.
FIBBS: What else?
WILLS: There's the hemiunibal spherical rod end.

FIBBS: The hemiunibal spherical rod end? Where could you find a finer rod end?
WILLS: There are rod ends and rod ends, Mr Fibbs.
FIBBS: I know there are rod ends and rod ends. But where could you find a finer hemi-unibal spherical rod end?
WILLS: They just don't want to have anything more to do with it.
FIBBS: This is shattering. Shattering. What else? Come on, Wills. There's no point in hiding anything from me.
WILLS: Well, I hate to say it, but they've gone very vicious about the high-speed taper-shank spiral flute-reamers.
FIBBS: The high-speed taper-shank spiral flute-reamers! But that's absolutely ridiculous! What could they possibly have against the high-speed taper-shank spiral flute-reamers?
WILLS: All I can say is they're in a state of very bad agitation about them. And then there's the gunmetal side-outlet relief with handwheel.
FIBBS: What!
WILLS: There's the nippled connector and the nippled adaptor and the vertical mechanical comparator.
FIBBS: No!
WILLS: And the one they can't speak of without trembling is the jaw for Jacob's chuck for use on portable drill.
FIBBS: My own Jacob's chuck? Not my very own Jacob's chuck?
WILLS: They've just taken a turn against the whole lot of them, I tell you. Male elbow adaptors, tubing nuts, grub screws, internal fan washers, dog points, half dog points, white metal bushes—
FIBBS: But not, surely not, my lovely parallel male stud couplings.
WILLS: They hate and detest your lovely parallel male stud couplings, and the straight-flange pump connectors, and back nuts, and front nuts, and the bronze draw-off cock with handwheel and the bronze draw-off cock without handwheel!
FIBBS: Not the bronze draw-off cock with handwheel?
WILLS: And without handwheel.
FIBBS: Without handwheel?
WILLS: And with handwheel.
FIBBS: Not with handwheel?
WILLS: And without handwheel.
FIBBS: Without handwheel?
WILLS: With handwheel *and* without handwheel.
FIBBS: With handwheel *and* without handwheel?
WILLS: With or without!
   [*Pause.*]
FIBBS [*broken*]: Tell me. What do they want to make in its place?
WILLS: Brandy balls.

(*Harold Pinter: Plays 2*, London: Methuen 1981.)

(2) Popular Mechanics

Raymond Carver

Early that day the weather turned and the snow was melting into dirty water. Streaks of it ran down from the little shoulder-high window that faced the back yard. Cars slushed by on the street outside, where it was getting dark. But it was getting dark on the inside too.

He was in the bedroom pushing clothes into a suitcase when she came to the door.

I'm glad you're leaving! I'm glad you're leaving! she said. Do you hear?

He kept on putting things into the suitcase.

Son of a bitch! I'm so glad you're leaving! She began to cry. You can't even look me in the face, can you?

Then she noticed the baby's picture on the bed and picked it up.

He looked at her and she wiped her eyes and stared at him before turning and going back to the living room.

Bring that back, he said.

Just get your things and get out, she said.

He did not answer. He fastened the suitcase, put on his coat, looked around the bedroom before turning off the light. Then he went out to the living room.

She stood in the doorway of the little kitchen, holding the baby.

I want the baby, he said.

Are you crazy?

No, but I want the baby. I'll get someone to come by for his things.

You're not touching this baby, she said.

The baby had begun to cry and she uncovered the blanket from around his head.

Oh, oh, she said, looking at the baby.

He moved towards her.

For God's sake! she said. She took a step back into the kitchen.

I want the baby.

Get out of here! She turned and tried to hold the baby over in a corner behind the stove.

But he came up. He reached across the stove and tightened his hands on the baby.

Let go of him, he said.

Get away, get away! she cried.

The baby was red-faced and screaming. In the scuffle they knocked down a flowerpot that hung behind the stove.

He crowded her into the wall then, trying to break her grip. He held on to the baby and pushed with all his weight.

Let go of him, he said.

Don't, she said. You're hurting the baby, she said.

I'm not hurting the baby, he said.

The kitchen window gave no light. In the near-dark he worked on her fisted fingers with one hand and with the other hand he gripped the screaming baby up under an arm near the shoulder.

She felt her fingers being forced open. She felt the baby going from her.

No! she screamed just as her hands came loose.

She would have it, this baby. She grabbed for the baby's other arm.

She caught the baby round the wrist and leaned back.

But he would not let go. He felt the baby slipping out of his hands and he pulled back very hard.

In this manner, the issue was decided.

(*The Stories of Raymond Carver*, London: Picador 1985.)

(3) 'Down the mine' (1937)

George Orwell

When you go down a coal-mine it is important to try and get to the coal face when the 'fillers' are at work …

The time to go there is when the machines are roaring and the air is black with coal dust, and when you can actually see what the miners have to do. At those times the place is like hell, or at any rate like my own mental picture of hell. Most of the things one imagines in hell are there – heat, noise, confusion, darkness, foul air, and, above all, unbearably cramped space. Everything except the fire, for there is no fire down there except the feeble beams of Davy lamps and electric torches which scarcely penetrate the clouds of coal dust.

When you have finally got there—and getting there is a job in itself: I will explain that in a moment—you crawl through the last line of pit props and see opposite you a shiny black wall three or four feet high. This is the coal face. Overhead is the smooth ceiling made by the rock from which the coal has been cut; underneath is the rock again, so that the gallery you are in is only as high as the ledge of coal itself, probably not much more than a yard. The first impression of all, overmastering everything else for a while, is the frightful, deafening din from the conveyor belt which carries the coal away. You cannot see very far, because the fog of coal dust throws back the beam of your lamp, but you can see on either side of you the line of half-naked kneeling men, one to every four or five yards, driving their shovels under the fallen coal and flinging it swiftly over their left shoulders. They are feeding it onto the conveyor belt, a moving rubber belt a couple of feet wide which runs a yard or two behind them. Down this belt a glittering river of coal races constantly. In a big mine it is carrying away several tons of coal every minute. It bears it off to some place in the main roads where it is shot into tubs holding half a ton, and thence dragged to the cages and hoisted to the outer air.

It is impossible to watch the 'fillers' at work without feeling a pang of envy for their toughness. It is a dreadful job that they do, an almost superhuman job by the standard of an ordinary person. For they are not only shifting monstrous quantities of coal, they are also doing it in a position that doubles or trebles the work. They have got to remain kneeling all the while – they could hardly rise from their knees without hitting the ceiling—and you can easily see by trying it what a tremendous effort this means. Shovelling is comparatively easy when you are standing up, because you can use your knee and thigh to drive the shovel along; kneeling down, the whole of the strain is thrown upon your arm and belly muscles. And the other conditions do not exactly make things easier. There is the heat—it varies, but in some mines it is suffocating—and the coal dust that stuffs up your throat and nostrils and collects along your eyelids, and the unending rattle of the conveyor belt, which in that confined space is rather like the rattle of a machine gun. But the fillers look and work as though they were made of iron. They really do look like iron—hammered iron statues—under the smooth coat of coal dust which clings to them from head to foot. It is only when you see miners down the mine and naked that you realise what splendid men they are. Most of them are small (big men are at a disadvantage in that job) but nearly all of them have the most noble bodies; wide shoulders tapering to slender supple waists, and small pronounced buttocks and sinewy thighs, with not an ounce of waste flesh anywhere. In the hotter mines they wear only a pair of thin drawers, clogs and knee-pads; in the hottest mines of all, only the clogs and knee-pads. You can hardly tell by the look of them whether they are young or old. They may be any age up to sixty or even sixty-five, but when they are black and naked they all look alike. No one could do their work who had not a young man's body, and a figure fit for a guardsman at that; just a few pounds of extra flesh on the waist-line, and the constant bending would be impossible. You can never forget that spectacle once you have seen it—the line of bowed, kneeling figures, sooty black all over, driving their huge shovels under the coal with stupendous force and speed. They are on the job for seven-and-a-half hours, theoretically without a break, for there is no time 'off'. Actually they snatch a quarter of an hour or so at some time during the shift to eat the food they have brought with them, usually a hunk of bread and dripping and a bottle of cold tea. The first time I was watching the 'fillers' at work I put my hand upon some dreadful slimy thing among the coal dust. It was a chewed quid of tobacco. Nearly all the miners chew tobacco, which is said to be good against thirst ...

(*Inside the Whale and Other Essays*, London: Penguin 1962.)

(4) 'A public-house man'

William Trevor

Any weekday suits, he wrote from Hill Street, W1. *Between 10 a.m. and midday, or if you find it more convenient, between three o'clock and five.*

Shortly after midday he went out to lunch, to the Caprice in the days of his splendour, to the Trattoria Toscana later on. Generally he had not returned by three, but his secretary, Mrs Bartlett, would be there, efficiently holding the fort.

Marchant Smith resembled, almost perfectly, an egg placed on top of a much larger egg. A great domed head, mostly hairless, sloped elegantly down to pick up the line of his shoulders. The ovoid continued, the rotund stomach beneath the striped blue cloth of jacket and waistcoat seeming almost corseted. He was, though stout, neatly made all the way down to his notably small feet.

'I don't see why not,' he said one December morning after we had spoken for no more than twenty minutes in his partitioned office, I seeking employment, he empowered to offer it. Five hundred pounds a year, he then apologetically revealed. It wasn't much, not even in 1959.

Marchant Smith was a double-barrelled name without a hyphen, no doubt created by its present bearer. He was known as Marchant among his friends at his own preference, his given Christian name not being to his liking. Notley's—the advertising agency of which he was the copy chief—was the only one that had held out any hope when I tentatively wrote to a number of them to offer my services. A mammoth concern in St James's might have taken me on if I'd agreed to do six months' selling in Selfridge's and another six months on the road. At J. Walter Thompson's I failed the writing test. Only Notley's welcomed my ignorance of the commercial world and of the craft for which I was presenting myself. On 11 January 1960 I reported there for duty ...

(*Excursions in the Real World*, London: Penguin 1993.)

Passages 3 and 4 are extracts from longer essays. Both are well worth reading in their entirety.

9 Doing the Right Thing: Formal Writing

THREE PERIODS

9.1 Defining formal writing

Personal writing thrives on individuality and difference; formal writing asks you to conform to long-established and widely accepted practice. In personal writing you 'do your own thing'; in formal writing you should know what the 'right thing' is and be able to deliver it on request. Formal writing is impersonal, observing recognised codes and standardised usage.

This chapter deals with three formal documents that may be of immediate concern: the application form, the curriculum vitae (CV), and the covering letter that generally accompanies the form or CV.

9.1.1 Job application form

The application form is the opening shot in a campaign to get you 'that job'. Forms tend to follow a standardised pattern:
- personal details (e.g. marital status)
- educational records (exam results etc.)
- employment record (e.g. work experience)
- general information (e.g. hobbies)
- supplementary information (e.g. reasons for seeking this job)
- availability, and names of referees.

Some forms may contain an additional questionnaire, often of the multiple-choice variety; e.g.

Of the following, which contributed *most* to the level of success you attained at school?

(i) teachers	☐	(v) ambition	☐
(ii) home encouragement	☐	(vi) a competitive streak	☐
(iii) luck	☐	(vii) a good memory	☐
(iv) personal application	☐	Tick *one* box only.	

Since all application forms tend to seek the same basic information, it makes sense to keep your personal job-search file: it will save you hunting down a detail that has slipped your memory. More importantly, a file will help you keep a systematic, readily available record of progress and ensure consistency should you find yourself, for example, applying twice to the same organisation within the space of months.

When completing a form:
- Photocopy the original and do a rough version.
- Read *all* instructions and then *all* the questions before starting to complete.
- Use *black pen* for the fair copy; only type if you are certain you can do a first-class job.
- Make sure your handwriting is legible; often capital letters are stipulated.
- Think carefully about ways to 'stretch' your information to fill the space available.
- Think hard about hobbies and interests: it is surprisingly easy to overlook activities simply because they are such a familiar part of our lives.
- List *genuine* interests only, and be prepared to explain them at an interview (e.g. if you put down 'reading' you should be able to talk about three books you've read recently).
- Choose your referees with care (preferably people of some standing), and be sure you have their permission to list their names.
- Check that all information you supply (e.g. referees' titles, addresses, phone numbers, qualifications) is correct.
- Have your spelling checked by someone reliable.
- Think particularly hard if asked to supply 'additional information that you feel may be of interest' (it might be just the opening you need!).
- Photocopy the completed form and store it in your file: you may need to check what you said if you're called to an interview.
- Address the envelope with the same care you gave to the form.

TASK 9.1.1 A

Job application form-filling

Fingal O'Flaherty's Irish Shebeens Ltd operates a string of successful pubs throughout Europe and is recruiting bar staff to fill permanent jobs.

Complete the organisation's application form below. You may need to blend fact and fiction in some responses. Take into account the guidelines set out above on form-filling.

Circulate and evaluate the completed forms.

Fingal O'Flaherty's Irish Shebeens Ltd

Application for employment—bar staff

Confidential

Please attach photograph here

Please complete section 1 in CAPITAL LETTERS and the remainder in your own handwriting. Tick boxes (✓) as appropriate.

Section 1. Personal details

Surname: _____

First name(s): _____

Sex: _____

Address (for correspondence): _____

_____

_____

Telephone number: _____

Home address (if different from above): _____

_____

_____

Telephone number: _____

Date of birth: _____

Place of birth: _____

Nationality: _____

Weight: _____

Height: _____

Marital status: _____

Have you any physical disabilities or handicaps? If so, give details. _____

_____

Have you ever had any serious illness? If so, give details. _____

_____

What languages do you speak or write fluently? _____

Do you hold a full current driving licence? _____

Have you had any serious car accidents? _____

Has your driving licence ever been endorsed? If so, give details. _____

_____

Have you ever been arrested or charged by the Gardaí? If so, give details. _____

_____

How did you learn of this vacancy? _____

Have you previously applied for employment with this company? _____

If so, when? _____

Have you lived outside Ireland for a period of more than three months? If so, give details.

_____

List, in order of preference, *three* European countries in which you would like to be based:

1. _____

2. _____

3. _____

List the European countries you have visited, stating the approximate amount of time spent in each.

_____

_____

_____

_____

_____

_____

How often do you mix socially with a group of friends?—

(i) most days ❑

(ii) once or twice per week ❑

(iii) once or twice per month ❑

(iv) rarely ❑

Tick one box only.

Section 2. Education record
In chronological order, including examination results.

School	Dates	Examination results

Section 3. Employment record

Company	Dates	Position held	Reason for leaving

Section 4. General information
(i) Interests, games, hobbies:
Give details of achievements.

(ii) Why are you interested in working for us?

_____
_____
_____
_____

(iii) Please use the space below to provide any additional information that you feel might be of interest.

_____
_____
_____
_____
_____
_____
_____
_____
_____
_____
_____
_____
_____
_____
_____
_____
_____
_____

(iv) How soon could you start working if offered a job? _____

(v) Please give the names, addresses and telephone numbers of your school or college principal and *two* other people (not relatives) to whom we may apply for references.

Name: _____
Address: _____
_____
Telephone number: _____

Name: _____
Address: _____
_____
Telephone number: _____

Name: _____
Address: _____
_____
Telephone number: _____

If you are now employed, a reference will be sought from your employer, but not unless a conditional offer has been made to you and you have accepted it.

Applicant's signature: _____
Date: _____

9.2 The CV

Large organisations filling vacancies use application forms as a preliminary screening stage. Perhaps six promising candidates might be selected for interview. An alternative method of recruitment is to invite applications that include a CV. In this instance, two documents are required: your CV and a covering letter.

The CV should always be typed or word-processed; increasingly, the covering letter will be as well—though watch out for specific requests to use handwriting.

As far as the applicant is concerned, the CV should act as a passport to the next stage—usually, a call to an interview. The CV must provide a prospective employer with the basic information that would be found in any application form. The *way* that information is presented may flatter you or it may give an impression of haste, carelessness, untidiness etc. Essentially, you are selling yourself on paper, so you need to think hard about the image you want to project.

Despite a small library of books advising you 'how to write the perfect CV', together with the availability of computer programs offering ready-made formats for a CV and covering letter, employers still complain of CVs and letters that are

- carelessly spelt ('My interessests include the challange of overseas travel')
- thoughtlessly addressed ('Dear The Personal Manager')
- poorly expressed ('I am most confident in my communicatory dexterities')
- wildly exaggerated in their claims ('fluency' in a language should mean that you could be interviewed in that language)
- too long (padded out with standard words such as 'dedicated', 'efficient', 'reliable')
- written on inappropriate paper (e.g. Snoopy notepaper).

Great care should be taken over the composition and presentation of your CV. At the same time you should recognise that a CV which receives more than a minute of the employer's attention is probably doing quite well. You could spend time and money producing the CV bible—an elaborately bound volume on expensive paper with table of contents, copies of certificates, declarations of this and that; but it is questionable whether the booklet would serve your cause better than the standard page of good-quality white paper that an employer can skim-read. Be honest, brief, factual, and neat.

In planning your CV, follow closely the format of an application form:

- name (use CAPITAL LETTERS or **bold type** to help it stand out)
- address
- phone number (including area code)
- date of birth
- education record, in chronological order, including exam results
- employment record (with dates)
- general information (interests, achievements etc.)

- references (you may wish to supply names, addresses and phone numbers of two or three referees, or you may wish to save space by stating that references are available on request).

Don't
- make false claims (you may be caught out at the interview)
- include *minor* details or out-of-date information
- abbreviate dates (Aug. 93) or words (exc. Fr. lang. skills)
- allow yourself even *one* mistake (ask someone reliable to check spelling, word usage etc.).

Do
- display your wares attractively, making artful use of space, headings, type size, underlining, bold type, and boxing. Without resorting to gimmicks, you can do an effective selling job on one page with these simple materials
- use a word-processor and good-quality printer—if only because you must be prepared to edit your CV to suit different job specifications, omitting there, adding here
- remember to work in extra skills such as foreign language competence, computer skills, ability to drive
- make a conscious effort to *match* your qualifications to the demands of the job you're applying for
- attach a small photograph of yourself to the top right corner of your CV; it's a courtesy that most interviewers will appreciate
- make a couple of photocopies of each version of your CV, and store them in your job-search file.

Sample CV

CURRICULUM VITAE

Name: ELAINE O'SULLIVAN
Address: 23 Hill View, Douglas, Cork
Telephone: (021) 696044
Date of birth: 13 December 1977

EDUCATION:

1989–1995	Douglas Comprehensive School, Cork
1992	Junior Certificate (copy of certificate enclosed)
1995	Leaving Certificate

Subject	Level	Grade
Irish	O	B3
English	H	C1
Mathematics	O	C2
French	H	C3
Geography	H	D1
Home economics	O	C1
Chemistry	O	C2

1995–1996 College of Business Studies, Douglas, Cork
NCVA Post-Leaving Certificate course in Business Studies—Secretarial. (Modules taken: office procedures, typewriting, word-processing, shorthand, bookkeeping, reception studies, communications, French.)

1996 National Vocational Certificate Level 2 (Distinction)

WORK EXPERIENCE:

1992–1996 Harry's, Hill Street, Douglas: waitressing and reception
1996 B. O'Brien, Solicitor, Bandon, Co. Cork: secretarial duties

ACHIEVEMENTS:

TYO Achiever of the Year (1993)
Secretary, School Council (1995)
Manager, School Bank (1994–1995)
Assistant patrol leader, Girl Guides
Medals for Irish dancing
Au pair in Bordeaux (July–August 1995)
Full driving licence

INTERESTS:

Dancing and drama (active member of Douglas Players)
Girl Guides
Swimming
Travel
Bee-keeping

REFERENCES:

Available on request

Above all, remember the aim of your CV—to make *you* stand out from all the other applicants: in today's market, a small ad in a national daily for an 'ordinary' job may produce fifty replies. What have *you* got that others might not possess?

TASK 9.2 A

Compile a CV

Select a newspaper job advertisement that seems to match your qualifications. Taking account of the advice above, produce a CV that will earn you an interview.

9.3 THE COVERING LETTER

As far as the applicant is concerned, the covering letter provides the opportunity (*a*) to communicate personality and (*b*) to highlight areas of the CV that might appeal to the employer. Even within the limits of the conventional 'I wish to apply …' letter it should be possible to convey something of your approach to job-hunting in general and of your attitude to this job in particular.

It is up to you to make the most of your *USPs*—unique selling points. What have *you* to offer this employer that is uncommon, if not unique?

Discreet self-promotion is a major function of the covering letter. Modesty may be a virtue, but not in this context.

It should be possible, with a little research, to address your letter to a named person rather than to, say, the Personnel Officer or 'Dear sir/madam'. You may have decided to send your CV and a covering letter to a number of firms that are not advertising vacancies but that will, you hope, keep your application on file should a vacancy occur; in such cases it requires very little initiative on your part to phone the firms to ask for the *name* of the person who deals with recruitment.

When writing your letter,
- always go through the rough draft, fair copy and proof-reading process
- don't necessarily trust your own proof-reading expertise: be prepared to seek help
- follow normal letter-writing conventions regarding
—address (your own and your addressee's)
—date
—opening ('Dear …')
—closing ('Yours sincerely' or 'Yours faithfully').

Note that section 10.1 contains detailed guidance on ways of laying out a business letter.
- Use good-quality, unlined white paper and leave generous margins.
- Aim for three or four paragraphs (see below).
- Set yourself a strict *one-side* limit.
- Fold and post it in a clearly addressed, plain white envelope that matches the size of your paper.

The contents of your letter should include:

(1) Introduction: Your standard formal application: 'I wish to apply for the position of ... advertised in ... of 6 May 1996.' This sentence might be your first paragraph.

(2) Body: Open-ended, but should feature

(a) evidence that you are aware of the company's business and of the job's demands

(b) mention of any previous connection or tie you may have had with the company

(c) CV highlights and their relevance to the post advertised

(d) unique selling points that might not have fitted the CV format

(e) any compelling reasons you may have for applying to this particular company.

Two or, at most, three paragraphs should be enough.

(3) Conclusion: Mention your CV and your availability for interview: 'I enclose a CV containing details of my education, qualifications, and experience. Should you wish to interview me I could attend at any time to suit your convenience if given reasonable notice.'

This is sufficient for a final paragraph: there is no need for 'Looking forward to ... ' or tired formulas such as 'Thanking you in anticipation of ...'

Before stating your availability, check your commitments.

TASK 9.3 A

A covering letter

Write a covering letter to accompany the application form you have completed for Fingal O'Flaherty's Irish Shebeens Ltd. In the body of your letter seek to highlight anything that might be taken as evidence of your

flexibility

sociability

reliability.

Circulate the letters, encouraging readers to correct any errors detected and to comment on style and content.

Supplementary tasks

1. Write a letter to a local employer seeking appropriate work placement from 2 to 16 February next. Identify key areas in which you would particularly look forward to receiving experience. Accompanying your letter is your CV.

Your letter might be a modified version of the covering letter outlined earlier in this chapter. Remember that you are asking a favour. As an incentive, you might point out that you will not expect remuneration!

2. In a recent newspaper, find an advertised job that matches the qualifications you possess or are in the process of acquiring. Apply for it with your CV and a covering letter.

3. Draw up a list of local organisations that recruit by means of an application form. Organise members of the group to obtain samples of the forms, either by personal visit, phoning, or letter. Circulate the collected forms. List and discuss the variations between them.

4. Write a letter to a potential referee asking him or her to act on your behalf if requested.
5. Obtain and complete a FÁS registration form.
6. A good way to begin the CV process is to put yourself through an informal skills self-audit. Read through the list of skills below. In the spaces provided, add any further skills you possess that aren't included. Tick the appropriate boxes.

Skills I possess

	Can do	Like doing	Do well
Problem-solving	☐	☐	☐
Listening sympathetically	☐	☐	☐
Motivating others	☐	☐	☐
Organising	☐	☐	☐
Selling	☐	☐	☐
Drawing	☐	☐	☐
Cooking	☐	☐	☐
Acting	☐	☐	☐
Singing	☐	☐	☐
Dancing	☐	☐	☐
Making music	☐	☐	☐
Researching	☐	☐	☐
Negotiating	☐	☐	☐
Making others laugh	☐	☐	☐
Making things	☐	☐	☐
Growing things	☐	☐	☐
Mending things	☐	☐	☐
Making friends	☐	☐	☐
Teaching	☐	☐	☐
Analysing	☐	☐	☐
Arguing a case	☐	☐	☐
Persuading	☐	☐	☐
Looking after children	☐	☐	☐
Caring for the elderly	☐	☐	☐
Taking decisions	☐	☐	☐
Driving	☐	☐	☐
	☐	☐	☐
	☐	☐	☐
	☐	☐	☐
	☐	☐	☐
	☐	☐	☐

You may bring to light qualities and talents you'd forgotten you possess. Perhaps you'd like to highlight some of these skills in your covering letter or at an interview. Are some of them directly relevant to the job you're applying for?

Chapter review
   1. What are the five most important points to watch for when completing
      (a) a job application form
      (b) a CV
      (c) a covering letter?
   2. Explain USP.
   3. What do the words 'curriculum vitae' mean?

10 'BUSINESS ENGLISH'

SIX PERIODS

10.1 THE 'DONE THING'

'Business English' usually refers to writing we associate with the work-place: business correspondence, faxes, memorandums, reports etc. The term is sometimes used without obvious affection. Report-writing (to take one example) is, for most of us, a chore but an absolutely necessary chore if businesses are to operate efficiently.

We can't deal in one chapter with *all* the varieties of writing that might be labelled 'business English': correspondence alone would include circular letters (or circulars), form letters, and letters of collection, complaint, enquiry, adjustment, and quotation. Instead we'll examine a *selection* of the documents most commonly encountered in the work-place, aiming to become familiar with the 'done thing' as far as content, format, style and language are concerned.

10.1.1 BUSINESS CORRESPONDENCE

The traditional business letter written on a good-quality A4 sheet with handsome printed letter-heading is yielding ground to such innovations of modern technology as fax transmission and electronic mail (e-mail). The 'paperless office' has long been a cliché; the new generation of lightweight, portable, powerful computers is marketed as 'an office in a box'.

The ordinary postal service is disparagingly styled 'snail mail'. Slow it undeniably is by comparison with fax and e-mail: their speed, efficiency, flexibility and cost-effectiveness are very appealing to the business world. The phone and the advent of faster, easier and cheaper travel (encouraging face-to-face meeting) also continue to erode the primacy of the business letter.

Yet even as we enter the era of the 'information superhighway' it is hard to see the letter being replaced. It will continue to serve as a documentary record and confirmation of an oral agreement. The e-mail business letter observes to some extent the conventions of layout and tone that have long governed the handwritten or typed letter. Arguably, the ability to produce a formal, professional-looking business letter may become a *more* desirable skill within the framework of the new technology.

10.1.2 Layout

The current fashion in business letters is for what is sometimes called 'blocked' style, and we'll concentrate on that style. It means that all lines, including the first line of each paragraph, start at the left-hand margin, with an extra line space to separate the paragraphs, instead of the traditional 'indented' style, in which the first line of a new paragraph is indented a number of spaces.

'Blocked style' is often used in conjunction with 'open punctuation', a term which means that punctuation is used only in the *body* of the letter.

Business letters follow a well-established format. The essential elements are:
(1)   the sender's address
(2)   a *reference*
(3)   the date
(4)   the receiver's (or inside) name, title, and address
(5)   the *salutation* or greeting
(6)   the heading
(7)   the body of the letter
(8)   the close
(9)   the signature, name of signatory, and (often) position held by the signatory
(10) notification of enclosed documents.

10.1.3 A sample letter explained

Here's a business letter in the 'blocked' style with open punctuation:

① Anna Dare Designs Ltd
Springfield House
Douglas
Cork
Tel (021) 392561 · Fax (021) 366321

② Our ref AD/CRD

③ 14 February 1996

④ Mr Eamon Donoghue
Sales Manager
Kilkenny Carpets
Bennetsbridge
Co. Kilkenny

⑤ Dear Mr Donoghue

⑥ PURCHASE OF CARPETING FOR LORD MAYOR'S OFFICE

⑦ Thank you for arranging my visit to your showrooms on Thursday 11 February last. I was impressed by the range and quality of the stock on display.

Your old-gold Wilton might prove suitable for the Lord Mayor's newly refurbished office. Since the choice will to some extent be determined by cost, I should be grateful if you would send me, as soon as possible, a quotation for supplying and fitting old-gold carpet and underlay. I enclose measurement details.

I am glad to have had the opportunity to meet you and look forward to receiving a competitive quotation.

⑧ Yours sincerely

Anna Dare

⑨ Anna Dare
Design Consultant

⑩ Enc

Notes

(1) On a printed letter-heading, additional technical information (e.g. company registration, VAT number) may be found in small type at the bottom of the sheet.

(2) The reference will usually give the author's and typist's initials. Alternatively, it may be numerical, referring to a filing system. In replying to a letter it is customary to quote the correspondent's reference.

(3) The natural order for the date is day, month, year. Avoid abbreviations, and never use all-numeral forms (14/2/1996). There is no need for a full stop at the end of the date or other 'displayed' lines.

(4) The inside name and address should include the addressee's courtesy title (e.g. Mr, Ms, Dr; note that *none* of these requires a full stop, since in each one the abbreviation contains the final letter of the original word), designation (e.g. Sales Manager), and, occasionally, qualifications (e.g. BA). Initials or first name should precede the surname, and all should be accurate. 'Esq.' (short for 'esquire') was once common after a man's name; it is never used in conjunction with Mr.

(5) In the letter above, the name of the addressee is known to the sender: 'Dear Mr Donoghue'. In greeting, the rule is to err on the side of formality. Use 'Dear Sirs' when writing to a company. If in doubt about the sex of your correspondent, use either 'Dear Sir' *or* 'Dear Madam' rather than 'Dear Sir/Madam'.

(6) The heading is there to help the reader see at a glance what the letter is about, so it should be short and should stand out, either through the use of capital letters or underlining.

(7) It is hard to be prescriptive about the *body* of a letter. The three Golden Rules are:
- Be clear.
- Be concise.
- Be courteous.

In the sample letter you will notice that the body consists of the 'classic' *three* paragraphs:

(i) the *background* against which the letter is being written, typically a phone call, meeting, or letter received

(ii) the 'meat' or reason for writing the letter (e.g. to request or give information)

(iii) the 'rounding off', often a courteous reminder of an expected outcome.

(8) The close in business letters is generally either 'Yours faithfully' or 'Yours sincerely'. Use the former with 'Dear Sirs,' 'Dear Sir' and 'Dear Madam'; use the latter when the salutation contains a name. Beware 'sincerely': it causes problems for poor spellers.

(9) A signature may be hard to read, hence the practice of typing below it the name and designation of the signatory. If the name doesn't clearly signal the writer's sex (e.g. Pat Reynolds) it may save embarrassment to put a courtesy title in brackets after the name (e.g. Mrs).

(10) A single enclosed document is indicated by 'Enc.', more than one by 'Encs.'

10.1.4 Style and content

- *Language* and *tone* should be formal, projecting a professional but not 'stuffy' image. In informal, spoken language you might say, 'Give me a bell when you can.' In a formal letter this becomes 'I look forward to receiving a phone call in the near future.'
- The effort to be formal sometimes produces 'commercialese' or jargon that is assumed to be business-like: 'Re yours of 14th inst., we beg to inform you ... Assuring you of our best attention at all times ...' In place of such absurd prefabricated phrases, use direct, unpretentious language that both you and your reader will understand.
- Conciseness, remember, is a Golden Rule. Most letters err on the side of wordiness. In this context, 'short is beautiful,' whether it be words, sentences, or paragraphs.
- Longwindedness is a particular problem in *rounding off* letters. Use standard endings such as: 'I look forward to hearing from you soon' (*never* 'Hoping to hear from you soon,' which is not a *complete* sentence) *or* 'Should you require further information, details or assistance, please do not hesitate to contact us,' *or* 'I hope this information may be of use to you.' *Never* write 'Thanking you in anticipation'—another incomplete sentence.
- Starting the body of a letter also causes difficulties. Avoid openings such as: 'I am writing to ask/inform you ...' (It is *obvious* you are writing!) *or* 'Referring to / With reference to / Following on from your letter/phone call ...' (all risky usages, tending to result in long, incoherent, grammatically incorrect sentences). It is safer to begin: 'Thank you for your letter/phone call of ...'
- It is good practice to *draft* a letter, especially if it is to contain several points. Whether informing, explaining, requesting, or complaining, follow a *logical* order.
- Anything less than 100 per cent correct is not good enough. Check and double-check grammar, spelling, punctuation, and layout. It is inexcusable to address Dr Derek Taunt as Dr Derek Gaunt or Dr Derek Daunt.
- 'Same' is misused in the belief that it is brisk and business-like: 'I am in receipt of your order and will forward same to our Delivery Department.' Here, as so often, 'same' should be replaced with the appropriate pronoun: 'I have received your order and will send it to our Delivery Department.'

TASK 10.1.4 A

A faulty letter

Discuss any errors of layout, style, content, spelling, punctuation or grammar you detect in the following letter. Then, working on your own, rewrite the letter so that it is *perfect*.

KERRY OUTDOOR CENTRE
Anascaul
Co. Kerry

Tel. 68325

21/5/95

Dear Mr. B. Smith,

Thanking you for your esteamed enquiry dated 3 May ult. which we apologise for the delay in answering same but I have been unusualy busy of late. We are always pleased to wellcome school groups to the centre, actually we've had lots of school groups since having opened the centre 2 years ago and much satisfaction has been expressed with the service provided by us. Our charges as per enclosed brochurewhich you shall find herewith are we beleive very reasonable and include full board and lodging, expert instruction and a coach (driven by your's truely!) from the point of collection to the centre and of course back again. They havent gone up since we opened.
Hoping you find everything you want in the brochure. Trusting all this meets with your approval and that we shall be able to do business to our mutual satisfaction.

                         Yours Faithfully

                         Michael O'Kennedy

                     Michael O'Kennedy (Director of centre)

PS I forgot to mention that our limit is 48. NB We can't acommadate mixed groups.

10.2 ROUTINE BUSINESS LETTERS

In this section you are asked to write two of the commonest types of business letter:
    (a) a letter of *enquiry* eliciting a letter of reply
    (b) a letter of *complaint* eliciting a letter of *adjustment* (dealing with a complaint).

10.2.1 LETTERS OF ENQUIRY AND REPLY

- In making any enquiry it is essential to be *precise* in stating your question (or questions) so that you get the information you seek.
- Make sure the recipient has all the information needed to answer the letter fully.
- A letter of reply will usually begin by stating that it is a response to an enquiry received.
- A reply containing numbered headings is often a very *clear* way to present information.
- Whether enquiring or replying, re-read what you have written, imagining *you* are the recipient.

10.2.2 Letters of complaint and adjustment

- When complaining, be courteous, reasonable, and firm. *Never*, however justifiable the complaint, resort to rudeness or abuse. The fault, just possibly, might be yours!
- Supply *details* to support your complaint: dates, times, numbers, makes, documents etc.
- Politely suggest appropriate redress: refund, replacement, repair etc.
- A reply to a complaint may *accept* or *deny* responsibility. Either way, maximum tact is necessary.
- Whether accepting or denying responsibility, an expression of regret for the inconvenience to the complainant is customary.
- Loss of goodwill or of custom and damaging publicity (even if only by word of mouth) are always possibilities if a complaint is not handled properly. If acknowledging responsibility, apologies must accompany a refund, replacement, or discount.

TASK 10.2.2 A

Daily business post

This activity is best carried out in pairs, but in small groups it may be managed singly. As a group, compile a list of businesses that might typically be associated with your vocational area. For example, if the area was tourism the list might comprise hotel, guesthouse, tourist information office, a range of leisure or sporting amenities (tennis village, equestrian centre, golf course), travel agent, coach hire operator, Bord Fáilte, bank, etc. All listed organisations should be of the kind that engage in correspondence.

The list should contain as many businesses as there are pairs, and there should be just *one* example of each business. Each pair 'becomes' one of the listed organisations and should start by giving it a name and designing an appropriate letter-heading and simple logo.

Each 'business' should now compose a letter of enquiry to send to another of the listed businesses. A little organisation will be needed to ensure that every business receives a letter. The letters, which should be as realistic and as professionally produced as possible, may initiate a correspondence or may pick up the threads of an existing correspondence, perhaps referring back to earlier letters. Twenty minutes should be allowed for composition.

The completed letters should be delivered to the addressees, who should begin by correcting any errors detected. Once the contents have been digested, letters of reply should be written, delivered, and corrected by the recipients. Fifteen minutes might be allotted for replies.

On completion of the round, matters arising from the letters should be discussed by the group.

At the group's next session, follow a similar procedure for letters of complaint and adjustment. Pairs should keep their original businesses but choose different recipients.

This simulation could be extended and developed, either by further rounds of letters (replies to replies), by experimenting with other kinds of letters (e.g. letters of collection), or by incorporating telephone role-playing arising out of the correspondence.

10.3 Memos

The word 'memorandum' derives from the Latin for 'something to be remembered'. It is most often used in the abbreviated form 'memo'.

A memo is an internal letter sent to a colleague or colleagues working within the same organisation. It therefore contains no address. It may once have been used to jog memory but nowadays it serves a variety of purposes, notably

- to request or convey information
- to float suggestions
- to issue instructions
- to report on decisions or actions taken
- to confirm arrangements.

The layout of a memo is usually decided for you, since most businesses use a standard printed form, similar in some respects to the telephone message pad. To encourage brevity, the memo form is usually *small* (typically, A5 size) and follows a standard format:

QUAYSIDE REMOVALS
Tramore Road
Waterford

Memorandum

From: Shane Keane
To: Jim Bolger
Date: 3 October 1996
Ref.: SK/OM

Subject: WORK EXPERIENCE PLACEMENT

1. Have accepted two students from Southgate Community College for work placement.
2. Names: Ken O'Connor (16) and Hugh Barrett (17).
3. Dates of work experience: 17–28 October next.
4. Suggest we meet my office 10 a.m. tomorrow to discuss what we could give them to do.

SK

Note

- No formal salutation or close is needed.
- Reference is as for letters: author's and typist's initials.
- Date, subject heading and enclosures are shown as in letters.
- Since the sender is a colleague of the receiver, initials often replace a signature.

Memos, which may be typed or handwritten, are almost always short and informal in style. Because they are short there is sometimes a danger of seeming dictatorial, particularly when giving instructions. The Three Cs of letter-writing are just as applicable here: be clear, concise, and *courteous*. If clarity would be improved by *numbering* the points (as in the sample above), then use numbers.

TASK 10.3 A

Memo writing

1. Write a memo, copies of which are to be distributed to *all* staff, in which you complain about the abuse of office phones in making and receiving personal calls during business hours. Make clear the cost to the company in time and money, and warn of the need to take further action if no improvement occurs. Be firm but diplomatic.
2. You are the personal assistant to the Personnel Manager, who has been absent all day at a conference. Write her a memo outlining details of an inter-office meeting and two appointments you have set up for her later in the week.
3. Your boss, the chief buyer for a large department store, has asked you to make arrangements for him or her to spend three days in Paris viewing the spring collections. Compose a memo outlining your provisional travel and accommodation bookings and asking if you may now confirm them.

10.4 E-MAIL

Electronic mail or e-mail is exactly that: mail sent electronically. Strictly that term also fits fax, which means sending facsimiles of documents electronically. But there are differences in the equipment used and in the ways in which messages are sent, and it is best to consider them separately.

E-mail is a 'postal' system based on computers linked via *modems*, which convert 'computer language' (digital signals) to 'phone language' (sound) and back again.

Messages typed on one computer are transmitted through the national or international telephone network to other computers using an electronic mailbox that stores the messages until they are collected by the receiver.

E-mail offers organisations the possibility of *internal* and *external* communication. For example, a university spread over a large college site or a hospital with departments in different areas of a city might make constant use of the free *internal* network to replace traditional memos, notices, letters etc. An example of *external* communication might be the formation of a cluster of, say, a dozen schools from EU member-states to undertake a joint project based on their exchange of data via e-mail. By subscribing to a common computer network, each school obtains its own mailbox (for receiving messages) and has access to the mailboxes of other schools (for sending messages). Entry to the network is by way of the public phone system.

E-mail scores in the following ways:
- It is faster and more reliable than the postal service.
- It can be sent at times when rates are cheapest.
- It can be circulated simultaneously to a number of receivers.
- It can be collected at a time that suits the receiver: the message is stored until it is accessed.
- It can be sent and received wherever a traveller has access to a portable computer and phone.
- It can transmit data in its many formats—text files, spreadsheet figures, data-base entries, raw code or entire computer programs—directly from one computer to another via modems.
- Confidentiality can be ensured.

10.4.1 Fax

It is almost as hard now to imagine any organisation operating without fax as it would have been to imagine the same company ten years ago operating without a telephone. With 'teleworking' becoming an attractive option for many, the number of fax machines in homes is rapidly increasing.

It is easiest to think of the fax system as *remote photocopying*. The machine is connected to the public phone system. A fax machine generally offers, in an A4-sized package,
- a phone
- a photocopier
- an answering machine
- fax transmission to anywhere in the world where there is a compatible fax machine connected to a telephone.

Fax messages score in the following ways:
- They travel faster and more reliably than the post.

- They can be sent when rates (the same as for phone calls) are cheapest.
- They can be viewed at the recipient's convenience.
- They can be sent throughout the world.
- Fax machines at present cost less than such domestic appliances as a fridge or television and will probably drop further in price while becoming more sophisticated in use.
- Fax machines reproduce anything that a photocopier accepts.

A typical fax 'cover sheet' looks like this:

Fingal O'Flaherty's Irish Shebeens Ltd
16 Paul Street · Drogheda · Co. Louth
Phone (041) 38503 · Fax (041) 38507

Fax message

To: _____
Number of pages, incl. this one: _____
Address:_____
Subject: _____
Date: _____

Fax number: _____
From: _____

Message: _____
_____
_____
_____
_____
_____
_____
_____
_____
_____
_____
_____
_____
_____
_____
_____

> **TASK 10.4.1 A**
>
> **Faxing**
>
> Using the sample fax sheet above, compose a fax from Jim Griffin in head office to Walter Zwingli, an architect based at 14 Rue du Palais, Versailles, France (fax number 0033 1 3952137). The purpose of the fax is to arrange a joint inspection of a promising site for an Irish pub in Versailles.

10.5 Reports

We first meet reports at school:

History
Exam: 48%   Place: 24   Effort: 4
Paul has worked hard and is usually co-operative and well behaved. If he revises strenuously he should achieve a C grade in the summer.

On this evidence a school report
- is a short, formally written document
- is intended for a specific readership (parents and pupil)
- gives information about performance over a period
- states results achieved
- analyses conduct and motivation
- aims to offer objective assessment
- makes recommendations for the future.

The simple two or three-line school report is, in nature, function, aim, and even format, very similar to the large volume totalling hundreds of pages that reports, at the request of the Government, on a natural disaster or serious accident.

Reports may be orally presented but are more often formally written; they investigate a topic on behalf, usually, of a limited readership, convey information, make available findings and conclusions, state results, offer analyses and make recommendations, and aspire to be factual and objective.

Writing reports is a routine professional chore for any teacher as it is for civil servants, members of the Gardaí and Defence Forces, those working in the caring professions, insurers, surveyors … You may find it hard to think of a job that does *not* involve report-writing.

Reports fall into three basic categories:

(1) **Routine reports:** These are submitted at regular intervals, often on printed forms. School reports and hospital reports on a patient's progress might be put in this category.

(2) **Short, special reports:** These reports are commissioned, often by the management or by a company's customer, to carry out an investigation into a

specific set of circumstances in the hope that a more informed decision may be taken as a result of the report's findings. The time limit is often short (a few weeks), and in layout and style the report usually follows well-established conventions. A safety officer, for example, might be asked to produce a short report on the desirability or otherwise of upgrading safety equipment in an area of a factory.

(3) **Long, detailed reports:** Elaborate reports appearing in the form of a printed book with table of contents, numerous appendixes etc. are obviously expensive to produce and are therefore within the reach only of large companies and state bodies. Months, even years may go into the preparation of such reports. The Arts Council, for example, might commission a person or a small group to prepare a report on the state of the arts in Ireland in the year 2000. Environmental impact surveys might also fall into this category.

10.5.1 SHORT, SPECIAL REPORTS

Since the form of report most of us are likely to encounter in our working lives is the short report, consisting of about 500 words, that's the one we'll concentrate on here.

What are its elements?

(1) **Report heading or title** (e.g. 'Enhancement of External Appearance of St Kame's College').

(2) **Definition of terms of reference**—the subject, limits and purpose of the report, together with the name of the commissioning agent or body. If a purpose of the report is to make recommendations, this will usually be stated; for example: 'As requested by the Board of Management, to examine ways in which the approach to, grounds and façade of St Kame's College might be made more attractive and to make practical recommendations.'

(3) **Procedure**—statement of the *method* by which the authors propose to carry out the investigation or research. The process might include:

(i) issue of a questionnaire
(ii) interviews
(iii) personal observation
(iv) practical experiments
(v) reading up on relevant literature.

(4) **Findings**—the presentation in logical, objective and impersonal style of the results of a questionnaire, interviews, observation etc. Findings will usually be issued in a layout using sub-headings and a system of numbering and indentation. Such a system is invaluable when readers need, in discussion, to refer to items in the text.

(5) **Conclusions:** These are the author's opinions or inferences, based on the findings and presented, like them, in systematic fashion, with the most important topping the list. Conclusions should be fair and reasonable and should not betray bias.

(6) **Recommendations:** If required by the terms of reference, these should be laid out systematically following the method established in steps 4 and 5. As proposals for

action to be taken, they will normally be ranked in *descending* order of priority. They should obviously take account of what is, in the context, feasible and practical.

(7) ***Signature, designation, and date.***

Good report-writing means observing the ABC that underlies so much of what constitutes good writing:

A stands for **accuracy**—of information and fact, as well as of spelling, punctuation, and grammar. It might also stand for ***appropriateness*** of material to its readers as well as of vocabulary and tone.

B stands for **brevity**. Enough said.

C stands for **clarity**, particularly when making the recommendations—the part of the report that many readers will turn to first. They should be in no doubt about your meaning. Clarity can be assisted by page layout, by good signposting, by generous use of space: remember that even a *short* report consisting of a solid block of text may be off-putting. **C** also stands for **comprehensiveness** (omitting nothing of significance) and **consultation** (it's always a good idea to run your conclusions and recommendations by others before committing yourself).

D (if it were to be added) stands for **drafting**. It is almost inconceivable that a worthwhile report could be written that hasn't gone through at least *one* draft. Typical stages in the preparation of a report will include:

Notes
Notes logically arranged
Rough draft
Fair copy

TASK 10.5.1 A

Writing a special report

Unquestionably the best way to practise report-writing is to write a real report, and a short discussion in the group might bring to light matters in your own environment that might usefully be reported on and where recommendations might be made and implemented.

If your group can identify a situation that calls for a report and can arrange for the report to be formally accepted and considered, proceed as follows:

(1) Decide as a group the terms of reference.
(2) Set a word limit (e.g. 500–600 words).
(3) Agree a deadline (e.g. three weeks).
(4) Divide into pairs. Each pair should agree on a method of procedure. Select whichever means of acquiring information best suits the circumstances.
(5) Research in pairs. Decide on findings, conclusions, and recommendations.
(6) Write up the report *individually*.
(7) Discuss the different versions of the report. Which one makes its case most convincingly?
(8) Submit it!

If your group is unable to identify a real problem to report on you might agree on an *imaginary* problem that calls for a report. For example, the school or college authorities might have commissioned reports on the disturbing outbreak of graffiti or the sudden increase in vandalism or falling standards in punctuality. If a grateful past pupil made a huge benefaction to the school or college out of his or her lottery winnings, a report might be commissioned on ways in which the money should be spent—on the library? on upgrading or acquiring new sports facilities? on the canteen? on facilities for socialising (e.g. common rooms)? on an information centre that might set the school or college firmly on the information superhighway?

Alternatively, a series of financial cutbacks in the Government's provision for your sector might mean the removal or pruning of certain services in your school or college, and reports might be written (*a*) to investigate areas where cutbacks could be made or (*b*) to explore ways of fund-raising in order to *preserve* existing services.

This chapter has merely dipped into a very large subject. Remember that businesses, bosses, teachers and textbooks all have their own preferences, support one usage rather than another, and favour a particular 'house style'. The new technology is bringing about major changes in the handling of paperwork. Sooner rather than later it will begin to shrink the mountain of letters, memos, minutes, management reports, drawings and faxes that accumulates under even a modest-sized company in the course of a year. So much is happening so fast that it is very hard to predict where 'business English' will be by the end of the century.

Supplementary tasks

1. Contact three local businesses—one large, one medium-sized, one small—to enquire what changes have taken place in the *patterns of their correspondence* over the past two or three years. Compare the findings, and try to account for them.
2. Research the latest developments in the 'paperless office', in particular the growing links between telephone and personal computer. What impact are fax and e-mail having on conventional mail? (You may need to involve An Post in your researches.)
3. Find specimens of 'blocked' and 'indented' letters. Display the samples within the group, and discuss the differences and their effect.
4. Research and explain clearly the differences between circular letters (circulars) and form letters.
5. Assemble a range of fax sheets from an assortment of local businesses, and examine the differences in headings and layout.
6. Write an essay on the pros and cons of teleworking. Take into account the economic, enviromental and psychological consequences of the practice.

Chapter review

1. How is 'same' abused in business letters?
2. What purposes does a memo serve?
3. Explain how an e-mail message is sent, and list some of the advantages of e-mail over conventional mail.
4. What are the differences between routine reports, short, special reports, and long, detailed reports?
5. In the context of a report, what are terms of reference?

The Project: Process and Product

11.1 'Produce a project ...'

On a communications course, a project usually signifies a sizeable task, sometimes written, sometimes practical, that may take you weeks or even months to complete. It makes demands on your initiative, commitment, organisational and research skills, command of language, and presentational techniques.

The simplest kind of project—type A—offers a very broad *choice* of topic (often related to your vocational area) or asks you to supply your own title, given certain guidelines. Minimum and maximum *word length* may be prescribed. You may be reminded of the need to call on *research skills* and of the importance of *structure* in the completed work. There is often an obligation to incorporate *visual and graphical aids.*

So, if you were doing a course in the business or secretarial area, you might pick a subject such as the impact of new technology on the traditional office, calling your project 'The 21st-Century Office: From Manual to Microchip.' You might aim to have between 1,500 and 2,000 words (a double-spaced A4 sheet with generous margins will have about 250 to 300 words), to incorporate graphs, pie charts, photographs, and drawings, and to complete the undertaking in six weeks.

A more complex project—type B—might require you to choose a topic in the field of communications itself and in planning and preparing the project to show familiarity with a particular medium of communication. In this instance you might opt to research the launch and marketing of a computer program (sample title: 'Windows of Opportunity?') and give a slide show based on a study of the advertising campaign as illustrated by an exhibition, print advertisements, and television commercials.

Type B is in effect an oral presentation built round a series of slides. Type A projects may also, as we have seen in chapter 5, perform a dual role, originating as *written* work and supplying the material for subsequent *oral* presentation.

Both types give you considerable *freedom* and *choice*. Most students find this one of the attractions of preparing a project. Within broad limits you are free

- to *choose* your topic
- to decide *how you will treat it*.

You are in control of your own learning. You can suit your own interests. While sticking to deadlines, you can work at your own pace. You will not have a supervisor constantly peering over your shoulder. Your teacher will be available for consultation, but the intention is that you should have the opportunity to show resourcefulness and initiative.

This chapter focuses on the *process* by which any project is created. The stages by which a project is made are similar to those by which a report is written. In fact, sometimes the final stage of the project process is to write a report on how you went about the task of producing your project.

The task in this chapter is to create a project. As with chapter 5, no period allocation is recommended. Some groups may wish to study the contents together in the classroom; others may prefer to go through them individually.

11.1.1 THE PROJECT PROCESS

Begin by defining your 'terms of reference'. You need answers to the following basic questions:

- **What is the project about?** Give a very specific answer. Students sometimes choose topics that could only be satisfactorily dealt with in a large book. Having taken all available advice, summarise your project's scope in a couple of sentences.
- **For whom is the project intended?** To have an audience in view is usually a help. Too often, projects are produced in a vacuum, on the vague understanding that the readers will be the teacher and the examiner (sometimes these are one and the same person). A target audience of 'general readers' is not helpful. The author needs to know, for example, what level of existing knowledge to assume in the reader. If the project is to be publicly displayed, this may affect layout decisions.
- **When is the project submission date?** Human nature being what it is, deadlines are a necessary evil. You may find yourself asked to make interim progress reports. Be grateful for this intermittent pressure. At all costs, avoid having to write a project the night before the submission date. It just won't work.
- **How long should the project be?** Guidelines on length will usually be issued, perhaps as maximum or minimum word limits. Students often start by wondering how they will manage to find so many words to say on the topic and end by wondering how they are going to stay within the upper limit. Base your detailed planning on the minimum word count. Allow it to dictate the proportions of your preliminary outline.

- **Who might be able to help me?** At every stage of preparation you stand to benefit by consulting others. In choosing your topic, in researching it, and in drafting, avail of the advice of tutors, friends, family, local experts, colleagues, and librarians. Most people are flattered to be asked and will readily give any help they can. Look for constructive criticism rather than fishing for compliments. Act constructively when shortcomings are pointed out (as they surely will be!). Remember to thank those who give you advice.
- **Where will I find information?** Much depends on the nature of your project. Your information may come from fieldwork, from observation, interview, or questionnaire, from first-hand knowledge, or from your personal investigation. Or it may be derived from the findings of others as set out in books, magazines, newspapers, reports, charts, periodicals, maps, and documentaries (whether audio or visual). If you're mostly dealing with written source material and are unsure where to look, section 13.4 may give you a start. Remember to keep a record of all books and sources used: you will need to acknowledge all your debts in the project.
- **Are there 'special requirements'?** Be alert from the start to any built-in specifications, such as the insistence on visual aids. From the outset be mindful of how such aids can improve appearance, heighten impact, and save space.
- **What criteria will be used in assessment?**—i.e. where do the marks go? It may be that how you present your findings will count for more than what you find. This is not to devalue the importance of researching accurate and (wherever possible) original material but to emphasise the importance of communicating with your audience. Your topic may have been exhaustively researched and your sources impeccable, but if you present your message in a dull, unattractive form the reader may be tempted to switch off. Your aim should be to present your meaning so clearly and attractively that even someone who has no particular interest in the subject will want to read to the end.

TASK 11.1.1 A

Project forum

Discuss as a group the project requirements of your course. Include
- target audience
- deadline and interim assessments
- assessment criteria
- special requirements
- local sources of information.

Use this opportunity to clarify all aspects of the project. For example, is it possible to undertake group projects? Is it permissible to gather information in pairs or small groups and then to write up the findings individually? Are there rulings about how projects should be physically produced? Is everybody aware of the possibilities in choosing covers, binding, paper size and quality, typeface etc.? Is there a ruling that the project must be typed or word-processed? When you have a clear understanding of what will be required, make a bookmark setting out the essential information: dates, target audience, title (if known), etc. Use this bookmark as a memo to yourself of what needs to be done. Additionally, you might make a wall calendar so you can chart your progress.

11.2 GETTING THE IDEA

The first step is to choose your topic—one that is (let's assume) broadly related to your vocational specialisation. If you are extremely fortunate you may be able to pinpoint at once an aspect of your vocational studies you wish to research further. Just be a little cautious: will the topic stand a reasonable chance of interesting your audience? Indeed, will it continue to interest *you* over the weeks or months of preparation? Is it worthy of the amount of time and energy you will give to it? Are you sure you have the necessary personal resources and access to the essential external resources to complete the project successfully? If you answer 'yes' to these questions, count yourself lucky and proceed to the next section.

If, on the other hand, you have difficulty identifying a suitable topic, begin by brainstorming, either in a small group or by yourself. In a box in the centre of a page write the title of your vocational course. Think of the vocation in terms of

- work-place (both physical environment and personnel who inhabit it)
- working conditions and practices
- working patterns
- codes of behaviour
- roles and expectations
- career structures
- hierarchy and status
- equipment (including clothing)
- health and safety
- industrial relations
- sex equality
- research and development
- past and future
- communication flow
- motivation and incentive
- controversies
- recruitment, training, and in-service training.

Rapidly compile a list of possible topics, using these and any additional headings that occur to you. Having compiled a long list, go through it slowly and thoughtfully, eliminating those that strike you as dull or impracticable, or unsuitable for other reasons. Your own interest and curiosity are basic factors in determining choice.

It may help you to think of a reader who knows absolutely nothing about your vocational area. Imagine writing about the topics that remain on your list for such a reader. Could you make the topics interesting for him or her? Talk about your short-list to anyone who will listen. This often helps to clarify the pros and cons, highlighting aspects you may not yet have considered.

Make your choice—but don't throw away your short-list. It's just possible that you may wish to revise your decision and review the original options.

11.2.1 Getting the go-ahead

The temptation, once a decision is reached, is to launch straight into research. Again, exercise caution. Whether or not it is required, it would be sensible to outline your plans in a semi-formal proposal and to submit this to your course director, seeking approval and suggestions.

Your proposal does not have to be an elaborate document. You are seeking, in a sense, outline planning permission. You are in a position to make your *general* intentions known, but you yourself don't yet know where your investigations will lead and what their outcome will be.

You ought to be able to provide

- a provisional title
- the overall aim of the project
- a list of resources you may tap
- a plan of action.

Sample proposal:

Title: 'A New Future for St Peter's Church'.

Aim: To explore ways in which a church building, at present unused, might become an amenity for the local community.

Resources:

Access to St Peter's Church
Parish records
Architectural plans, drawings, and photographs
Secretaries of an assortment of local groups
Local historians
Questionnaires circulated to townspeople
Members of the urban district council

Plan of action:

1. Research the history of St Peter's Church.
2. Identify local groups interested in making use of the building (e.g. Flower Club, Amateur Drama Club, Citizens' Advice Bureau).
3. Ascertain from the relevant church authorities whether the building could be made available.
4. Assess the building's suitability for a variety of community uses.

If you were a tutor and one of your students submitted the above proposal to you, what suggestions or modifications would you make?

11.2.2 Getting going

Your tutor has approved your proposal. You are ready to start information-gathering.

Much of the data you assemble will come in the form of notes, taken either from printed originals or at interviews. You are likely to acquire documents, whether photocopies or originals. Invest in a selection of wallet folders and a couple of A4 pads. The folder is a convenient way of keeping paper resources under one cover—magazines, notes, jotters, booklets, letters, folded posters. Pens, computer disks, even cassettes may find their way into a folder.

From the very start, set aside a section of an A4 pad for listing all **sources** you have consulted. Get into the habit of listing a source *immediately after* you have made use of it: it is possible to waste hours afterwards trying to trace a missing source.

As soon as possible, organise your project into sections and sub-sections. If you are using a lever-arch file, divide it into corresponding sections.

Don't be afraid to consult experts, whether local, national, or international. At the very least it will give you practice in writing letters of enquiry. Correspondence with a renowned expert will always be interesting for the reader. You have nothing to lose but the price of a stamp.

Accuracy is vital. Statistics and information presented as factual should be checked and, if possible, cross-checked with another source. If you are reporting on interviews you've conducted you *must* convey your interviewee's opinions accurately. If you are quoting a source, the words in quotation marks must be *exactly* as spoken.

Set a deadline for the completion of your information-gathering—and stick by it! There has to be a cut-off point when you stop assembling (however much you enjoy it) and start sifting.

11.2.3 Getting sorted

Sorting means evaluating, discarding, and arranging what's left. Evaluate, above all, for *relevance*. You have to be firm with yourself: however much you may enjoy a particular anecdote or wish to share your pleasure in a certain photograph, the ultimate criterion must be, is it *relevant*? If it's not, discard it.

The remaining material must be arranged. Decide how to divide it into sections and how to order the sections (which should be appropriately headed and numbered). Assessors usually look at the candidate's ability to structure ideas in a *logical sequence*. In other words, an item of information should *follow from* an earlier item; a section should build on the sections that have preceded it. So keep tinkering with possible ways of arranging until you come up with a satisfactory solution.

Having mapped out the sections and having allocated to each section its basic information, plan out your paragraphs within each section. What you are aiming for is a *skeleton outline*—a detailed breakdown of the whole project, showing what topic each paragraph will deal with. Indicate in your outline where you hope to use graphics.

You may find it helpful to use a very large sheet of paper for your skeleton outline. You will then be able to see at a glance how many sections you're using, how they relate to each other, and how the proportions compare.

The preparation of a skeleton outline may be the most important stage of all. You are deciding on the *content* and *shape* and *look* of your project. If you do a good job now, the actual writing will almost be a formality. You alone can take the layout decisions, but you should look for a second opinion once you think you've formed an outline.

11.2.4 Getting it on paper

And so to writing, which, as usual, means drafting until you're satisfied, making a final fair copy, and then proof-reading. If you have access to a word-processor you will find it a convenient way of drafting and editing.

Remember that you will almost certainly be assessed on your style and *use of language*. As in writing reports and minutes, your style should be formal, objective, and impersonal. Re-read the advice given in section 10.5.1 about **accuracy**, **brevity**, and **clarity**. Keep the reader always in mind, particularly if using specialist terms. These will be familiar to you because you use them every day as part of your vocational training, but they may need to be explained for those who haven't the same background.

Your project should have
- a **title page**, clearly stating the title and author's name
- a **table of contents**, showing how the project is divided into sections and telling at a glance how it is organised
- a **bibliography** or list of the books and articles you have consulted. Entries are usually listed alphabetically by surname and should record: author or authors (surname and first name or initial), *title* (in italic if possible, otherwise underlined), publisher, and year of publication; e.g. Corner, J., and Hawthorn, J. (editors), *Communication Studies: an Introductory Reader* (fourth edition) (Edward Arnold, London, 1993)
- **acknowledgments** (of assistance received)
- **page numbers**.

You may wish to include an **introduction** (where you supply the background to your project and 'introduce' it to the reader) and/or an **appendix** or appendixes (in which you provide supplementary material or material that may have arrived too late for inclusion in the body). Don't use either simply to look 'professional'.

The completed project needs to be *'packaged'*. We know that consumers are impressed by attractive packaging, and your care should extend to the physical production of your project. Access to a computer page make-up program and laser printer will open up all sorts of presentation possibilities. A tight budget will restrict choice.

Consider carefully your options in
- method of production (from handwriting to laser printer)
- typeface and type size (bearing in mind title, headings, body etc.)
- paper size and quality
- cover and type of binding (is stapling the only solution?)
- graphics.

11.3 Graphics

Graphics take many forms but they all emphasise the *visual* rather than the *verbal*. Computer technology makes it easy to convert lengthy verbal analyses into charts or graphs. As a result newspapers and magazines make more and more use of visual aids. In preparing your project, explore the possibilities of expressing information *visually*. If you have access to a computer, you might begin by investigating its capabilities in this area.

Consider some advantages of graphics. They can
- overcome language barriers
- make complex information available to *all* intelligence levels
- compress a large amount of information into a small space
- clarify information that words struggle to convey (e.g. a diagram of a complex mechanism)
- enliven a page of text
- make information available at a glance
- catch attention, tempting us to read what we might otherwise ignore
- help us to pin information into our memories.

Among the most commonly used graphical aids are:

signs and symbols
diagrams
cartoons and cartoon strips
photographs
maps
drawings
tables
graphs
charts
pictograms

Here are samples of the kind of aids you might wish to use:

1. *Table*
Circulation of Dublin daily newspapers, 1985–95

	Irish Times	Irish Independant	Irish Press
1985	85,420	158,685	89,249
1986	85,611	153,362	78,328
1987	88,739	151,150	79,235
1988	86,337	154,296	63,904
1989	91,885	152,513	63,904
1990	93,187	149,620	60,635
1991	93,827	150,377	59,049
1992	94,021	150,121	52,167
1993	92,295	144,174	46,759
1994	93,066	144,023	38,806
1995	95,310	147,066	n.a.

(Sources: Audit Bureau of Circulation and JNRR-Lansdowne.)

2. Line graph:

Numbers of students in second-level education

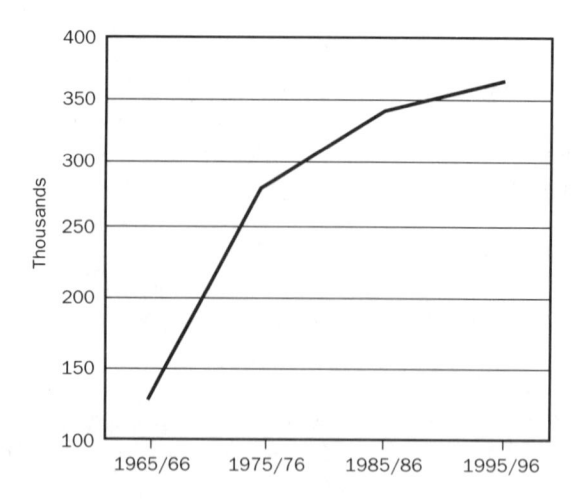

(Source: Department of Education.)

3. Bar charts—horizontal and vertical:

(i) *Horizontal*

Projected enrolment of students in second level

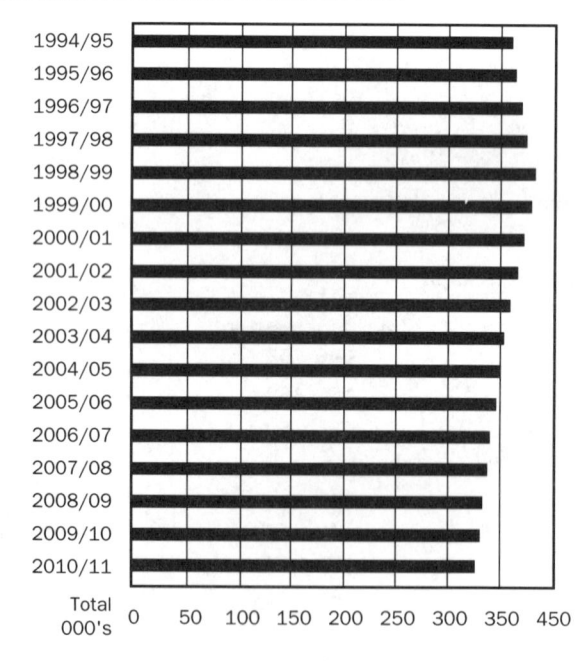

(Source: Department of Education.)

(ii) *Vertical*
Exchequer expenditure at second level

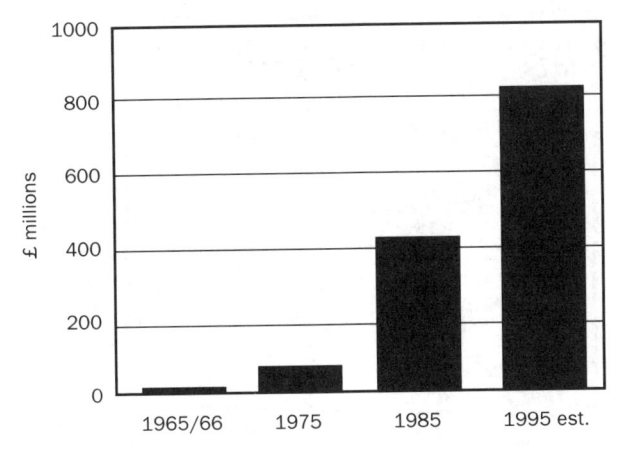

[Bar chart: £ millions vs year. 1965/66: ~20; 1975: ~80; 1985: ~440; 1995 est.: ~840.]

(Source: Department of Education.)

4. Pie chart:
Annual intake to post-second-level senior cycle programmes, 1994/95 (estimated)

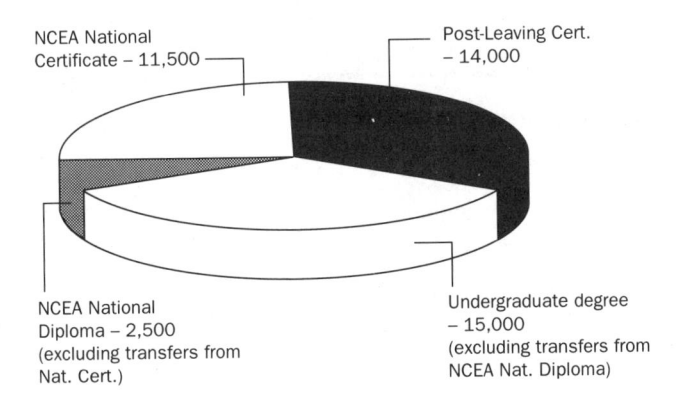

[Pie chart with segments:
- NCEA National Certificate – 11,500
- Post-Leaving Cert. – 14,000
- NCEA National Diploma – 2,500 (excluding transfers from Nat. Cert.)
- Undergraduate degree – 15,000 (excluding transfers from NCEA Nat. Diploma)]

(Source: Department of Education.)

5. Pictogram:
Some institutions of the European Union

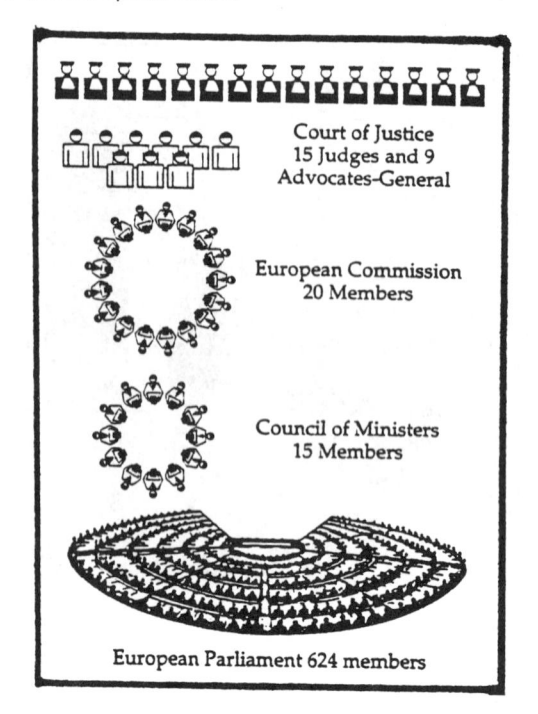

Court of Justice
15 Judges and 9
Advocates-General

European Commission
20 Members

Council of Ministers
15 Members

European Parliament 624 members

(Source: European Commission.)

6. Organisation chart:
Role of the Department of Education

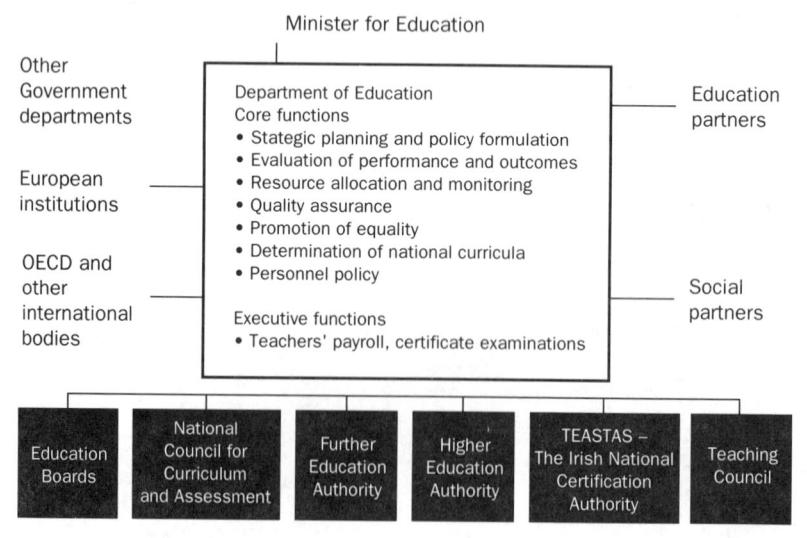

Minister for Education

Other Government departments

European institutions

OECD and other international bodies

Department of Education
Core functions
- Stategic planning and policy formulation
- Evaluation of performance and outcomes
- Resource allocation and monitoring
- Quality assurance
- Promotion of equality
- Determination of national curricula
- Personnel policy

Executive functions
- Teachers' payroll, certificate examinations

Education partners

Social partners

- Education Boards
- National Council for Curriculum and Assessment
- Further Education Authority
- Higher Education Authority
- TEASTAS – The Irish National Certification Authority
- Teaching Council

(Source: Department of Education.)

7. Flow chart:
Proposed framework for vocational qualifications

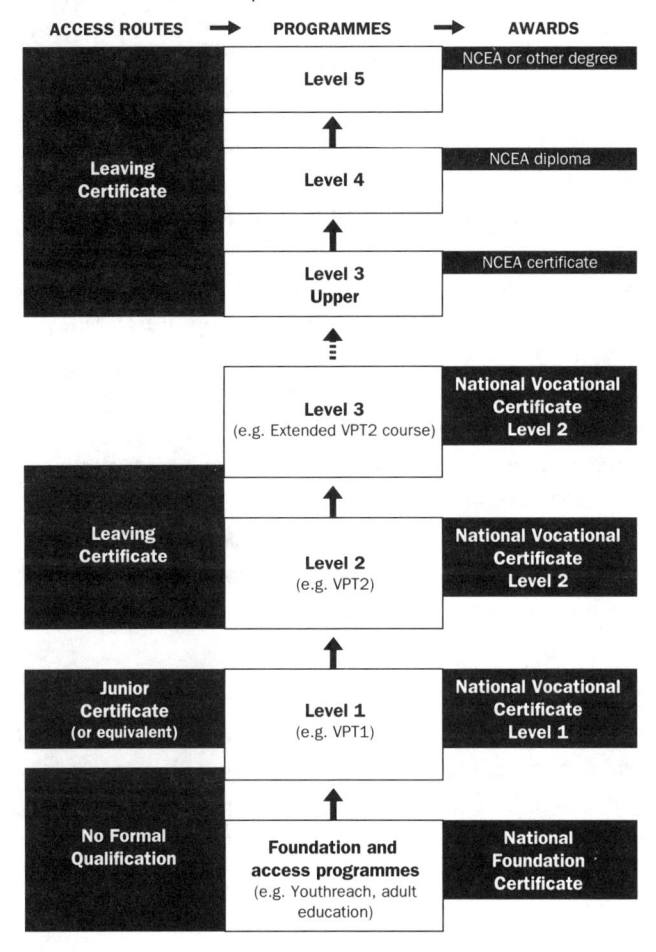

ACCESS ROUTES	PROGRAMMES	AWARDS
Leaving Certificate	Level 5	NCEA or other degree
Leaving Certificate	Level 4	NCEA diploma
Leaving Certificate	Level 3 Upper	NCEA certificate
Leaving Certificate	Level 3 (e.g. Extended VPT2 course)	National Vocational Certificate Level 2
Leaving Certificate	Level 2 (e.g. VPT2)	National Vocational Certificate Level 2
Junior Certificate (or equivalent)	Level 1 (e.g. VPT1)	National Vocational Certificate Level 1
No Formal Qualification	Foundation and access programmes (e.g. Youthreach, adult education)	National Foundation Certificate

(Source: NCVA, *Preparing for the New Europe*, 1992.)

The range of graphics from which you can choose is enormous. See what works in the world around you, in the print and electronic media you meet daily. Ask yourself if it could be adapted to suit your needs. Be inventive!

Supplementary tasks

1. An opinion poll taken the day after a budget asked the question, 'Do you think your standard of living will rise, fall or remain the same as a result of this budget?' Of those who responded, 12 per cent felt it would rise, 13 per cent felt it would fall, 73 per cent thought it would remain the same, and 2 per cent had no opinion. Express these results as a pie chart.

2. A national lottery has issued the following statistics at the end of a five-year period:

Year	Sales	Prizes
1990	£160 million	£90 million
1991	£240 million	£120 million
1992	£250 million	£130 million
1993	£265 million	£140 million
1994	£295 million	£150 million

Show the sales figures as a *horizontal* bar chart and the prize figures as a *vertical* bar chart.

3. In 1965 there were approximately 6,600 full-time teachers in second-level schools, in 1975 approximately 15,000, in 1985 approximately 19,000, and in 1995 approximately 22,000. Show this increase in a line graph.

4. Devise a pictogram to show the projected enrolment of students at second level in the horizontal bar chart on page 158 above.

5. Here are typical wedding costs (excluding the reception): stationery £150, rings £850, car hire £200, flowers £250, photography £400, church fees £150, groom's attire £280, bride's dress £680, going-away outfit £150, lingerie £50, cosmetics £40, attendants' outfits £350. Display this information in a format that has strong and clear visual impact.

Chapter review

1. List and explain five of the principal advantages of presenting information in visual form.
2. What specific advantages does the pie chart offer as a way of conveying statistics?
3. What are the limitations of a pictogram?
4. If you wished to include this textbook in a bibliography, how should the entry read?

Brush Up Your Basics: Writing Skills

12.1 Basic writing skills

This chapter is about reducing noise when we want to make clear *written* meanings. Sometimes the written messages we send are confusing, ambiguous, or even nonsense. Cloudy meanings on paper are often the result of fuzzy thinking. However, they may also be caused by ignorance of or lack of attention to what are called 'basic writing skills':
- handwriting
- punctuation
- spelling
- grammar
- vocabulary.

Here's a chance to brush up those skills. You'll find more about punctuation, spelling and handwriting than about vocabulary and grammar, simply because of pressure on space. Overall, the aim is to *remind* you of what you have forgotten rather than teach you anything new.

No period allocation is suggested for this chapter. Some individuals and groups may be perfectly satisfied with current practice; others may still be unsure of the difference between, say, a sentence and a phrase or between the comma and the full stop. The best method of studying the chapter is 'little and often'. If you want to undertake revision of punctuation, for instance, a fifteen-minute session devoted to a particular punctuation mark at the start of a series of periods is probably more useful than a whole period dealing with a range of punctuation marks. Tasks may be undertaken as a group or on a self-test basis.

Look on this positively as your last chance within the educational system to plug gaps or repair omissions. If the *motivation* is present, you may master now what has defeated you in the past (e.g. the correct use of the apostrophe). Perhaps the need to write a flawless letter of application is the spur you've always lacked.

Above all, remember that, whether learning or revising, the aim is to rid your writing of unwanted noise. Speech offers opportunities to clear up misunderstandings at once; a reader who may be thousands of miles away has no such opportunities.

12.1.1 HANDWRITING

Poor handwriting results in lower grades for course work, fewer marks in written exams, and lack of interest shown in application letters. The truth is that teachers, examiners and employers are only human and consciously or subconsciously will be influenced by handwriting that is hard to read.

Would you dream of sending an important message in a language or code with which your receiver is only partly familiar? This is what you're doing if you submit an illegible or semi-legible exam paper. At worst you'll have caused incomprehension; at best you'll have slowed down your reader, made concentration difficult, and put him or her in bad humour. The assumption may be made that you are aware of the problems created by your script, have it in your power to improve matters and have neglected to take remedial action. Wouldn't any examiner feel justified in marking you down?

Be honest: if you were faced with the scripts shown below would you not feel hostile towards A for the *apparent* reluctance to communicate with you? And grateful to B for the ease with which you can take his or her meaning?

A

B

> People don't talk like this, they talk like this. Syllables, words, sentences run together like a watercolour left in the rain. To understand what anyone is saying to us we must separate these noises into words and the words into sentences so that we might in our turn issue a stream of mixed sounds in response. If what we say is suitably apt and amusing, the listener will show his delight by emitting a series of uncontrolled high-pitched noises, accompanied by sharp intakes of breath of the sort normally associated with a seizure or heart failure.

Most of us associate reading with the *printed* word; handwriting is perceived as 'second-best' for clarity and speed of intake. Of course, printed type may lack the elegance, even beauty, of manuscript. It tells us nothing about the writer's age, eyesight, mood, or personality. There are times when printing, however clear, is inappropriate. Wouldn't some kinds of letter look distinctly odd in print? Even if you don't believe all that graphologists say they can deduce from a specimen of manuscript, you might be willing to agree that handwriting tells the reader *something* about the writer. Would you also agree that, while clarity in handwriting is important, a world in which handwriting was entirely uniform would be a much duller place?

TASK 12.1.1 A

Handwriting audit

On a sheet of unlined paper, write out the first paragraph of section 12.1.1 above ('Poor handwriting results ... hard to read'). Write fairly quickly, in your normal style.

Now, be judge of your own handwriting. Complete the following check-list, referring for evidence to what you have just written.

(1) My handwriting is
- very clear ☐
- clear ☐
- hard to read ☐
- very hard to read ☐

(2) My words are
- very large ☐
- large ☐
- average ☐
- small ☐
- very small ☐

(3) In appearance, my writing is
- very ornate ☐
- elegant ☐
- neat/plain ☐
- untidy ☐
- ugly ☐

(4) Words are spaced	very widely	☐	—consistent in size	Yes	☐
	adequately/evenly	☐		No	☐
	close	☐	Exceptions		
	too close	☐	—all clearly upper or lower case		
(5) My letters are				Yes	☐
—all equally legible	Yes	☐		No	☐
	No	☐	Exceptions		

Exceptions
—all leaning the same way
    Yes ☐
    No ☐
Exceptions

When you have completed the check-list, go into pairs and study each other's responses. How aware are individuals of the virtues and shortcomings of their handwriting?

Handwriting is a subject on which feelings run surprisingly high. In our teens it may be a sensitive issue, perhaps because handwriting is often seen as an expression of personality. Teenagers experiment with styles that 'suit', adding flourishes that seem to communicate individuality, copying features they admire in others' writing, and designing elaborate signatures.

Our main obligation in writing anything that others will read is *legibility*. If in your check-list you identified problem areas, are you content to continue causing noise to your reader? Noise reduction may in some instances be a very simple matter of using a different writing implement or different kind of paper; in others it may be a case of asking your local librarian to recommend a reputable teach-yourself manual. The initiative rests with you!

12.2 PUNCTUATION

Let's be clear *why* we punctuate. Without it we'd be faced, as readers, with this:

madonnasethersightsonhimjuliarobertsheld
himcloseyounggunstheworldoveridolisehimbut
ethanhawkecinemaslatestyounglionhdenieshispowers
ofattractionsorryabouttheshirtmanitsnotminequips
ethanhawkeasheamblespastmeonhiswaytomakeupthe
24yearoldactorisinlondonforpreciselythreehours
tobeinterviewedstyledandphotographedandheseems
nonetoohappyaboutthebrightlycolouredflower
patternedshirthehasbeenaskedtowearforour
photographsthisisliketotallynotmehesaystugging
attheoffendingitemalthoughhawkeiscurrentlythe
hottestyoungfilmstarinamericabecauseofhisrolesin
realitybitesandtheforthcomingbeforesunrisethe
leatheranddenimwearinggoateesportingactorisnot

> youraverageattitudetotingidolunlikethestudied
> broodingbrandoesquebratpackersofthe1980smatt
> dillonroblowetomcruiseemilioestevezkiefer
> sutherlandetalhawkeisengaginglyselfdeprecating
> andhedisplaysallthestyleandcasualinsoucianceof
> abonafide1990sfilmstarpuppyfatnotwithstanding

(*Sunday Times Magazine*, 9 April 1995.)

Ask a volunteer to read this aloud without preparation. How often does the reader stumble or falter and have to backtrack in order to make the letters make sense?

Writing, remember, post-dates speech and is a means of reproducing, through marks on paper, the stream of intelligible sounds we make when we talk.

Speech is an *unbroken* flow of sound: there is no speech equivalent of the white space that separates written words. If you listen to someone speaking an unfamiliar language, you have no way of knowing how many separate *words* are being spoken. Even in English it is possible to be confused about how the sound should be divided. *Oronyms* are streams of sound that may be separated in different ways: 'the stuff he knows' may be wrongly divided as 'the stuffy nose'.

The most basic punctuation we use in writing is the separation of one word from another. The reader's task is immediately easier:

> madonna set her sights on him julia roberts held him close young guns the world over idolise him but ethan hawke cinemas latest young lion denies his powers of attraction

To make the reader's job still easier, we indicate further separations, using full stops and commas, which divide sound into sentences and phrases:

> sorry about the shirt, man, its not mine, quips ethan hawke, as he ambles past me on his way to makeup. the 24 year old actor is in london for precisely three hours to be interviewed, styled and photographed, and he seems none too happy about the brightly coloured flower patterned shirt he has been asked to wear for our photographs. this is, like, totally not me, he says, tugging at the offending item.

Now let's add the capital letters that separate proper names and sentences, the quotation marks that separate direct speech, the hyphens, dashes, apostrophes, etc.:

> Madonna set her sights on him. Julia Roberts held him close. Young guns the world over idolise him. But Ethan Hawke, cinema's latest young lion, denies his powers of attraction. 'Sorry about the shirt, man, it's not mine,' quips Ethan Hawke, as he ambles past me on his way to make-up. The 24-year-old actor is in London for precisely three hours to be interviewed, styled and photographed, and he seems none too happy about the brightly coloured flower-patterned shirt he has been asked to wear for our photographs. 'This

is, like, totally not me,' he says, tugging at the offending item. Although Hawke is currently the hottest young film star in America, because of his roles in *Reality Bites* and the forthcoming *Before Sunrise*, the leather-and-denim-wearing, goatee-sporting actor is not your average attitude-toting idol. Unlike the studied, brooding Brandoesque brat-packers of the 1980s—Matt Dillon, Rob Lowe, Tom Cruise, Emilio Estevez, Kiefer Sutherland et al.—Hawke is engagingly self-deprecating, and he displays all the style and casual insouciance of a bona fide 1990s film star, puppy fat notwithstanding.

The final version offers us all the help we've been trained to expect of printed matter.

12.2.1 General issues

(1) Control: Punctuation offers the possibility of *controlling* your meaning when you commit it to paper. The absence of punctuation or faulty punctuation passes control to the reader, who must make the best meaning he can, acting on guesswork. Accurate, sophisticated punctuation enables you to be *clear* and to convey much of the effect (tone, emphasis, nuance, etc.) of the *spoken* word—what your reader might have *heard* in your voice had you spoken the words.

(2) Range: There are at least a dozen punctuation marks in common use. As a writer, you could get by without ever using some of them—for example, the semi-colon. But it would be like owning a 21-gear bike and restricting yourself to three or four of them.

(3) Taste rules OK? Like language itself, punctuation is always undergoing change. This makes it impossible to talk with certainty of rules. For example, the use of the full stop in abbreviations is no longer the simple rule it once was, as we'll see in section 12.2.2. Personal taste and fashion have always played a part in choice of punctuation. Fashion now favours a 'light' style, aiming to be clear but avoiding lots of commas, semi-colons etc.

(4) Separators: If your punctuation is suspect, it might help you to think of punctuation marks as *separators* or dividers, ranging from the paragraph that separates topics down to the commas that separate single-word items in a list.

12.2.2 Full stop (.)

The facts ...
The full stop has three functions:

1 (major): It brings a sentence in statement form to an end, like this. It *separates* one sentence from another.
Note
Each new sentence starts with a capital letter.

2 (minor): It shows *abbreviation*—for example e.g., i.e., etc., Co.

Note 1
The trend is to *drop* the full stop when the shortened form includes the *last* letter of the word abbreviated: Mr, Mrs, Dr.

Note 2
The initials of the names of organisations increasingly appear without full stops (e.g. RTE, ESB, FÁS, SIPTU).

3 (minor): A series of three full stops shows *omission*: e.g. in the 'Ethan Hawke' passage quoted above, the sentence 'But Ethan Hawke, cinema's latest young lion, denies his powers of attraction' could be shortened, if necessary, to 'But Ethan Hawke … denies his powers of attraction.'

TASK 12.2.2 A

Full stop self-test

Write out the following passage, putting in the full stops (and capital letters):

i know him we met at a party twenty years ago it was given by prof lee for her department she held it in the house in st paul street he arrived late so did i you could say it was fate, destiny, chance, etc

Note: Answers to all self-tests will be found at the end of this chapter.

12.2.3 QUESTION MARK (?) AND EXCLAMATION MARK (!)

The facts …
In addition to making *statements*, sentences may *question* or *exclaim* (express strong feelings, irony etc.):
What is a proper noun**?**
You've never heard of Ethan Hawke**!**
What a bright student you are**!**

 Both marks incorporate a full stop and are therefore powerful separators. Both are normally followed by a capital letter. In formal writing the exclamation mark is used sparingly; overuse diminishes its impact.

 In passages of direct speech, both marks are placed *inside* the quotation marks:
'Is a proper noun the name of a *particular* person, place or thing**?**' he asked. 'At last**!**' she exclaimed in relief.

Note 1
Remember that a question mark is **not** needed for *indirect* questions. It is often wrongly used with 'wonder':
I wonder what Madonna saw in Ethan Hawke? ✗
This merely *states* that there is wonder in my mind: no question is asked.

Note 2

For some reason, students often treat these marks as optional in written *dialogue*. It could be argued that they are never more needed than in, for example, a play script.

TASK 12.2.3 A

Question mark and exclamation mark self-test

Replace the asterisk with a question mark, exclamation mark, or full stop:

(i) 'Halt*' shouted the sentry* 'Who goes there*'

(ii) 'Ouch* Who threw that*'

(iii) I wonder if it's his*

(iv) What a shame* I don't think*

(v) He asked what I wanted*

12.2.4 CAPITAL LETTERS

The facts ...

Capital letters separate off—

(1) sentences, by capitalising the first letter:
   Young guns the world over idolise him.
(2) proper nouns from common nouns:
   '... the hottest young film star in **A**merica.'
(3) adjectives derived from proper nouns:
   '... brooding **B**randoesque brat-packers ...'
(4) passages of direct speech:
   He said, '**T**hat's it!'
(5) titles of all kinds (including those of people and organisations, books, newspapers, and magazines, and plays, films, and radio and television programmes):
   Reality **B**ites
   'The **L**ate **L**ate **S**how'
(6) the personal pronoun '**I**':
   I know them.

TASK 12.2.4 A

Capital letter self-test

Make a numbered list of all the capital letters needed in the following passage:

at st hilda's in galway, jane did spanish with miss o'brien on tuesdays and thursdays, using *spanish for starters*. 'i didn't learn much,' she confessed, 'and decided to quit at easter.'

12.2.5 COMMA (,)

The facts ...

Commas cause problems. Student writers recognise the mark's value as a separator but are often unsure about its exact *force* in keeping items or units apart. Commas, therefore, are sometimes found where a stronger separator (e.g. full stop or semi-colon) was required.

When writers become self-conscious about punctuation they tend to shake a seasoning of commas over a passage in the hope that some will settle in the right places. Regrettably, they sometimes fall where no comma ever went before.

Beware *underpowered* commas, *overused* commas, *misplaced* commas! With its wide range of applications, tempting flexibility, and ready availability, the comma is open to abuse.

Here are two common forms of comma-abuse:
I can't see her, is she wearing red? ✘
The thief, ran off. ✘

The first example is actually *two* sentences—a statement followed by a question:
I can't see her. Is she wearing red? ✓

In the second example the writer has separated a subject (thief) from its verb (ran off)—an unnatural separation:
The thief ran off. ✓

To help students distinguish between the need for full stops and commas, a 'voice test' is often recommended. This involves reading aloud and listening to the sound of your own voice. When you hear your voice dropping to a lower note and stopping, you probably need a full stop.
Drop + stop = .
When you hear your voice pausing fractionally and rising slightly in pitch, you probably need a comma.
Pause + rise = ,

A sentence might look and sound like this:
My   car,   an   ancient   green   Golf,   suffers   from   rust.

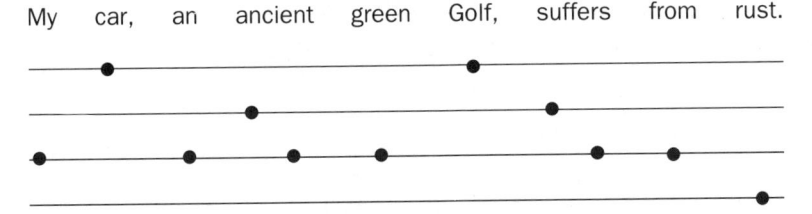

It has to be said that in order to hear clearly the rising inflection on commas you need to read aloud like a conscientious news reader or primary school storyteller.

What does the comma separate?
(1) Items in a *series or list*, whether single words (nouns, adjectives, verbs, adverbs) or groups of words (phrases or clauses):
   (*a*) Nouns:
      I bought tea, milk, bread, chocolate, cake and potatoes.
      (How would the meaning change if you removed the comma after 'chocolate'?)
   (*b*) Adjectives:

> The stranger was tall, dark, handsome and debonair.

(c) Adverbs:
> You should find it a truly, madly, deeply satisfying experience.

(d) Verbs:
> Hawke acts, writes, directs, models and promotes.

(e) Phrases:
> He looked up, smiled briefly, got to his feet, and strode to the door.

Note

An address is basically a *list* in which the items (house number, street, town and county) are separated by commas.

(2) People addressed, whether by name or other designation:
> 'Sorry about the shirt, man, it's not mine …'

(3) Direct or indirect speech when they occur in the same sentence:
> 'Do you', he enquired, 'come here often?'

(4) Descriptive, explanatory or parenthetical phrases or clauses that could be lifted out of the sentence without damaging the remainder or, alternatively, 'fenced off' within brackets or dashes:
> The film, a romantic comedy, appeals to the Slacker Generation, successors of the brat-packers.

(5) Question tags (strictly speaking, unnecessary additions):
> 'You saw it, didn't you?'
> 'It's a blow, isn't it?'

(6) Interjections (literally, bits 'thrown into' a sentence and therefore not essential to it) and sentence adverbs. The commonest are: yes, no, please, thank you, well, of course, too, however, oh, er, um, you know, like:
> There is, however, no evidence to support your, eh, thesis, you know.

(7) Participial (or '–ing') phrases:
> Feeling tired, she went to bed early.

Note

Beware of notoriously 'dangling' (or misrelated) participles, which can produce unintentional comedy:

Driving down the lane, the lost heifer gave me a real fright. ✗

This sentence needs to be recast:

The lost heifer gave me a real fright as I was driving down the lane. ✓

Finally, to demonstrate how commas can vitally affect meaning, explain clearly the difference between:

(i) The brother who works in the brewery is a bit of a chancer.

(ii) The brother, who works in the brewery, is a bit of a chancer.

Would the terms **defining** and **non-defining** assist your explanation?

TASK 12.2.5 A

Comma self-test

Write out this passage, putting in all necessary commas:

Crossing to the podium the speaker obviously nervous picked up her cue cards adjusted her glasses cleared her throat and began: 'Distinguished visitors honoured guests ladies and gentlemen it's been a moving exciting exhilarating evening hasn't it? However all good things er come to you know an end.'

12.2.6 SEMI-COLON (;)

The facts ...

Neglected and underused, this separator is stronger than a comma but weaker than a full stop. It is *not* followed by a capital letter. Think of its force as midway between that of a comma and a full stop. It is easy to use, helps to keep control of long sentences, and may enable you to make more sophisticated meanings on paper. It has two major functions:

(1) To separate groups of words or units of sense which could exist as independent sentences but are so closely connected in meaning that they are better coexisting as parts of the same sentence:

Outside, the house is restrained and severe; inside, it's a riot of colour.
Note 1
As is sometimes the case, the semi-colon here could be replaced with a conjunction such as 'but'.
Note 2
Here, as often, the semi-colon emphasises *contrast* between parts of a sentence.
Note 3
Used in this way, the semi-colon may delicately imply a connection the writer wouldn't dare state openly:

Nick won that year's prize; his father chaired the panel of judges.

(2) To organise individually long items into a coherent list, emphasising the parallelism and making the structure at all times clear to the reader:

The view from the summit was spectacular: to the east, glinting in the morning sunshine, the slate roofs of the small fishing village; to the south, the sparkling, apparently limitless Atlantic, dotted with tiny islands; on the western horizon, the gaunt lighthouse, rising sheer from the boiling sea; [note that this sentence could be expanded almost indefinitely while maintaining its clear basic structure]; and finally, hundreds of feet below her, the lake by which they had picnicked.

TASK 12.2.6 A

Semi-colon self-test

Rewrite this passage, inserting semi-colons:

His career was far from brilliant: a short period in the navy, ending in dishonourable discharge for theft some years doing nothing in particular in London and other large English cities a brief spell in Boston, where he held down a job in a fast-food outlet an unspecified time 'on the road' in Europe and then the abrupt return to Limerick.

TASK 12.2.6 B

Which of the following sentences need a semi-colon?

(i) This one isn't expensive that one will cost you a bomb.
(ii) Jim is here but Paula's out.
(iii) My wife is fond of rice I'm a potato person myself.

12.2.7 COLON (:)

The facts ...

The colon is sometimes confused with the semi-colon because of their resemblance. The colon's 'pause value' might be reckoned a little stronger than that of a comma but weaker than that of a semi-colon. It is not followed by a capital letter.

The colon serves two principal functions:

(1) To expand, amplify or develop information provided in the unit leading up to the colon:
The teacher was right: afternoon school had been cancelled. (*How* was she right? The section after the colon answers the question.)

(2) To introduce a list or sizeable quotation:
At this point I am reminded of Wilde's famous words: 'Education is an admirable thing, but it is well to remember from time to time that nothing that is worth knowing can be taught.'

Note

In both examples above, the colon means, in effect, 'namely,' 'that is,' 'as follows,' 'let me tell you more about what I've just said.' As with the semi-colon, there is strong interdependence between the words leading up to the colon and those that follow it.

TASK 12.2.7 A

Colon self-test

Convert the following eight sentence fragments into four sentences, using a colon to marry your pairs:

(i) Mae West put it neatly.
(ii) You're not going out wearing that.
(iii) A sleeping-bag, a torch, a pillow and a towel.
(iv) Attack, attack—and attack!
(v) One thing is certain.
(vi) Goodness had nothing to do with it.
(vii) Be sure to bring the following.
(viii) The plan couldn't have been simpler.

Be careful which member of the couple comes first!

12.2.8 Hyphen (-) and dash (—)

The facts ...
Although they look somewhat alike and may sometimes be mistaken for each other, these two marks serve different functions. The dash is very much a separator; the hyphen is mostly a joiner, though it does have one important separating function.

On typewriters and certain computers there is no provision for a dash, and so it has to be improvised; the best way of doing this is by typing two or three consecutive hyphens. Remember that there is never a space before or after a hyphen or a dash.

The hyphen has two principal functions:

(1) To create new meanings by joining existing words (or prefixes and words) to form new compounds: mother-in-law, commander-in-chief, semi-colon, multi-storey, devil-may-care.

Note 1
In very common compounds (blackboard, dustbin, outpatient) the hyphen may eventually disappear. It is sometimes hard to judge whether the hyphen is still necessary: some textbooks (text-books?) print 'semicolon', others 'semi-colon'.

Note 2
The hyphen's joining properties have obvious appeal to newspaper sub-editors pressed for space:
Ex-lover's bus-stop bust-up!

Note 3
Lazy writers sometimes take refuge in hyphens:
She had a 'why-don't-you-go-and-take-a-running-jump-at-yourself' expression on her face.
Could the writer have used *one* word in place of the hyphenated compound?

(2) To divide a word at the end of a line if the whole word won't fit. When separation takes place, the hyphen is placed after the *first* section of the word and is *not* repeated on the new line. The aim should be to hyphenate after a pronounceable syllable or series of syllables: e.g. auto-matic, sus-picion.

Note
Monosyllables, however long (e.g. cheese, rhyme, thought), are not divided.

The dash is much used informally, in notes, letters etc. It is often viewed with suspicion in formal writing, where it may be thought slapdash, the result of haste. In fact, it is a versatile mark and, depending on the circumstances, may be used to replace brackets, commas, colon and even semi-colon.

Its two main functions are:

(1) To separate with a pair of dashes—like these—something 'dropped into' a sentence, often parenthetically. Dashes can therefore substitute for brackets and, sometimes, commas (see section 12.2.5 above, function 4):
Emily Dickinson's poetry—familiar to thousands of Leaving Certificate English students—makes constant use of the dash.

Note

Here, as often, the dash gives a feeling of abruptness, of something that occurred to the writer after he or she had written the first three words.

(2) To tack on to the end of a sentence, after a single dash, an afterthought:
The dash in Dickinson's poetry suggests doubt, hesitancy, inconclusiveness—she even ends poems with dashes!

TASK 12.2.8 A

Hyphen and dash self-test

Rewrite this passage, which needs five hyphens and five dashes:

A half eaten apple it was a Golden Delicious sat on the sideboard and beside it lay a jam smeared book mine! Red faced with annoyance, I glared at my brother in law, who muttered something about having just got up a likely story! That's relations for you infuriating!

12.2.9 BRACKETS ()

The facts ...
Like the dash, brackets (which always appear in pairs) separate words inserted into a sentence as an aside, explanation, or amplification. Generally the insertion is of less importance than the rest of the sentence and might be removed without damaging the overall sense.

Brackets are handy for holding brief quotations or references if you don't want to break the flow of the reader's thought; but too many such interpolations may seem awkward.

Note
(When a complete sentence, like this one, is enclosed in brackets, the full stop comes *inside* the closing mark.) The full stop goes *outside* when a sentence closes with a bracketed phrase (like this).

TASK 12.2.9 A

Brackets self-test

Write out the phrases that might be enclosed in brackets in each of these sentences:
(i) The film's main characters are Stanley Robert de Niro and Iris Jane Fonda.
(ii) 'Cracker' RTE1, 10 p.m. is turning out to be exactly that!
(iii) In the Dáil the minister said it was her intention to set up an enquiry jeers and boos and to establish the truth prolonged catcalling and interruptions.

12.2.10 INVERTED COMMAS (" ")

The facts ...
Like brackets, inverted commas always appear in pairs. It is up to you whether you use double ("...") or single ('...'), so long as you are consistent. Their major function is to separate direct speech; minor functions are to mark off quotations, titles, and colloquialisms. All these functions have been illustrated in connection with other marks, allowing us to concentrate on *rules for direct speech*.

'Baby, it's cold outside.'

Reading this line with its inverted commas, you will assume it is either direct speech or a title (of a song, poem, etc.).

When a writer wishes to make it clear that the line was spoken, she has three options:

(1) He murmured, 'Baby, it's cold outside.'
(2) 'Baby, it's cold outside,' he murmured.
(3) 'Baby,' he murmured, 'it's cold outside.'

Spoken words may
  (*a*) be *introduced* with the identity of speaker and verb of speaking
  (*b*) be *followed* by the same information
  (*c*) be *interrupted* by the information.

A skilful writer will vary the three patterns.

The punctuation marks that help the reader by separating the words actually spoken from speaker ('he') and verb of speaking ('murmured') are:

(*a*)
—comma after the verb of speaking (murmured,)
—opening and closing inverted commas ('Baby ... outside')
—capital letter for start of words spoken (Baby)

(*b*)
—comma after the final word spoken (outside,')
—opening and closing inverted commas ('Baby ... outside')

(*c*)
—two sets of inverted commas to enclose the words spoken ('Baby' ... 'it's cold outside.')
—a pair of separating commas to enclose speaker and verb of speaking (, he murmured,)

Note 1
In version 3, 'it's' does *not* start with a capital letter, since it merely continues the direct speech. Most students find option 3 the most difficult to master.

Note 2
If you need to show speech within a speech, or if spoken words refer to a title, use *single* inverted commas for the enclosed speech or title:

"Baby," he murmured, "as the song says, 'It's cold outside'."

Alternatively, use single on the outside, double on the inside.

> **TASK 12.2.10 A**

Inverted commas self-test

Write out *two* versions of the following words, in the first of which Adam accuses Eve and in the second of which Eve accuses Adam:

Eve said Adam did it

> **TASK 12.2.10 B**

Punctuate this story:

guarding the gates of heaven stood st peter along came a lost soul who's there demanded st peter it is i replied the lost soul go to hell retorted st peter we've a rake of english teachers here as it is

Note: Show a change of speaker by a change of paragraph.

12.2.11 Apostrophe (')

The facts ...

Perhaps this mark should be renamed the 'catastrophe'. For most students it's the most troublesome mark of all. A recent newspaper survey found that nearly half of those surveyed did not recognise any difference between **it's** and **its** and 15 per cent did not know what an apostrophe is.

The apostrophe is often omitted where it is required (Yeats poems) or inserted incorrectly (Yeat's poems). Widespread uncertainty about its use may eventually lead to the apostrophe's disappearance. Already, words such as 'shan't' (which should, technically, contain at least one other apostrophe to show the omission of –ll in 'shall') have reduced to a single apostrophe (indicating the absence of which letter?).

The apostrophe is actually quite simple to use, particularly if you grasp one essential fact:
The apostrophe always shows that a letter (or letters) has been left out.

Letters are left out of words when we want
(*a*) to shorten or contract
(*b*) to show possession or relationship.

The first of these processes is easily shown:

they are → they're
you are → you're
it is → it's
cannot → can't
I would → I'd
one has → one's

Less obvious is how letters are lost in showing possession or relationship. Take possession:

the flag of the ship = the flag 'belongs to' the ship

In place of the cumbersome 'of the', English allows
the ship's flag

But what missing letter does the apostrophe replace? The answer lies in the distant past. The Old English (roughly 450–1150 AD) equivalent of 'ship's' was 'scipes'. The 'e' has dropped out—as it has in landes, godes, stanes, bearnes, daeges, and many others.

The possessive apostrophe means learning three rules:

Rule 1

's to show that something or someone 'belongs to' *one* possessor (the boy's foot)

Rule 2

s' to show that something or someone 'belongs to' *more than one* possessor
Remember, the *possessor* becomes plural—which in the great majority of English words means adding s, with the apostrophe coming *after* that s (the boys' father)

Rule 3

's to show possession by an *irregular plural*. A few very common words do *not* become plural by adding s; they are treated as if singular: the children's parents.
Other common irregular plurals are men, women, teeth, feet, mice, sheep, fish.

Warning!
(1) *Relationship* is often overlooked in such everyday phrases as a stone's throw, a fortnight's holiday, for God's sake, a month's notice, ten years' service.
(2) *Possessive pronouns* (mine, yours, his, hers, its, ours, theirs—belonging to me, you etc.) do *not* contain apostrophes; it would be as daft to write 'hi's books' as it would to write 'Your's sincerely'.
(3) *Notorious confusables* include who's (who is/who has) and whose (belonging to 'who'); it's (it is/it has) and its (belonging to 'it').
(4) *Simple plurals* without any hint of possession require *no* apostrophe:
Six TDs voted.
The 1990s saw great changes.
(5) *Proper names* conform to the three rules: Keats's letters, Dickens's novels. But sometimes long names ending in s simply add an apostrophe to show possession:
the theorem of Pythagoras → Pythagoras' theorem

TASK 12.2.11 A

Apostrophe self-test

We've seen 'the flag of the ship' become 'the ship's flag'. Do the same conversion on the following phrases:
(i) the star of the film →
(ii) the saddles of the horses →
(iii) the liberation of women →
(iv) the church of St James →
(v) the tails of the mice →

> **TASK 12.2.11 B**
>
> Put apostrophes into these sentences:
> (i) Whose bikes that? Isnt it yours?
> (ii) Micks mothers dogs left its muddy marks everywhere!
> (iii) For Heavens sake dont lose the childrens ball!

12.2.12 Phrases, sentences, and paragraphs

The facts ...

In primary school you were taught that a sentence is 'a group of words making complete sense' and a phrase is 'a group of words that in itself does not make complete sense, even though it might as an answer to a question.'

This is a short sentence. (Sentence)

A short sentence. (Phrase)

Single words may be sentences because they 'include' unspoken words:

Hello (you).

(You) Stop!

Writing separates into units of phrases, sentences and paragraphs as a way of assisting readers to grasp the meaning. Phrases are assembled to form sentences, sentences to form paragraphs about a topic. These are the blocks with which we build meaning.

TOPIC: The camel

INDENT PARAGRAPH START → The camel is well adapted to survive in a desert environment. Labelled "The Ship of the Desert", it can travel for days without drinking. *It stores up to twenty gallons of water in special cells in its stomach.* Its fatty hump acts as a food store. The camel's lips are covered *with thick skin*, allowing it to eat thorny desert plants.

SENTENCE: It stores up to twenty gallons of water in special cells in its stomach.

PHRASE: with thick skin

Formal writing, it used to be felt, should always be cast in sentences. Phrases were 'incorrect', and were to be found only in tabloid newspapers or advertisements. (Can you see why advertising favours phrases?) Attitudes now are more relaxed. It's recognised that a writer may wish to use phrases for a variety of reasons.

Good paragraphing is an indication of a tidy, orderly mind concerned to get its message across and genuinely eager to help the reader. Usually, a paragraph will announce its topic in an opening sentence. Sometimes the topic will be summed up in the paragraph's final sentence.

Paragraphs help the *visual* appearance of a page. Pages of unbroken type or handwriting put most readers off. The indentation made for the first line of a paragraph breaks up the solid mass. A line blank between paragraphs further relieves the reader's eye.

Paragraphs help readers to follow the flow of *dialogue* in a novel or short story. The modern practice is to show a change of speaker by a change of paragraph. The formula to remember is *NS = NP* (new speaker = new paragraph).

TASK 12.2.12 A

Phrase and sentence self-test
After each of the following write either **S** (sentence) or **P** (phrase):
(i) Stop that!
(ii) On your bike.
(iii) Out of the trees and into.
(iv) Let's be friends.
(v) The manager came in then.

12.3 SPELLING

First the *bad* news:
- English has at least forty-four different sounds but only twenty-six letters to spell them.
- The spelling of English shows how the words sounded when spoken five hundred years ago. Printers back then needed uniform decisions on what letters to choose to represent sound. Pronunciation has changed greatly over the centuries, but spellings have remained much the same—exhibits in a phonetic museum. 'Knight' (now pronounced 'nite') in the fifteenth century would have included a sounded 'k' and a guttural sound to render 'gh'.
- Modern English is not a phonetically written language, as any learner sorting out *ought, though, through, rough, trough* and *bough* will wearily tell you.
- Many attempts have been made to design an improved system of English spelling or to reform the existing system (e.g. 'Cut Spelling', which cuts out redundant letters as in 'th skils of riting') but without, so far, notable success.

Now the *good* news:
- A large majority (about 84 per cent) of English words follow regular patterns and rules (e.g. belong to 'families' such as catch, match, patch).
- Only about 3 per cent of English words are genuinely unpredictable, and since these are some of the words in commonest use (of, women, who, one, do), their very familiarity drums correct spellings into our heads.

If you are a weak speller you may not take much comfort from the good news. There is no doubt that English spelling causes headaches (how might an innocent learner expect

'ache' to sound?). Every few months the British press uses the appearance of yet another survey to deplore the further decline in spelling standards. Headlines announce:
50% of adults unable to spell 'withhold', 'occurred', 'innovate'!
34% of secretarial job applicants unable to spell 'truly'!
54% of adults unable to tell the difference between 'practice' and 'practise'!
Over 75% of university science students unable to spell 'occurrence'!

TASK 12.3 A

Spelling self-test

How do you rate your own spelling? Can you improve on the performance of 83 per cent of British adults who apparently can't spell the six words indicated by the following clues?

(i) Wanted: cheap ac—m———n for two students.
(ii) 'Yours faithfully' and 'Yours si———y' are the two closures most regularly used.
(iii) At times a referee must s-p—te or keep apart two boxers.
(iv) Don't poke your nose into my b—ness!
(v) The measurement from head to toe is your h——t.
(vi) Nowadays it is not always ne———ry to wear a tie in fashionable restaurants.

Even if you didn't manage to get one correct answer, does it matter? After all, the former Vice-President of the United States, Dan Quayle, showed very publicly his inability to spell potatoes—or should that be potatos? And isn't it true that Shakespeare did not spell his own surname the same way twice in any of the six surviving signatures?

Faulty spelling matters when
- it creates so much noise that meaning is either obscured or lost completely
- it communicates a damaging picture of the writer (careless, stupid, uneducated, rude etc.)
- it stands in the way of achievement (in exams, job-hunting, promotion etc.).

But we should not be too judgmental of incorrect spelling, because
- some of the greatest writers were terrible spellers (Scott Fitzgerald, for instance, could never get 'yacht' right)
- dyslexia (difficulty in learning to read) afflicts as much as 5 per cent of the population
- even the best spellers have blind spots and make mitsakes. Many a school report regrets that X has not benifited/benefitted from the excellent tuition on offer. (And the correct spelling is …?)

12.3.1 Spelling self-help

If your spelling is shaky, what can you do to help yourself?

(1) Discover exactly what mistakes you make. Very often the words a weak speller is most confident about are those that are wrong. Use teachers, family and friends as error-detectors.

(2) Keep a list, *correctly spelt*, of the *common* words that cause you difficulty. Go over it regularly.

(3) Use a dictionary if you are unsure of the full spelling but can get the first few letters. (Can you complete 'psy—a—ist'?)

(4) Study the *appearance* of words that cause you bother. Have you noticed how people who are unsure of a spelling will write the word down and say, 'That *looks* right'?

(5) Group troublesome words into *categories*, underlining the problem areas. For example:
- One doubled letter: exagg**e**rate
- Two doubled letters: embarrassed
- Misspelling through mispronunciation: library, interested, secretary …
- Specific letter problems: d**e**scribe, exist**e**nce, p**e**rsuade …

(6) Use a selection of the various rules available (see below) and home-made mnemonics (e.g. se**par**ate has a *pair* of '**a**'s)

(7) Use *all* the methods suggested and *keep using them*! You won't become an ace speller overnight.

Warning!
Whoever said 'Rules were made to be broken' must have had spelling in mind!

Rule 1
The ie/ei rule that everybody knows in part. Learn all *three* parts:
(i) i before e (believe)
(ii) except after c (receive)
(iii) or when pronounced other than ee (neighbours)
Notable exceptions: seize, friend.

Rule 2
When a word containing –ll is added to another word, –ll becomes –l:
skill + full → skilful
well + come → welcome
all + ways → always

Rule 3
Words ending in silent –e drop the e before a suffix starting with a vowel:
come + ing → coming
hope + ing → hoping
Notable exceptions: words ending in –ce or –ge:
notice + able → noticeable
outrage + ous → outrageous

Rule 4

–ly is a suffix used to make a great many adverbs:

beautiful + ly → beautifully

extreme + ly → extremely

The suffix is never –ley!

immediate + ly → immediatley ✘

Rule 5

Dis– and mis– are prefixes attached to many words. Don't be tempted to add or subtract letters when joining these prefixes to root words:

dis + appear → disappear ✓

dis + appoint → dissapoint ✘

mis + spell → mispell ✘

12.4 CONFUSIONS

English places at its speakers' disposal an enormous treasury of words. It is notoriously difficult to calculate exactly *how many* words are available for our use, and it's equally difficult to estimate the size of any person's vocabulary. (The first obstacle is to distinguish between our *active* vocabulary of words we actually use and our *passive* vocabulary of words we know but never use and mightn't even know how to pronounce.) The current edition of the *Oxford English Dictionary* contains about 300,000 entries, defining over half a million items.

Given the size of the English lexicon, it is not surprising that in sound and spelling some words are very alike and thus cause confusion. Is the title of Daniel Corkery's story 'The Breadth of Life', 'The Bread of Life', 'The Breath of Life', or 'The Breathe of Life'?

TASK 12.4 A

Confusables

The following sentences contain pairs of some of the most notorious confusables. Choose the correct word from each bracketed pair:

(i) The teacher was reluctant to [except/accept] my excuse.

(ii) The introduction of a new player had the desired [effect/affect] of producing a goal.

(iii) The [compliment/complement] brought an instant blush to his cheeks.

(iv) Slouched posture and glazed expression clearly signalled his [disinterested/uninterested] attitude to the proceedings.

(v) A [continuous/continual] stream of spectators poured from the racecourse.

(vi) Nobody likes to [loose/lose].

(vii) Customers appreciate the [personal/personnel] touch in most services.

(viii) The opposition stands accused of lack of [principle/principal].

(ix) *All [Quite/Quiet] on the Western Front* is a rare example of a famous book that became a famous film.

(x) Job applications should always be written on good-quality [stationery/stationary].

(xi) I can't decide [weather/whether] to go or to stay.

(xii) Time [past/passed] all too quickly, and soon it was time to leave.

(xiii) 'It won't come [off/of],' she complained, tugging furiously at her boot.

(xiv) Who said the emperor wasn't wearing any [cloths/clothes]?

With the best will in the world, our use of language sometimes gives rise to *ambiguities*. A very simple sentence, 'He likes me better than you,' could have two quite different meanings. As could 'You can't have too many on a committee.'

A notice posted in a shop window, 'LOST—a small, red-faced woman's wrist-watch' would surely be improved by a little re-arranging: LOST—a woman's small, red-faced wrist-watch.'

The above example belongs with those lists of 'howlers' regularly reproduced in magazines and on notice-boards and reportedly taken from student essays, insurance claim forms, newspaper headlines etc.

TASK 12.4 B

Put it another way

Rewrite, rearrange or reword the following statements so that any ambiguities are removed. Try to keep adjustments to the minimum and be sure that the reader receives the message the author intended:

(i) An invisible car came out of nowhere, struck my car, and vanished.

(ii) The pedestrian had no idea which direction to go, so I ran over him.

(iii) We never allow a dissatisfied customer to leave the premises if we can avoid it.

(iv) The lecturers for tomorrow will be found pinned to the notice-board.

(v) Coming home, I drove into the wrong house and collided with a tree I didn't have.

(vi) The other car collided with mine without giving warning of its intentions.

(vii) The guy was all over the road; I had to swerve a number of times before I hit him.

(viii) In my attempt to kill a fly I drove into a telephone pole.

(ix) The telephone was approaching fast; I was attempting to swerve out of its path when it struck my front end.

This chapter has tried to raise your consciousness of the ways in which it is possible to eliminate unwanted noise in written communication. Chapter 8 suggested one very important way in which you can remove noise: intelligent proof-reading. If we all took the trouble to *check* and *double-check*, we might save a great deal of confusion.

Answers

12.2.2 A. I know him. We met at a party twenty years ago. It was given by Prof. Lee for her department. She held it in the house in St Paul Street. He arrived late. So did I. You could say it was fate, destiny, chance etc.

12.2.3 A. (i) ! . ? (ii) ! ? (iii) . (iv) ! ! (v) .

12.2.4 A. At St Hilda's in Galway, Jane did Spanish with Miss O'Brien on Tuesdays and Thursdays, using *Spanish for Starters*. 'I didn't learn much,' she confessed, 'and decided to quit at Easter.'

12.2.5 A. Crossing to the podium, the speaker, obviously nervous, picked up her cue cards, adjusted her glasses, cleared her throat and began: 'Distinguished visitors, honoured guests, ladies and gentlemen, it's been a moving, exciting, exhilarating evening, hasn't it? However, all good things, er, come to, you know, an end.'

12.2.6 A. ... discharge for theft; ... large English cities; ... fast-food outlet; ... in Europe; ...

12.2.6 B. (i) and (iii).

12.2.7 A. (i) + (vi); (v) + (ii); (vii) + (iii); (viii) + (iv).

12.2.8 A. A half-eaten apple—it was a Golden Delicious—sat on the sideboard and beside it lay a jam-smeared book—mine! Red-faced with annoyance, I glared at my brother-in-law, who muttered something about having just got up—a likely story! That's relations for you—infuriating!

12.2.9 A. (i) (Robert de Niro) (Jane Fonda). (ii) (RTE1, 10 p.m.). (iii) (jeers and boos) (prolonged catcalling and interruptions).

12.2.10 A. (i) 'Eve', said Adam, 'did it.' (ii) Eve said, 'Adam did it.'

12.2.10 B. Guarding the gates of Heaven stood St Peter. Along came a lost soul. 'Who's there?' demanded St Peter.

'It is I,' replied the lost soul.

'Go to hell,' retorted St Peter. 'We've a rake of English teachers here as it is.'

12.2.11 A. (i) the film's star; (ii) the horses' saddles; (iii) the women's liberation; (iv) St James's church; (v) the mice's tails.

12.2.11 B. (i) Whose bike's that? Isn't it yours? (ii) Mick's mother's dog's left its muddy marks everywhere. (iii) For Heaven's sake don't lose the children's ball.

12.2.12 A. (i) sentence; (ii) phrase; (iii) phrase; (iv) sentence; (v) sentence.

12.3 A. (i) accommodation; (ii) sincerely; (iii) separate; (iv) business; (v) height; (vi) necessary.

12.4 A. (i) accept; (ii) effect; (iii) compliment; (iv) uninterested; (v) continuous; (vi) lose; (vii) personal; (viii) principle; (ix) quiet; (x) stationery; (xi) whether; (xii) passed; (xiii) off; (xiv) clothes.

PART 4

WORDS WE READ

13 READING FOR A PURPOSE

FOUR PERIODS

13.1 'NOBODY READS ANY MORE'

Do we live in a post-literate world? Has the age of the printed word given way to the age of the (tele)visual image? Does the new technology spell The End for the book? Who wants pulp fiction when you can have virtual reality?

Somebody must be reading. Retail book buying in Ireland is worth about £123 million a year. Irish publishers in the mid-1990s employ about 450 people and publish some 800 titles annually. In the United States, cradle of the digital technology that is revolutionising publishing, some 100,000 new titles are published each year. Americans bought over 1,000 million books in 1994, many of them from bookshops that double as bars or cafés. American books, particularly college textbooks, now often come accompanied by a computer disk or CD-ROM, but so far there seems to be no real justification for the gloomier predictions about the book's future.

In part 4 we'll consider the *purposes* for which people read. This chapter looks at the *functional* reading we do in a *social* context—reading we're *obliged* to do as workers, car owners, income tax payers, or just concerned citizens. It offers advice if your purpose in reading is to *find* a particular piece of information in a world that sometimes seems bewilderingly overstocked with the commodity. Chapter 14 is about the reading we do for ourselves, when our purpose is to pass time pleasurably.

People are certainly reading. What do *you* read?

TASK 13.1 A

Taking written meanings

Over the past twenty-four hours you have almost certainly seen a great many words written in all sorts of places—words written on buses, walls, desks, cereal packets, even, conceivably, in the sky!

Give yourself three minutes to jot down where you have *actively read* words since this time yesterday. Be as specific as possible. Pool the results.

You will probably be surprised by
- the amount of reading you've done
- the *variety* of places where you've come across written words.

Your joint list may include some of the different forms of writing discussed in part 3: letters, faxes, memos, notices, minutes, notes, projects, reports etc. After all, we mostly write to be read. The group's list may feature:

newspapers	computer instructions
cheques	catalogue
magazines	invitations
telephone call card	hoardings
recipes	labels
coin	'for sale' signs
leaflets	timetables
brand names	film subtitles
signposts	brochures
phone directory	envelopes
posters	television commercials
menu	novels
Bible	

Whether you've been *devouring* a bedtime thriller, *scanning* the television guide in search of a programme, *flipping through* a magazine in a waiting room, *referring to* a notice posted in a corridor, *leafing through* the pages of your diary, *browsing through* titles in a bookshop, *skimming through* a bank statement, or *poring over* an application form, you've been taking meanings made by others: receiving messages.

Think how your daily life would be altered if you were unable to receive written messages. It is often said that adults who are unable to read don't go out as much as those who can. Why might this be so?

Of course you haven't simply been a *taker* of meaning, a mere passive *receiver*. As has so often been stressed, communication is a *two-way* process. The act of reading involves you *actively* in the making of meaning.

We talk of words *making sense* to us. We also talk of *making sense* of something. Written words *make sense* to us, but we also *make sense* of them.

A simple example: the *context* in which we read affects the meaning we place on words. If the light is poor and the driver is tired and in a hurry, she may create a false meaning from a signpost. Instead of taking the meaning intended she will have made her own different meaning. It's a common experience that the same words read in different moods may produce quite different effects. So we *interact* with written words.

There are
- different kinds of text to be read
- appropriate ways of reading them.

At the start of our schooldays, classrooms are places where
- we learn to read.

They later become places where
- we read to learn.

Much of the reading we do in the course of our lives is to learn, to find information, to keep abreast of events and ideas, and to share knowledge and experience with others. Reading of this kind is done, in a sense, to profit ourselves: as a result we might invest wisely, pay less tax, reject suspicious 'free offers', or become more knowledgeable about ourselves, our society, our jobs, the world we live in and the big issues of the age.

13.1.1 FOUR WAYS OF READING

Because so much of our early reading is school-related and seems always to be accompanied by the instructions 'slowly and carefully', it's easy to forget that other ways of reading exist and may be more appropriate to the *purpose* in hand. We should think of

(1) **scanning**—*very fast* 'at-a-glance' reading, for example of notice-boards, timetables, schedules, and directories, to find a particular piece of information

(2) **skimming**—*fast*, superficial reading, for example of magazine and newspaper articles, junk mail, brochures, advertisements, to get the gist or a general overview

(3) **normal reading**—at moderate cruising speed, of novels, letters, or newspapers

(4) **close reading**—slow, intensive study of manuals, complicated documents, poetry, or demanding novels.

To sign a contract you've merely *scanned* would be foolish. To *pore over* a Christmas cracker joke, hunting for hidden subtleties, would be equally foolish. There are different sorts of text, written for quite different purposes, and as readers we need to choose an appropriate style of reading. In practice we often use a mixture of styles—for example, skimming and then backtracking to read normally. Let's look more closely at each of the four ways.

13.1.2 SCANNING

'Scan: to look at all parts of, esp. quickly.'

We scan horizons in search of objects, rooms in search of individuals, a page in search of a bit of information (name, number, address, statistic). The purpose is to find the desired information as fast as possible. An exam candidate, given the question paper, will often, before doing anything else, scan it anxiously to see if expected names or topics feature. Following this preliminary scan the candidate will skim-read the questions before finally settling down to close reading and choosing.

In scanning, we skip over unimportant words to get to those we want to meet.

TASK 13.1.1 A

Scan test

You are looking for a new boat that you can carry on a car roof-rack—something weighing about 125 lb would be ideal. Scan the specifications below to find which of the four models best suits your needs.

SPECIFICATIONS

Model	12'K	14'K	14'R	16'M20
Centre line	12'1"	14'1"	13'8"	16'3"
Seats	3	3	3	4
Beam	56"	57"	62"	70"
Bow height	27.0"	$27^1/2$ "	30"	32"
Transom height	15"	15"	16"	16"/21"
Transom width	51"	51"	54"	62"
Person cap.	3	4	4	5
Person cap. lbs.	410	500	590	800
Weight cap. lbs.	570	680	830	1150
H.P. cap	10	15	25	40
Approx. wt. lbs.	100	128	175	250

13.2 SKIMMING

Skimming is fast reading to get the drift. Often we skim-read to discover if we are sufficiently interested to go back and read carefully. Researching a project, we might skim-read a chapter or two from a book to see if it is relevant to our needs. Skimming by definition means a surface reading, homing in only on topic sentences (which are often at the beginning of paragraphs), seeing where the writer is going, gleaning what the writer's overall drift might be.

TASK 13.2 A

Skim test

In an airport bookshop a few minutes before your flight is called you are hurriedly searching for something to read. You skim the blurbs (brief back-cover descriptions) of three paperbacks looking for tough crime-writing that's just a bit different. How long does it take you to decide which of the following fills the bill?

The Real McCoy

The world knows him as Paul Grinstead. A bit of a loner. Even an oddity. Little do they suspect. By night, he's the Iceman. And the Iceman cometh. A small Cornish fishing village is traumatised by a series of horrific slayings, each bearing the hideous trademark of ... the Iceman! Can Chief Inspector Noah McCoy stop the slaughter?

The Fax of Life
An unusual pencil ... a mysterious fax from Vancouver ... a shot in the dark—three clues from which boozy ex-journo Bill Castle must unravel the mysteries leading to the sudden demise of glamorous ex-starlet Lucinda Laverty while holidaying in the high Pyrenees. Set in the luxurious playgrounds of Europe's super-rich, this spellbinding adventure story will have you biting your nails right to the last page.

All Gone
In the sleazy depths of the Miami underworld a deadly spider spins a web of fiendish cunning. But is the fly as innocent as he looks?

Yes, he's done it again. Never content with the conventional, author Sam Pappenheimer tells his riveting story entirely in ... baby talk! Another tour-de-force from the James Joyce of crime!

13.2.1 NORMAL READING

This is the natural, casual way we read material that makes no great demands on our concentration. Normal reading speeds vary greatly, and it may help you to know whether you are a slow or fast reader. If you are very slow you might consider taking action to improve your speed. Books teaching speed-reading techniques are readily available, and you might have a look at some in your local library before you decide to buy. Two cautions: first, comprehension is always more important than speed (not much point in reading without understanding!); second, you will not become a super-efficient fast reader overnight: improvement will take *regular* hard work.

The test that follows does not offer precise scientific measurement but it may give a rough idea of where you stand on a reading speed scale.

TASK 13.2.1 A

How fast do you read?

You are about to read a passage of 537 words. It will contain a good deal of information presented in a light, journalistic style. You are unlikely to meet unfamiliar words. It is vital that you read the passage at your normal reading rate. *Do not rush or compete.* Read to get a reasonable understanding but don't fuss about small details.

The group leader will issue your times if you put up a hand or say 'Finished' when you have completed the passage. Make a note of your time, close the book, and wait until the last person has finished.

Remember, *normal* reading, starting ... *now!*

Six days a week an Englishman named Roy Dean sits down and does in a matter of minutes something that many of us cannot do at all: he completes the crossword puzzle in the *Times*. Dean is the— well, the dean of the British crossword. In 1970, under test conditions, he solved a *Times* crossword in just three minutes and forty-five seconds, a feat so phenomenal that it has stood unchallenged for twenty years.

According to a Gallup poll, the crossword is the most popular sedentary recreation. The very first crossword, containing just thirty-two clues, appeared in the New York *World* on 21 December 1913. It had been thought up as a space filler by an expatriate Englishman named Arthur Wynne, who called it a word-cross. (Remember what I said about inventors never quite getting the name right?) It became a regular feature in the *World*, but nobody else picked it up until April 1924, when a fledgling publishing company called Simon and Schuster brought out a volume of crossword puzzles, priced at $1.35. It was an immediate hit and two other volumes were quickly produced. By the end of the first year the company had sold half a million copies, and crossword puzzles were a craze throughout America—so much so that for a time the Baltimore and Ohio Railroad installed dictionaries in each of its carriages for the convenience of puzzle-solving travellers who had an acute need to know that Iliamna is the largest lake in Alaska or that oquassa is a kind of freshwater fish.

Despite this huge popularity, the most venerable papers on both sides of the Atlantic refused for years to acknowledge that the crossword was more than a passing fad. The *Times* held out until January 1930, when it finally produced its first crossword (devised by a Norfolk farmer who had never previously solved one, much less constructed one). To salve its conscience at succumbing to a frivolous game, the *Times* printed occasional crosswords in Latin. Its namesake in New York held out for another decade and did not produce its first crossword until 1942.

Only one other word game has ever challenged the crossword puzzle for popularity and respectability and that's Scrabble. Scrabble was introduced by a games company called Selchow and Righter in 1953, though it had been invented, by one Alfred Butts, more than twenty years earlier in 1931. Butts clearly didn't have too much regard for which letters are used most often in English. With just ninety-eight tiles, he insisted on having at least two of each letter, which means that q, j and z appear disproportionately often. As a result, success at Scrabble generally involves being able to come up with obscure words like 'zax' (a hatchetlike tool) and 'xi' (the fourteenth letter of the Greek alphabet).

Butts intentionally depressed the number of s's to discourage the formation of plurals, though he compensated by increasing the number of i's to encourage the formation of suffixes and prefixes. The highest score, according to Alan Richter, a former British champion writing in the *Atlantic* in 1987, was 3,881 points. It included the word 'psychoanalyzing', which alone was worth 1,539 points.
(Bill Bryson, *Mother Tongue*, p. 222–4 (adapted).)

When the last person has finished and noted his or her time, answer the following ten questions by ticking the appropriate box. (The answers will be found at the end of this chapter.) A score of 7 or more would indicate that you have read with adequate understanding; lower than 7 would suggest that you may have sacrificed sense to speed.

		True	False
(i)	Six days a week Roy Dean does the *Guardian* crossword.	☐	☐
(ii)	Crosswords were invented by an Englishman called Gallup.	☐	☐
(iii)	The publishing company of Selchow and Righter brought out a volume of crossword puzzles in April 1924.	☐	☐
(iv)	The *Times* occasionally printed Latin crosswords.	☐	☐
(v)	The first crossword contained thirty-two clues.	☐	☐
(vi)	The highest recorded Scrabble score is 1,539 points.	☐	☐
(vii)	The Baltimore and Ohio Railroad placed dictionaries in each of its carriages.	☐	☐
(viii)	Zax is the fourteenth letter of the Greek alphabet.	☐	☐
(ix)	Alfred Butts insisted on having at least two tiles of each letter in Scrabble.	☐	☐
(x)	The first crossword to appear in the *Times* was set by a farmer.	☐	☐

Your time minutes	seconds	Words per min. (approx.)	Rate
1	00	530	Very fast
1	05	489	
1	10	454	
1	15	424	Fast
1	20	398	
1	25	374	
1	30	353	
1	35	335	
1	40	318	
1	45	303	Above average
1	50	289	
1	55	277	
2	00	265	
2	05	254	Average
2	10	245	
2	15	236	Slow
2	20	227	
2	25	219	
2	30	212	
2	35	205	
2	40	199	
2	45	193	
2	50	187	
2	55	182	
3	00	177	

To find out your approximate reading speed, check your given time against the table above.

13.3 CLOSE READING

Here is a paragraph chosen fairly much at random from the middle of a book that, in hardback, spent a record 237 weeks in the British list of top ten non-fiction best-sellers:

The success of the unification of the electromagnetic and weak nuclear forces led to a number of attempts to combine these two forces with the strong nuclear force into what is called a grand unified theory (or GUT). This title is rather an exaggeration: the resultant theories are not all that grand, nor are they fully unified, as they do not include gravity. Nor are they really complete theories, because they contain a number of parameters whose values cannot be predicted from the theory but have to be chosen to fit in with the experiment. Nevertheless they may be a step towards a complete, fully unified theory.

The basic idea of GUTs is as follows. As was mentioned above, the strong nuclear force gets weaker at high energies. On the other hand, the electromagnetic and weak forces, which are not asymptotically free, get stronger at high energies. At some very high energy, called the grand unification energy, these three forces would all have the same strength and so could just be different aspects of a single force. The GUTs also predict that at this energy the different spin-$1/2$ matter particles, like quarks and electrons, would also all be essentially the same, thus achieving another unification.
(Stephen Hawking, *A Brief History of Time*, p. 74.)

Huge numbers of people own copies of this book. How easily would they have read the passage above? Why might those of us who are not astrophysicists or cosmologists have to take our time to get the gist of the passage, let alone comprehend fully the author's meaning?

It might seem unfair to select part of a complex argument in a highly specialised field. Specialist areas seem to acquire their own vocabularies to exclude the non-specialist. Legal documents, books on education and officialese in its many different forms are some types of reading that almost seem designed to baffle the lay person.

You might imagine that a novelist would ensure that his or her words could be read fluently and without frequent backtracking. But novels vary enormously in their accessibility. Here are the opening sections of two twentieth-century novels:

Strether's first question, when he reached the hotel, was about his friend; yet on his learning that Waymarsh was apparently not to arrive till evening he was not wholly disconcerted. A telegram from him bespeaking a room 'only if not noisy,' reply paid, was produced for the inquirer at the office, so that the understanding they should meet at Chester rather than at Liverpool remained to that extent sound. The same secret principle, however, that had prompted Strether not absolutely to desire Waymarsh's presence at the dock, that had led him thus to postpone for a few hours his enjoyment of it, now operated to make him feel he could still wait without disappointment. They would dine together at the worst, and with all respect to dear old Waymarsh—if not even, for that matter, to himself—there was little fear that in the sequel they shouldn't see enough of each other. The principle I have just mentioned as operating had been, with the most newly disembarked of the two men, wholly instinctive—the fruit of a sharp sense that, delightful as it would be to find himself looking, after so much separation, into his comrade's face, his business would be a trifle bungled should he simply arrange for this countenance to present itself to the nearing steamer as the first 'note' of Europe. Mixed with everything was the apprehension, already, on Strether's part, that he would, at best, throughout, prove the note of Europe in quite a sufficient degree.
(Henry James, *The Ambassadors*, 1903.)

'Morning, Jeeves,' I said.

'Good morning, sir,' said Jeeves.

He put the good old cup of tea softly on the table by my bed, and I took a refreshing sip. Just right, as usual. Not too hot, not too sweet, not too weak, not too strong, not too much milk, and not a drop spilled in the saucer. A most amazing cove, Jeeves. So dashed competent in every respect. I've said it before, and I'll say it again. I mean to say, take just one small instance. Every other valet I've ever had used to barge into my room in the morning while I was still asleep, causing much misery: but Jeeves seems to know when I'm awake by a sort of telepathy. He always floats in with the cup exactly two minutes after I come to life. Makes a deuce of a lot of difference to a fellow's day.

'How's the weather, Jeeves?'

'Exceptionally clement, sir.'

'Anything in the papers?'

'Some slight friction threatening in the Balkans, sir. Otherwise, nothing.'

(P. G. Wodehouse, *The Inimitable Jeeves*, 1923.)

Why is one passage so much harder to read than the other? Why does one demand close reading while the other may be read normally?

Close reading is the method we use to deal with material that is difficult (for whatever reason) or that we need to master fully. Obvious though it may sound, the first and basic requirement for close reading is *concentration.*

Good concentration is the product of many factors, such as

- the right *physical environment* (e.g. quality of light, temperature, form of seating, work surface etc.)
- the right *time of day* (most of us feel that we function better at some times of day than at others)
- the right *frame of mind* (mood, psychological state, motivation)
- the right *preparation* (having to hand the necessary 'tools', such as pad, pen etc.)
- the right *state of health* (a blinding headache does not assist concentration!)
- *freedom from distraction* (callers, phone, extraneous noises).

Close reading, particularly when learning is an objective, will usually need to be accompanied by *writing*, either in the form of *text-marking* (underlining, margin annotating, highlighting) or *note-taking*.

A further recommendation is intelligent use of skimming. Instead of making several unsuccessful assaults on a difficult opening sentence and then allowing your mind to wander (always a tempting option) it is often wiser to skim through the whole passage to get the gist and then re-read slowly, stopping to underline or make notes. If the passage is lengthy (say, a chapter), it may be helpful to read the opening and closing paragraphs, which will usually introduce or summarise the chapter's contents.

The best test of close reading is our ability to summarise in our own words what we have just read. Not surprisingly, the formal summary has long been a feared question in English-language exams. It is very hard to disguise failure of understanding or lapse of attention.

TASK 13.3 A

Summarise in your own words ...

Here is a moderately difficult passage from a book about language. First, skim-read it to get the general drift. Then re-read the passage closely to understand the argument in detail. You may wish to highlight or underline key words or key phrases. When you are satisfied that you have fully grasped the meaning, close the book and summarise the substance in your own words. Aim to complete the task in about 150 words, which is roughly a quarter of the original's length.

Exchange completed summaries within the group and discuss any significant variations. Could this passage be adequately summarised using a much smaller word allowance?

Journalists say that when a dog bites a man that is not news, but when a man bites a dog that is news. This is the essence of the language instinct: language conveys news. The streams of words called 'sentences' are not just memory prods, reminding you of man and man's best friend and letting you fill in the rest: they tell you who in fact did what to whom. Thus we get more from most stretches of language than Woody Allen got from *War and Peace*, which he read in two hours after taking speed-reading lessons: 'It was about some Russians.' Language allows us to know how octopuses make love and how to remove cherry stains and why Tad was heartbroken, and whether the Red Sox will win the World Series without a good relief pitcher and how to build an atom bomb in your basement and how Catherine the Great died, among other things.

When scientists see some apparent magic trick in nature, like bats homing in on insects in pitch blackness or salmon returning to breed in their natal stream, they look for the engineering principles behind it. For bats, the trick turned out to be sonar; for salmon, it was locking in to a faint scent trail. What is the trick behind the ability of *Homo sapiens* to convey that man bites dog?

In fact there is not one trick but two, and they are associated with the names of two European scholars who wrote in the nineteenth century. The first principle, articulated by the Swiss linguist Ferdinand de Saussure, is 'the arbitrariness of the sign', the wholly conventional pairing of a sound with a meaning. The word 'dog' does not look like a dog, walk like a dog, or woof like a dog, but it means 'dog' just the same. It does so because every English-speaker has undergone an identical act of rote learning in childhood that links the sound to the meaning. For the price of this standardised memorisation, the members of a language community receive an enormous benefit: the ability to convey a concept from mind to mind virtually instantaneously. Sometimes the shotgun marriage between sound and meaning can be amusing. As Richard Lederer points out in *Crazy English*, we drive on a parkway but park in a driveway, there is no ham in hamburger or bread in sweetbreads, and blueberries are blue but cranberries are not cran. But think about the 'sane' alternative of depicting a concept so that receivers can apprehend the meaning in the form. The process is so challenging to the ingenuity, so comically unreliable, that we have made it into party games, like Pictionary and charades.

The second trick behind the language instinct is captured in a phrase from Wilhelm von Humboldt that presaged Chomsky: language 'makes infinite use of finite media.' We know the difference between the forgettable *dog bites man* and the newsworthy *man bites dog* because of the order in which 'dog', 'man' and 'bites' are combined. That is, we use a code to translate between orders of words and combinations of thoughts. That code, or set of rules, is called a generative grammar...

(Steven Pinker, *The Language Instinct*, p. 83–4.)

The arrival of the information superhighway at our front doors will make efficient reading a more and more desirable competence to have. In the search for increased efficiency the most important point to remember is that there is no such thing as 'the *best* way to read'. Instead we should think of *appropriateness*, of finding and using the *method* that suits the *material* and our *purpose* in reading it.

13.4 Finding written information

Say you are researching your project or a mass media assignment. You are hunting for a particular piece of statistical information. Where do you start looking?

At present, you would probably think first of the reference section of your local library. But in the not-too-distant future you will be able, more and more, to search for the information by accessing data-banks, and you won't have to leave your home, because you will be connected to the Internet or some similar system.

Massive changes are taking place in the ways information is available to us. However, this section will concentrate on the traditional places to look for written information, since it will probably take some time for the personal computer to become a standard item of household equipment.

It is important to have some ideas about *where* to look. The human mind is extraordinary but even the most brilliant can contain only a tiny amount of the sum of human knowledge. The answers we want are out there somewhere; the person who can quickly discover exactly where is an asset to any organisation.

A comprehensive guide to Irish sources of information would fill many pages and would include the output of Government departments and other state bodies, health boards, local authorities, banks, big companies, trade unions, and a great range of political and cultural organisations. Specialist journals, professional and learned periodicals, yearbooks and directories would all have to be listed.

The following recommendations are highly selective, therefore, but they may suggest practical steps to take if you find yourself in an informational cul-de-sac.

13.4.1 Phone and directory

Since somebody, somewhere will have at his or her fingertips the information you are seeking, you are, if you think about it, only a phone call away from the answer.

The phone is an invaluable aid to any information-seeker. A direct phone approach to an expert in the area you are researching may require courage to make but could steer you in the right direction. If you explain your problem clearly and courteously, you may be surprised how forthcoming, friendly and helpful the response will be. Large organisations have information officers, whose job is to supply informational guidelines to the public and who may be able to send you printed information. You have very little to lose by an approach.

The phone directory itself is full of information. We tend to think just of the central section of alphabetised names, forgetting the Golden Pages (try skimming the introductory pages to see what they contain), the state services directory, and the information on telecommunications in the opening section. Next time you pick up a directory, flick through the volume to check what it now contains.

13.4.2 LIBRARIES

Your *local public library* is an obvious first stop in finding written information. Remember,
- membership of your local branch gives you access to books in other branches through inter-library loans
- consulting the library staff at the start may save you a lot of time and frustration; besides, advising borrowers is part of the service they willingly provide
- in seeking advice, it will help if you know what it is you want to know!
- books in the reference section are not generally available on loan
- if you are collecting information for an assignment, don't forget to record the basic details of books you consult: you may need them for your bibliography.

Your geographical area may contain other libraries that could be of use to you. Schools, colleges of art, RTCs, universities, specialist organisations, dioceses and many more may be willing to facilitate you—if your approach is right.

Bookshops are in the business of *selling* books (new or second-hand), but browsing through the shelves may sometimes be a valuable exercise. Ask the assistants where books covering your area of interest may be found, and scan what's available. If you turn up something that looks genuinely interesting but is beyond your means, record the details and ask your local library to acquire it.

13.4.3 CENTRAL STATISTICS OFFICE

This is the Government agency responsible for the collection and publication of most official economic and social statistics. Its principal offices are now in Cork, though some of its activities are still carried out in Dublin.

We are all part of the statistical data assembled by the CSO: our births, marriages and deaths are recorded in *Annual Reports on Vital Statistics*. Other areas in which the CSO publishes statistical information include

—agriculture, forestry, and fisheries
—building and construction
—demography
—industry
—labour

—prices
—services (including distribution)
—tourism and travel
—trade
—transport
—household budgets.

All CSO publications can be consulted in the CSO libraries in Cork and Dublin, which are open to the public. They contain a large selection of statistical publications and yearbooks of other countries. Information may also be obtained by phoning the CSO and asking for the information officer.

13.4.4 ENCYCLOPAEDIAS

An encyclopaedia may be a book or series of volumes containing information on all branches of human knowledge (e.g. *Encyclopaedia Britannica*) or a work providing exhaustive information on just *one branch* of knowledge (e.g. *The Royal Horticultural Society Encyclopaedia of Gardening*).

An up-to-date encyclopaedia will contain useful and authoritative material and will also supply references to other relevant books.

13.4.5 IPA YEARBOOK

As the name suggests, a yearbook is published annually and contains the most recent available information on its subject. A film yearbook, for example, records and reviews films released over the previous twelve months and lists all those who collaborated in producing them.

A yearbook that might be of use to you is the one issued annually by the Institute of Public Administration, *Administration Yearbook and Diary*. It is too expensive for most individuals to buy but any sizeable organisation or enterprise will own a copy and your local library should have a copy in the reference section.

The IPA Yearbook is, in its own words, 'a comprehensive directory of Irish life, covering the private as well as the public sector. Its information ranges from health boards to major companies; Government departments to voluntary agencies; professional organisations to merchant banks; advertising agencies to third-level institutions; independent radio stations to religious orders; EU institutions to statistics covering Ireland's agriculture, industry, trade, public finances, social welfare, health and education.'

From the IPA Yearbook you can learn the current salaries of public representatives and officials, the sunrise and sunset times for Dublin in the current year, and the dates of public holidays. Above all, it contains names, addresses, and phone and fax numbers. Here is a sample section of one page:

An English equivalent of the IPA Yearbook is Whita*ker's Almanack*, which was first published in 1868 and is an invaluable guide to world affairs. Like *the IPA Yearbook, it is* extensively revised each year and contains information that is both comprehensive and up to date.

Chapter review
1. Name the four ways of reading listed in this chapter, and clearly state the purpose of each.
2. Show how the same words read in different moods may produce quite different effects. Provide examples to illustrate the phenomenon.
3. Explain why any modern state needs a statistics-collecting agency.
4. What is the IPA Yearbook?

Supplementary tasks

1. As a group, compile a list of libraries and bookshops in your area.
2. Find out how much this year's edition of the IPA Yearbook costs.
3. How many yearbooks, directories and encyclopaedias does the reference section of your local library contain?
4. As a group, compile a list of useful reference works in your vocational area. Include magazines and newspapers.
5. Ask each member of the group to provide three quiz-type questions seeking information that may be found in a current phone directory (e.g. what is the phone number of Valentia Observatory?). Put the questions together to form a quiz and issue it to all members of the group, to be completed by an agreed deadline.

Answers

Task 13.2.1 A. (i) false; (ii) false; (iii) false; (iv) true; (v) true; (vi) false; (vii) true; (viii) false; (ix) true; (x) true.

READING FOR PLEASURE

THREE PERIODS

14.1 ATTITUDES TO READING

Reading—of novels, poems, or plays—is a central activity in most classrooms where English is taught. It's a rare student or teacher who stops to ask *why*. Whether we're aware of it or not, we carry round with us certain beliefs about the value of reading and don't often bring them into the open for examination. The general feeling seems to be that 'reading is good for you.' Children are frequently rationed in their television allowance; do parents ever insist that their children read for entertainment at, say, weekends only?

TASK 14.1 A

Why read?

Using a selection of the following starters, hold a series of rounds:

(i) Reading is good for you because …
(ii) A well-read person is someone who …
(iii) Reading is enjoyable/not enjoyable because …
(iv) A classic is …
(v) Mostly, I read because …
(vi) A book I've re-read once/twice/many times is …
(vii) Jobs that involve a lot of reading include …
(viii) The way I usually choose books is …

Appoint a recorder to keep a note of points that recur or are surprising, and use them as a basis for further discussion.

14.1.1 Books—a load of crap?

When we read for ourselves, by choice rather than by necessity, we do so for all sorts of reasons—as your rounds no doubt revealed. Here is one reader's honest admission:

When getting my nose in a book
Cured most things short of school,
It was worth ruining my eyes
To know I could still keep cool,
And deal out the old right hook
To dirty dogs twice my size.

Later, with inch-thick specs,
Evil was just my lark:
Me and my cloak and fangs
Had ripping times in the dark.
The women I clubbed with sex!
I broke them up like meringues.

Don't read much now: the dude
Who lets the girl down before
The hero arrives, the chap
Who's yellow and keeps the store,
Seem far too familiar. Get stewed:
Books are a load of crap.
(Philip Larkin, 'A Study of Reading Habits'.)

The poet, Philip Larkin

TASK 14.1.1 A

Reading habits

Spend about ten minutes discussing Larkin's poem. You might explore responses to these questions:
1. Does this poem throw any light on reasons for reading?
2. Do you relate in any ways to the reading experiences described here?
3. Does the photograph of the poet (who was librarian in Hull University) enhance enjoyment of the poem?
4. What kinds of pleasure might any reader get from this poem?

14.2 Who is reading what?

Reading has been a widespread pastime for a mere two hundred years or so. Its current popularity has to do with such factors as near-universal literacy, the paperback revolution, and increased leisure time. Modern bookshops are carefully designed to promote comfortable browsing: they are warm, well-lit, spacious, sometimes open outside normal working hours, and employ assistants with specialist knowledge who will advise customers against a background of classical music. Books themselves are packaged to achieve maximum attractiveness. The £1 classic is an amazing bargain. Public libraries are user-friendly and accessible; book clubs and mail order make buying easy and inviting.

The range of what is available in print is mind-boggling. Books, magazines and newspapers exist in all shapes and sizes, catering for the most specialised tastes and interests. Looking at the staggering array in a city bookshop, you might wonder who buys what.

TASK 14.2 A

Organising a reading questionnaire

As a group, design a short questionnaire to obtain information about reading habits. You might wish to survey such areas as

- *what* people read (fact or fiction? books or magazines?)
- *how much* people read (a book a week/month/year?)
- *where* and *when* people read
- *how often* people *buy* books or magazines
- *how much* people spend on their reading
- which *authors* and *genres* are popular
- *how people choose* books or magazines
- *how people developed the habit* of reading
- *who belongs* to book clubs, libraries etc.

Making up a questionnaire is not easy. Begin by deciding who to aim it at—each other, fellow-students, family and friends, members of the local community? On what *scale* will you conduct your survey? How many questionnaires should each researcher be expected to have completed?

Questions need to be clearly framed and designed to elicit the required information. They may include

(a) those demanding simple 'yes' or 'no' answers

(b) those requiring a short factual statement

(c) those offering a set of possible answers from which to choose; e.g. 'Do you buy books—

regularly? ❏
seldom? ❏
never? ❏

When consensus has been reached on a range of questions to use,

- arrange for the making and distribution of copies
- agree a date by which completed questionnaires should be returned
- persuade two volunteers from the group to collate the findings and make a short informal oral report to the group
- set a date for this feedback session.

TASK 14.2 B

The final stage of the questionnaire process is to review the exercise.

- What has the survey revealed about reading tastes, habits, patterns and trends?
- Is it possible to make any generalisations based on the group's research?
- Do the findings contain any surprises?
- In which of the areas surveyed would you welcome more information?
- Have your questions been effective in obtaining information?
- Do your findings correlate in any way with the weekly best-seller lists compiled by the Booksellers' Association and printed in the newspapers? Here is a sample list:

HARDBACKS

General

THIS WEEK		LAST WEEK	WEEKS ON LIST
1	**Rogue Trader / Nick Leeson** (Little, Brown £16.99) How Baring's man in Singapore got there — and what went wrong	—	1
2	**The One that Got Away / Chris Ryan** (Century £14.99) Story of the only member of the Bravo Two Zero team to evade capture	3	34
3	**Immediate Action / Andy McNab** (Bantam Press £15.99) Successor to Bravo Two Zero; account of SAS which raised MOD hackles	1	18
4	**The X-Files Book of the Unexplained / Jane Goldman** (Simon & Schuster £15.99) Surveys weird phenomena dramatised in TV series	2	18
5	**Emotional Intelligence / Daniel Goleman** (Bloomsbury £14.99) How to gain control of your emotions and focus their energy for success	7	6
6	**Elizabeth / Sarah Bradford** (Heinemann £20) Long and well-received life of the Queen	4	5
7	**Maxwell: The Final Verdict / Tom Bower** (HarperCollins £16.99) Last year of tycoon's life analysed by persistent Maxwell-watcher	—	3
8	**Notes from a Small Island / Bill Bryson** (Doubleday £15.99) Withering survey of Limey products such as Marmite and Farleigh Wallop	8	21
9	**The Nemesis File / Paul Bruce** (Blake £15.99) Former SAS soldier's controversial revelations about secret ops	5	7
10	**One and Two Halves to K2 / James Ballard** (BBC Books £15.99) Alison Hargreaves' husband takes their children to the scene of her death	6	2

Fiction

THIS WEEK		LAST WEEK	WEEKS ON LIST
1	**Primary Colors / Anonymous** (Chatto £15.99) Philandering presidential candidate's rise — by a White House insider?	—	1
2	**The Hundred Secret Senses / Amy Tan** (Flamingo £15.99) Five-year-old's half-sister arrives in the US from China, bringing ghosts	1	3
3	**Cross Channel / Julian Barnes** (Cape £13.99) New stories from a writer as lauded in France as he is here	2	7
4	**The Horse Whisperer / Nicholas Evans** (Bantam Press £14.99) Rugged man soothes traumatised horse and high-powered owner	7	22
5	**Last Orders / Graham Swift** (Picador £15.99) Why won't deceased butcher's wife help scatter his ashes?	9	5
6	**X-Files 3: Ground Zero / Kevin J Anderson** (HarperCollins £9.99) Agents Mulder and Scully investigate inexplicable human incinerations	4	11
7	**In the Presence of the Enemy / Elizabeth George** (Bantam Press £16.99) Kidnap of journalist's daughter may bring down the government	3	4
8	**The Bloody Ground / Bernard Cornwell** (HarperCollins £14.99) Fourth Starbuck chronicle of derring-do in the American civil war	5	13
9	**The Moor's Last Sigh / Salman Rushdie** (Cape £15.99) Family mayhem ensnares heir to Indian spice fortune	—	18
10	**The Ghost Road / Pat Barker** (Viking £15.99) Completes a first-world-war war trilogy about a shellshocked survivor	8	16

PAPERBACKS

General

THIS WEEK		LAST WEEK	WEEKS ON LIST
1	**Unofficial X-files Companion / Ngaire Genge** (Macmillan £9.99) The truth is in here: character profiles and in-jokes to keep ardent x-philes happy	2	10
2	**The State We're In / Will Hutton** (Vintage £7.99) Journalist calls for radical reform of our political system	1	8
3	**Fingerprints of the Gods / Graham Hancock** (Mandarin £6.99) Did a civilisation flourish 15,000 years ago?	3	3
4	**Bravo Two Zero / Andy McNab** (Corgi £5.99) Story of an SAS patrol behind Iraqi lines in the Gulf war	4	64
5	**Writing Home / Alan Bennett** (Faber £7.99) Playwright's autobiographical diaries, reviews and reminiscences	5	21
6	**The Truth is out There / Brian Lowry** (HarperCollins £9.99) Compendium of facts, figures, summaries, from TV hit The X-files	8	4
7	**Long Walk to Freedom / Nelson Mandela** (Abacus £8.99) Autobiography of ANC leader, now South Africa's president	7	20
8	**Wild Swans / Jung Chang** (Flamingo £7.99) Modern China seen through the lives of three women; the 1992 NCR winner	9	121
9	**An Anthropologist on Mars / Oliver Sacks** (Picador £6.99) Essays from the further reaches of the mind from the author of Awakenings	—	2
10	**The Celestine Prophecy Experiential Guide / J Redfield and C Adrienne** (Bantam £7.99) Explores therapeutic value of Redfield's novel	—	3

Fiction

THIS WEEK		LAST WEEK	WEEKS ON LIST
1	**Behind the Scenes at the Museum / Kate Atkinson** (Black Swan £6.99) This year's Whitbread winner had the critics raving	1	7
2	**The Rainmaker / John Grisham** (Arrow £5.99) Out-of-work young lawyer fights giant medical-insurance scam	2	5
3	**Trainspotting (film tie-in edition) / Irvine Welsh** (Minerva £6.99) Rejacketed version of Leith low-life story, now a controversial, funny film	3	2
4	**Trainspotting / Irvine Welsh** (Minerva £6.99) Highs and lows of Edinburgh junkies from author of The Acid House	4	4
5	**Snow Falling on Cedars / David Guterson** (Bloomsbury £5.99) Murder on Pacific island awakens tensions submerged since Pearl Harbor	5	25
6	**Ladder of Years / Anne Tyler** (Vintage £5.99) Wife leaves family to reinvent herself in another town — but can she escape?	6	3
7	**A Breath of Fresh Air / Erica James** (Orion £5.99) Widowed in her thirties, Charlotte returns to Cheshire village life	10	2
8	**Kiss the Girls / James Patterson** (HarperCollins £5.99) Two serial killers keep in touch in an unhealthy competition	8	3
9	**The Juror / George Dawes Green** (Bantam £5.99) Single-mother juror in murder trial is stalked by the mafia	7	6
10	**Miss Smilla's Feeling for Snow / Peter Hoeg** (Flamingo £5.99) Atmospheric Danish thriller in which boy falls to death — was he pushed?	—	35

The Sunday Times, 3 March 1996

14.3 THE BOOK INDUSTRY

Printed words were available for mass consumption long before the products we associate today with mass communication—television, radio, films etc. The book industry is a legitimate area for research if your communications course includes an assignment on the mass media. For example, a *written report* based on the kind of questionnaire carried out in section 14.2 above might satisfy requirements. Similar questionnaires could lead to reports on, for instance,

- magazine buying and reading
- cinema and video viewing
- radio listening
- musical tastes
- library borrowing patterns
- audiobook buying
- CD-ROM publishing.

Alternatively, you might consider and report on ways in which books are *marketed*. Consult a recent best-seller list from a newspaper; have you been aware of media publicity for any of the titles? Take account of promotional methods such as

- blurb
- advertising (including signing sessions, author's appearances on radio and television programmes)
- reviewing.

Below is a typical advertisement for a best-seller.

- What does it suggest about the book's contents?
- What expectations does it create?
- What techniques does it use to sell the book?

14.3.1 A SAMPLE REVIEW

Reviewing, whether of a book, a live performance, a film, or a television programme, is often an option on a communications course. The same reviewing techniques apply, whichever medium you are dealing with. All reviews set out to answer three basic questions:

(1) What is this work about?
(2) How is it done?
(3) Does it succeed?

Question 1 asks you to say a little about the *story* and *plot*. In some ways you're like a reporter answering the traditional five Ws + H: Who? what? why? when? where? how?

Once you've dealt with these essential questions (remembering not to give away *all* the secrets of the plot!) you need to move on to say something about the work's *theme*—its core idea, its central point. Reviewers sometimes leave the theme until last, making it part of their summing up. Has the work's creator really got something interesting and worthwhile to say?

Question 2 is about method or **technique**. *How* has this artist chosen to tell her story? What kind of **settings** and **characters** has she chosen? What is distinctive, different and recognisable about her *style*? From what **point of view** is the story presented? How is *language* handled?

Question 3 asks you to reveal your personal **opinion**. Do you think this novel, play or film worked? What features particularly appealed to you? Was it an unqualified success or merely a partial one? Don't be afraid to let your feelings show but in the interests of fairness remember not to blame an artist for failing to do what he or she never set out to do! (Incidentally, since your reader will understand from the start that the whole review is *your* opinion, there is no need to keep using phrases such as 'In my view' or 'I think'.)

Here is a review of a recent American novel that has been made into a film. Does it observe the guidelines set out above? Can you see places where the reviewer might have given more examples from the novel? Does the review seem fair? Does it communicate clear opinions about the book? Why not read the book and see if you agree with those opinions?

Billy Bathgate by E. L. Doctorow (Picador 1990).
Billy Bathgate *is the story of a fifteen-year-old boy who realises the dream of every Bronx street kid of his acquaintance by becoming a member of the notorious Dutch Schultz gang in the New York underworld of the early 1930s. The reader follows Billy's fortunes from the moment when his juggling first earns him Schultz's attention to the inevitable bloody conclusion in the sleazy back room of a New Jersey chophouse. In between, we experience with extraordinary vividness the day-to-day life of organised crime: its routine boredom, superficial glamour, frustration, occasional horrific outbursts of violence, and, above all, uncertainties. And the story, a cunning blend of fact (the real-life atrocities of Schultz made tabloid headlines) and fiction, doesn't quite end in the Palace Chophouse ...*

Countless gangster films have made us familiar with the clothes, the accents, the automobiles, the speak-easies, the molls, the guns. What new angle can E. L. Doctorow possibly offer?

In telling his grim story he has made a decision that is both surprising and traditional: the tale of the Schultz gang's decline and fall will be told by Billy. Doctorow's choice of an adolescent boy as his narrator reminds us of two famous earlier American novels, Huckleberry Finn *and* Catcher in the Rye. *Like Huck and Holden Caulfield before him, Billy is for much of the time a fascinated spectator, an onlooker who is drawn into the action almost despite himself. He is keenly aware of the dangers of his chosen vocation but he is a born survivor, quick-witted, brave, physically nimble, and exceptionally keen-eyed. He tells his story of life with Schultz like it was—which was mostly fast and furious. The novel's opening rush of words transmits the breathless excitement and is typical of much that follows:*

'He had to have planned it because when we drove onto the dock the boat was there and the engine was running and you could see the water churning up phosphorescence in the river, which was the only light there was because there was no moon, nor no electric light either in the shack where the dockmaster should have been sitting, nor on the boat itself, and certainly not from the car, yet everyone knew where everything was, and when the big Packard came down the ramp Mickey the driver braked it so that the wheels hardly rattled the boards, and when he pulled up alongside the gangway the doors were already open and they hustled Bo and the girl upside before they even made a shadow in the darkness.'

The pace, the tone, the style and the substance of Billy Bathgate *are all suggested in this passage, which almost seems written with the camera in mind. You glimpse here one of the novel's undoubted strengths—its attention to the minute details of what could be seen, heard, smelt etc. Through Billy's words, Doctorow gives us the opportunity to experience the past as if it were the living present, showing us the crowded streets, the night club, the small-town upstate hotel, the brothel, the hospital—all through the wondering eyes of Dutch's protégé.*

At the centre of the book is Billy's relationship with the murderous Schultz, complicated by his dangerous infatuation with the Dutchman's mysterious girl-friend, Drew Preston. For many readers the dominant memories will be of Schultz's mad rages: Doctorow describes in unsparing detail and in frank language a number of lurid, clumsy killings; and the showdown itself, in the Palace's stinking men's room, takes place in slow motion so that the reader can feel at first hand the full terror of the cornered gangsters.

The Schultz that Billy serves is a mobster in decline, a relic of a vanished era when brute strength and willpower alone guaranteed supremacy. It is almost possible to feel some sympathy for the monstrous Dutch as he grapples with the faceless law, the smooth new Mafia operators, and the fickleness of his henchmen. But never for very long. The mortally wounded Schultz (whose real name was Arthur Flegenheimer) babbling in his hospital bed is pitiful. Here, the book seems to say, is a nobody who through terror briefly became a somebody, only to be reduced in the end to a nobody. Billy, whose feelings for Schultz alternated between nervous love and stricken horror, is finally relieved to be set free of the threat of violence.

Billy Bathgate *is an enormously impressive novel. It is by turns exciting, funny, erotic, tender, frightening, savage, and entertaining. It offers an entirely convincing picture of the vanished past of a great city and a credible portrait of a major gangster. The racy speech patterns in which the story is told take a little time to get used to, but once the rhythm is established and the lack of punctuation is accepted, the reader is whirled along to the tantalising conclusion. For where is Billy now and what has he become?*

14.3.2 A STORY TO RELAY (FOR TASK 6.1 A)

The circus was visiting the little town of Ballygoblabla. In McDermott's bar, Phil the fiddler sat drinking pints and boasting to the lion-tamer. 'As true as I'm sitting here,' he said, 'there's not the animal born that I couldn't tame with my fiddle.'

'I will bet you', said the lion-tamer, whose name was Barry, 'five thousand pounds that you couldn't tame my three lions.'

'You're on!' said Phil, and away they all went to the Big Top to see the outcome.

Phil sauntered into the middle of the cage, tucked his fiddle under his chin, and began to play a graceful, haunting lament. 'Send in a lion,' he called.

With a roar that made the onlookers' blood run cold, the first lion, Basil, tore into the cage, saw the fiddler, crouched to spring—and then, abruptly, sank back on its haunches, propped his head on his forepaws, and began to listen.

'Number two!' called Phil, never letting up on the lament.

In came the second lion, Claude, and didn't the same thing happen? There on the sawdust lay Basil and Claude, entranced by the doleful lament.

Triumphantly, Phil called for the third—Rodney. Into the ring he padded, paused for the merest fraction, bounded over to Phil, and devoured him and his fiddle.

Indignantly, Basil and Claude went over to Rodney. 'What did you have to go and do that for? We were *listening* to that!'

Putting his large, furry forepaw to his ear, Rodney roared, 'Eh?'

(If for any reason this story proves unsuitable, substitute one of your own. Stories with whipcrack endings work well.)

Supplementary task

This chapter's single supplementary task is a *challenge*. Five books are listed below. All should be readily available in paperback; they can be found in libraries, in second-hand bookshops, and on the shelves of friends. The challenge is: over the duration of your course, read them.

Miss Smilla's Feeling for Snow by Peter Høeg (Flamingo 1994). An unusual title for a very unusual thriller, which begins in Copenhagen, ends on the Arctic ice-cap, and has a Greenlander as its irresistible heroine.

Schindler's List by Thomas Keneally. If you were moved by the Spielberg film you'll find the original book far more harrowing, since you get to know the principal characters so much better than a film allows.

The Shipping News by E. Annie Proulx (Fourth Estate 1993). Mostly set in Newfoundland and told in a highly original style, this acclaimed story is heart-warming, funny, and packed with extraordinary people and information. Get over the first three pages and you'll be hooked.

The Secret World of the Irish Male by Joseph O'Connor (New Island Books 1994). A collection of newspaper and magazine articles loosely strung together to form an opinionated, rude, perceptive and very, very funny book that culminates in the author's 1994 World Cup diary. An audio version (read by Joseph O'Connor) is also available.

A Snail in My Prime: New and Selected Poems by Paul Durcan (Harvill 1993).

PART 5

MASS COMMUNICATION

THE MASS MEDIA

TEN PERIODS

15.1 MASS COMMUNICATION

Mass communication involves public meanings produced like industrial commodities and sent to audiences that may number millions (see p. 5). Think of a British Sunday newspaper printing almost 5 million copies, and remember that the number of its *readers* may at least *double* the number of *buyers*.

Individual members of the audience *construct their own meanings* from the messages they receive but they don't, as a rule, send messages back. Up till now we've been used to thinking of communication as a *two-way* process; in mass communication, audience feedback is rare. True, audiences may let a film company know what they think (or might have thought) of its product by staying away in droves, and anyone may write a letter of congratulation or complaint to a newspaper, but genuine *interaction* between the few who produce mass meanings and the many who receive them is *not* a characteristic of this form of communication.

TASK 15.1 A

A definition to test

'Mass communication is the practice and product of providing leisure entertainment and information to an unknown audience by means of corporately financed, industrially produced, state-regulated, high-technology, privately consumed commodities in the modern print, screen, audio and broadcast media' (Tim O'Sullivan et al., *Key Concepts in Communication*, p. 131).

1. This is a packed definition. Begin by separating out the elements. Does every member of the group understand what is meant by each element? Is there, for example, a shared understanding of what is meant by 'an unknown audience' or 'state-regulated'? Discuss any difficulties.

2. Is the definition comprehensive and completely accurate? Does it fit all mass media products? In what sense, for example, are films 'privately consumed'? Discuss any modifications members of the group might wish to propose.

Our definition makes clear that **mass communication happens through the mass media**. These are listed as 'print, screen, audio and broadcast', in which categories belong books, newspapers, magazines, films, television, radio, CDs, photographs, cartoons, advertisements, and popular music, as well as other less obvious forms of mass communication that you may have identified in discussion.

15.1.1 WHO NEEDS MEDIA STUDIES?

TEACHER [*brightly*]: Good morning, all! Today we're going to decode an episode of 'Baywatch' as an example of— [*Class groans.*]

SEÁN: 'Baywatch' is *entertainment*. It's meant to be *enjoyed*. Why do we always have to *analyse* everything?

Replies to Seán's question might include:

- 'The media are *everywhere*: shouldn't we try to understand how they may, consciously or unconsciously, *influence* us?'
- 'Nothing about the media is quite as simple as it seems. Lesson 1 in media studies is that the media always provide us with a *version of reality* rather than, as it might at first appear, reality itself. So we need to learn to recognise the differences.'
- 'The media use *codes and conventions*; the cinema's flashback is a very simple example. By learning more about those codes and conventions, won't we increase our receptiveness, extend our range of understanding, and heighten our enjoyment?'
- 'The media exercise enormous *power*—to persuade, to indoctrinate, to shape attitudes. We need to learn to interrogate the messages they send us, even to resist them, instead of passively accepting them.'
- 'The media's output varies hugely in *quality*; we should learn to distinguish between the good, the bad, and the downright insulting.'
- 'Throughout the world the camera and the microphone are now an integral part of the democratic process. It's impossible to understand our society without analysing the media.'
- 'The more you know about the way the media are, the ways they operate, the directions in which they're developing, the better you will be able to handle a future in which, thanks to new technologies, society will be even more media-saturated than it is at present.'

> **TASK 15.1.1 A**
>
> **Stock responses**
> Briefly discuss the responses above. Do they offer adequate reasons for media studies courses? Are there other, more compelling reasons? Among those sketched above, which do you find the most persuasive?

15.1.2 How should we study the media?

If you studied the media as part of your Junior Certificate English programme, you probably compartmentalised for convenience: first, newspapers; then advertising; next, television etc. At that level the print media may receive more attention than the electronic, just because they fit more easily into the conventional textbook and curricular time slots.

Here, our approach will be in terms of **key concepts**, which apply equally to all media. This should free the group to follow its own media interests. You may opt to focus on a particular medium because, say, it is locally based (e.g. a visiting film production or a radio station) and there is easy access to resources. At the same time the conceptual framework allows you to range widely in search of supporting evidence from other media. The core concepts encourage cross-referencing, helping us to recognise what texts from different media have in common and how they share a language.

15.1.3 Five key concepts

(1) Ownership and control
(2) Audience
(3) Access
(4) Selection
(5) Ideology

To some extent these concepts overlap. It is impossible, for instance, to separate the issue of control from the concept of audience (who are, some believe, the true 'controllers' of the media).

These five concepts are among the most regularly studied but they are not the full story. For example, there is no room for genre and narrative. In treatment, more space has been given to ownership and control than to the others, because this area may have received little attention at secondary level.

Groups may decide to spend more time on some concepts than others, depending on the availability of resources and facilities and the level of general interest. It is always illuminating to hear from media practitioners themselves, and it should be possible to persuade some to talk to the group. A visit to a newspaper office, television studio, recording studio or film set is always highly instructive.

If members of your group are actively engaged in media production (e.g. music or video making), draw on their experiences within the overall conceptual framework and see how theory integrates with practice. After all, professionals and amateurs face exactly the same basic problems, such as funding, selection, finding an audience etc.

If your study should happen to coincide with a controversy focused on the media, be prepared to follow the story (local, national, or international) through to its conclusion. National newspapers now have specialist media correspondents and weekly sections devoted to the latest technological developments.

In the sections that follow, some tasks are labelled 'R2D2'. This stands for

Research—e.g. consult written information in libraries, make direct approaches to media producers or institutions for information etc.

Report—make a brief statement to the group on the results of your enquiries.

Discuss—as a group, assessing the researcher's report.

Develop—follow up in writing or in further research as indicated by the group discussion. You may have hit on the makings of a good written assignment!

Tasks mostly leave it to you to decide which *medium* you wish to focus on. Beware of concentrating exclusively on television: it is the dominant medium at present, but this should not blind us to other possibilities.

15.2 Ownership and control

Who *owns* the media? Can you name three international media moguls? Do they in fact exercise day-to-day *control* over their television stations, newspapers, film and recording companies? How might the average media reader recognise such control?

Rupert Murdoch is an owner of a giant transnational media conglomerate. Suppose you were a popular novelist. Your latest blockbuster might be published in hardback by a Murdoch company in Britain, the United States, and Australia. It would almost certainly be reviewed in many Murdoch-owned newspapers throughout the world and promoted on Murdoch-owned television channels. It might very well be serialised in Murdoch-owned magazines before being published in paperback by another Murdoch company. A Murdoch film company might then buy the film rights and make the film of the book, which would in turn be reviewed and promoted in Murdoch-owned print and on Murdoch-owned satellite and cable television. Some time after its cinema release the film would doubtless appear on television, and it might even spawn a television series.

Is it any business of the general public that one person should own so many media institutions throughout the world? Are there any undesirable consequences of such monopoly? To what extent is owner-control regulated by the state? Is state regulation of cyberspace actually possible, assuming international agreement were reached? Are these questions worth asking, and if so, where do we look for answers?

If you accept the widely held view that the media are **'consciousness industries'**, that is, large businesses that profoundly influence the way we perceive and interpret our world, then the questions are definitely worth asking.

The degree of *power* wielded by the media and those who own them is hotly debated, often within the media themselves. At one extreme are those who argue that the media *set the agenda* for society, determining how we think and act, how we see each other (i.e. stereotypically), how we vote, how we spend money, how we decide what is normal, what we talk about. In Ireland it could be argued that for thirty years the 'Late Late Show' has set a liberal agenda, opening up issues (e.g. divorce, celibacy in the priesthood) that otherwise might have remained closed.

At the other extreme are those who maintain that the media simply *reflect* the way things are, have (advertising apart) no deliberate manipulative, persuasive or propagandist aims, and function simply as bringers of entertainment, education, and information. Gay Byrne, Marian Finucane and others like them are *conduits* through whom the public express their opinions rather than *opinion-formers*. Ownership and control, therefore, are not serious issues: it is no more important to know who owns *Hot Press* than it is to know who owns the local chipper.

TASK 15.2 A

Setting the agenda? (R2D2)

'During the 1970s and 1980s, *The Late Late Show* set the headlines for most people's conversations in pubs, workplaces and shops during the following few days' (Gemma Hussey, *Ireland Today*, p. 350.)

What issues did the 'Late Late Show' raise in the seventies and eighties? Ask those who watched. Does the programme continue to set headlines in the nineties? If not, what broadcasts (if any) fulfil the same function? In your view, do broadcasting personalities (local, national or international) influence public opinion?

Be as specific as possible in discussing these questions. You may need to research audience figures.

The debate on ownership and control of the media generates a lot of heat, not least among politicians who, in a democratic system, often find themselves at odds with media personnel and practice. We are living through a global telecommunications revolution, so you are likely to have plenty of opportunity to study the issues as they arise and are dealt with. They may surface in the efforts of an overseas press baron to add Irish titles to his stable, in the acquisition by a media mogul of exclusive rights to television coverage of your favourite sporting events, or in a referendum held by one of our European neighbours to test public opinion on monopolisation.

15.2.1 THE IRISH MEDIA BACKGROUND

Before deciding where you stand on the various controversial media issues you should have a clear understanding of the current position in the Irish media, together with some knowledge of how Ireland is situated in relation to immediate neighbours (Britain and other European countries) as well as to more distant same-language media providers (United States or Australia).

To be aware of the major developments in the Irish print and electronic media during the twentieth century would be helpful: it's easy to forget that public service broadcasting in Ireland is still very young, with radio coming on air in 1926 and television in 1961. A useful introduction to the background of the Irish media is *Headlines and Deadlines* by Aileen O'Meara and Kathleen O'Meara. This has a handy appendix containing lists of national and regional newspapers and of local radio stations. The Green Paper on Broadcasting, *Active or Passive?: Broadcasting in the Future Tense* (1995) deals in sixteen short chapters with the main issues facing broadcasting and provides much useful background material. Chapter 16 deals with concentration of ownership and, like most other chapters, ends with a series of questions to debate.

Any discussion of ownership and control in Ireland must start by recognising that the dominant broadcast media (RTE radio and television) provide a public service and belong to the state sector. The institutions that produce newspapers, books, films, posters, magazines, comics, plays, popular music and advertisements belong in the commercial sector.

In a sense, all those who pay television licences 'own' the national broadcasting service, controlling it through their public representatives, the Government, who select nine of their fellow-citizens to serve a five-year term as the RTE Authority.

In 1994 approximately £50 million of RTE's annual budget came from licence fees, £70 million from television and radio advertising, and a further £18 million from commercial enterprises (Aertel, *RTE Guide* etc.) and other broadcasting income. Consult the most recent RTE annual report for the latest figures.

On this £140 million budget RTE supports two television channels (with a third, Teilifís na Gaeilge, in the offing), four national radio networks, and a limited local radio service (in Cork).

RTE does not yet face competition from indigenous privately owned television, although as long ago as 1988 the Independent Radio and Television Commission (IRTC) was set up to license an independent third television channel. Commercial radio, on the other hand, is a reality, with twenty-one independent stations currently operating in different parts of the country, all regulated by the IRTC.

TASK 15.2.1 A

The IRTC (R2D2)

Find out as much as you can about the IRTC, its composition, the names of members, the organisation's remit, its budget, whereabouts, successes and failures, and current activities. What was the story of Century Radio? What can you find out about its successor, Radio Ireland, and the consortium behind it? What provision for independent broadcasting is currently under consideration?

TASK 15.2.1 B

Local radio (R2D2)

How did local radio come into being? Find out what you can about the origins, development and current standing of a local radio station (e.g. Radio Kerry, Highland Radio). Research ownership, financing, audience, programme mix, attitudes towards RTE, and plans for future development.

Other Irish media, notably the publishing, film and music industries, have to make their independent way in the capitalist market. The patterns of ownership and control are particularly interesting in the Irish-owned newspaper business.

TASK 15.2.1 C

The press (R2D2)

Who owns the national daily papers? How did they come into the hands of the present owners? How secure does the future seem? What recommendations has the Commission on the Newspaper Industry made to 'guarantee the plurality of ownership' of the press? Dividing up the research among pairs, find out about the history of Irish newspapers, and assess what the future might hold.

15.3 OWNERSHIP AND CONTROL: THE CONTEXT

Even the most powerful media owners, whether corporate or individual, do not operate in a vacuum. Their control is subject to a variety of forces, of which the most obvious are:
- (i) state regulation
- (ii) self-regulation
- (iii) economic factors
- (iv) advertising
- (v) media personnel
- (vi) media sources
- (vii) audience.

15.3.1 STATE REGULATION

The relationship between the media and the state is always worth studying. Under totalitarian regimes the media operate within very tight bounds and give out the ruling party line. In a democratic society there is usually some tension between the media, whether independent or state-sponsored, and the elected politicians.

Media producers in Ireland are subject to the Constitution and to the law. For example, RTE and local radio are regulated by the Broadcasting Authority Acts, 1960–1979. In recent years the most controversial demonstration of the state's power to control broadcasters has been the section 31 Ministerial Order issued in 1989 that banned broadcast interviews with members of a number of organisations, including Sinn Féin. The ban was lifted in 1994.

Official state censorship of the media is now comparatively rare. The Office of the Film Censor certifies films according to five classifications (general, PG, over 12, over 15, and over 18), very occasionally banning outright (e.g. *Natural Born Killers* in 1995). In 1993, of 131 full-length films presented for censorship, 130 were passed without cuts; the remaining film was cut, was referred to the Appeal Board by its distributor, and failed to obtain a licence. In 1989 the role of the Film Censor was extended to include the regulation of videos under the Video Recordings Act, 1989. Books may still be banned by a Censorship Board whose main concern in the recent past seems to have been to deny entry to visually obscene magazines.

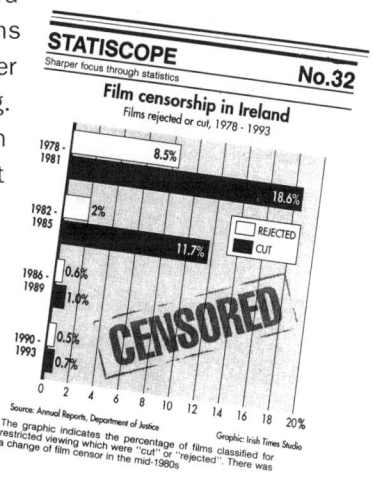

Media personnel have to be constantly mindful of legal boundaries in relation to copyright, libel, defamation, slander, official secrets, privilege, etc. As we approach the twenty-first century, those boundaries are undergoing review. The Commission on the Newspaper Industry included such legal issues as libel, privacy and press freedom in its remit, as well as the possible introduction of a press council to investigate complaints. Developments abroad, such as the extraordinary amount of publicity granted to a number of recent American trials, may have an impact on our legal parameters.

15.3.2 SELF-REGULATION

However determined media personnel may be to track down 'the truth in the news', in practice they submit to self-regulation. Media institutions supply internal guidelines recommending self-control, consultation upwards, innate common sense, and careful judgment. Professional bodies issue advice on standards of practice, an example being the National Union of Journalists' Code of Conduct, some extracts from which you might consider discussing:

'A journalist shall strive to ensure that the information he/she disseminates is fair and accurate, avoid the expression of comment and conjecture as established fact and falsification by distortion, selection or misrepresentation.

'A journalist shall obtain information, photographs and illustrations only by straightforward means. The use of other means can be justified only by over-riding considerations of the public interest. The journalist is entitled to exercise a personal conscientious objection to the use of such means.

'Subject to the justification by over-riding considerations of the public interest, a journalist shall do nothing which entails intrusion into private grief and distress.

'A journalist shall protect confidential sources of information.'

The advertising industry has its own regulatory body, the Advertising Standards Authority of Ireland, which aims to ensure that all advertisements are legal, decent, honest, and truthful. The ASAI investigates complaints about commercial advertisements and periodically makes available the results of its adjudications. In 1993/94 it received 490 complaints, the great majority either in the press or outdoor categories, and 221 were investigated. Of these complaints, 137 (62 per cent) were upheld.

Would you have challenged this description of New Pampers baby wipes, and if so, on what grounds? 'The softest, gentle wipes for the happiest babies.' How would you have gone about establishing a significant softness differential between the Pampers product and a number of competing products? In 1995 the ASAI Complaints Committee concluded that 'it was not possible to determine that the claim to be the "softest" had been adequately substantiated and that in the circumstances claims to outright superiority in terms of softness should not be made.'

Advertisers using the broadcast media are also subject to the RTE Code of Standards for Broadcast Advertising. This section from appendix 4 deals with the advertising of alcoholic drinks:

'Alcoholic drink advertising on RTE must not encourage young people or other non-drinkers to begin drinking—it must be cast towards brand selling and identification only. Bar locations for product or pack shots—including the presence of bar staff—are acceptable. Bar, party or social scenes featuring alcoholic drink must be handled with restraint—crowded situations and excessive heartiness and enjoyment may not be shown or implied. Only small numbers may be depicted—not more than six people, inclusive of staff and this must be obvious to viewers. Sound effects, background music, singing, laughter etc. must be kept to a reasonable minimum' (*Broadcasting Guidelines for RTE Personnel*, p. 133.)

Media personnel practise what is in effect self-censorship. The Irish media sometimes congratulate themselves for showing a degree of self-restraint in exposing the private lives of public figures that is markedly absent, for example, from certain British newspapers.

Print and broadcast media codes diverge when it comes to showing political bias. Whereas RTE is required by the state to remain impartial in its treatment of political matters, newspapers openly support political parties. A glance at the headlines will often clearly reveal the paper's affiliations.

(TASK 15.3.2 A)

Bias and impartiality (R2D2)

What is the political bias of each of the national daily papers? Which of the British dailies that are big sellers in Ireland support Conservative politics and which Labour? In Northern Ireland, which newspapers represent the voices of unionism and nationalism? Find out the exact responsibilities of RTE when dealing with news and current affairs. In your experience, do broadcasters ever display political bias? Record some interviews with Government and opposition spokespersons from RTE1's 'Morning Ireland', and assess the interviewer's objectivity.

15.3.3 ECONOMIC FACTORS

Media organisations are subject to the laws of the market, just as other industries are. If customers ignore the product, the producer is in trouble. In its century-long history, the cinema has probably attracted more attention to its budgeting than any other medium. The asking prices of stars, spectacular overspending on the latest blockbuster and the gigantic profits to be made on merchandising are standard fare in television, radio, newspaper and magazine coverage of the cinema. The recent boom in the number of Irish-made feature films (15 in 1994) and television drama series (9 in 1994) made in Ireland has fuelled public interest in media spending and is itself the result of attractive tax incentives made available from 1993.

We should ask ourselves:
(i) How do the media finance their operations?
(ii) How do economic considerations affect the nature of what is produced?

The second question is both more interesting and harder to answer. If the publishers had devoted unlimited means to the production of this textbook, what would be different about it? To what extent do financial considerations determine what we read, listen to, or watch? In each of the media, what are the tell-tale signs of cost-cutting? In the broadcast media, what evidence of limited funding is to be found in programming and programme-making? Could or should the money RTE spent staging three successive Eurovision song contests have been better used in other areas? What are the *cheapest* and *dearest* forms of television and radio?

TASK 15.3.3 A

She who pays the piper ...
In your experience, is there any evidence to suggest that media providers tailor their products to avoid offending those who put up the money (e.g. major advertisers, investors, sponsors)? Discuss.

TASK 15.3.3 B

From prequel to sequel
What evidence is there that media organisations *minimise* financial risk by relying on tried and tested formulas instead of trying new approaches? In discussing the question, consider a range of media. Does one medium sometimes try to cash in on the success of another?

TASK 15.3.3 C

Newspaper costings (R2D2)

Newspaper sales are falling, yet the choice in the shops is greater than ever. In the crowded market, which papers are most expensive, and why? Investigate a range of dailies—'tabloid' and 'quality', Irish and English. Look at price differences and try to account for them. What are consumers getting for their money? You may need to take into account such factors as circulation, ratio of advertising to sales revenue, VAT, and length

15.3.4 ADVERTISING

Advertising is right at the heart of media provision. For example, at present it foots over 51 per cent of the bill for our national broadcasting service. Its cousin, sponsorship (or indirect funding), contributes huge sums to rock tours, symphony concerts, sporting occasions, youth theatres, the training of media personnel, and the underwriting of media events.

The Green Paper on Broadcasting finds no evidence that television and radio's heavy indebtedness to advertising revenue has 'compromised the editorial integrity of broadcasters' (p. 185). We've touched on the RTE Code of Standards in relation to alcoholic drink; other areas dealt with in the code include subliminal advertising, the avoidance of undue stridency, inertia selling, the advertising of medicines and treatments, and the child audience. The code seems comprehensive in scope. Does it keep the advertisers under control?

Advertising is nothing if not subtle, and it possesses certain advantages. The point is often made that advertisers will lavish more time, talent and money on a thirty-second advertisement than the programme-makers have at their disposal for the surrounding half-hour—and it shows! Some of today's best-known film directors served their apprenticeship making commercials and have sometimes returned to this medium to direct 'prestige' productions.

Frequently we watch or read advertising without being fully conscious of the fact. Top of RTE's TAM ratings in 1993 was not the Eurovision Song Contest nor the Republic's crucial football match with Northern Ireland but the 'Late Late Toy Show' (10 December), presenting a range of commercial products. Are television's film programmes basically trailers, its holiday programmes thinly disguised commercials for tour operators?

Large numbers of children watch the 'Late Late Toy Show', and concern is often expressed about the vulnerability of children in the broadcasting market, particularly when the distinction between programme and commercial matter is allowed to become blurred. But adults may also prove blind to persuasive intent: it can be very easy to miss the small type that reads 'Advertising feature'!

Without advertising revenue, it is generally agreed that many media products would be prohibitively expensive. But are the interests of advertisers gradually taking precedence over those of viewers, listeners and readers? In ways that may not be immediately obvious, does advertising control much media output?

TASK 15.3.4 A

Advertising rates (R2D2)

Obtain advertising rate cards from a range of national and local newspapers. Clarify the different types of advertisement (e.g. display, classified). Compare costs of, say, a full-page colour advertisement between a range of newspapers. Find out approximately the proportion of overall revenue provided by advertising for each of the papers you select. Are discounts available? Find out the costs of broadcast advertising on RTE and local radio. Account for the variations in charges. How do broadcast charges compare with those for cinema and outdoor advertising?

TASK 15.3.4 B

Colour supplement ads

Obtain a copy of a colour supplement from a 'quality' and a 'popular' British Sunday newspaper. Compare, contrast and account for the *range* of products, facilities and services advertised in the two supplements. Estimate in each case what proportion of the magazine is taken up by advertisements.

15.3.5 MEDIA PERSONNEL

To what extent are media organisations owned or controlled by the people who work in them? How influential are those famous faces and voices in determining what emerges from the printing presses and screens?

By their nature and scale, most media involve collaboration, often between a great many people. Some years ago the *Irish Times* ran a headline, 'What weighs ten tons and takes 520 people to produce?' The answer was—one day's *Irish Times*. Within the work force, who takes control? Can even top reporters be sure that the story they submit will appear exactly as they wrote it? What considerations might cause a story to be altered?

15.3.6 MEDIA SOURCES

Our knowledge of what is happening in the world around us comes mostly from broadcast news and current affairs programmes; newspapers increasingly are used to fill in the details. Where do the media (including independent radio, which is obliged to give 20 per cent of its time to news and current affairs) get the news and information they pass on to us?

The heavy reliance by news gatherers on comparatively few sources—Government, Gardaí, courts, emergency services, city and county councils—is often viewed suspiciously. Is there not a danger that sources may *manage* the news, feeding misinformation, suppressing sensitive information, being 'economical with the truth', putting a favourable 'spin' on events, distorting figures, setting an agenda that suits special interests?

Media sources are powerful simply because they have ready access to the public ear. While it is true that much radio, both national and local, is now 'talk-driven', with the voices of ordinary people regularly heard, at news times and in formal discussions we find ourselves listening to the usual line-up of establishment figures: politicians, bishops, judges, and chief executives.

There is always a risk that media sources may abuse their power. Two of the most familiar phrases in news bulletins are 'sources close to ...' and 'a Government spokesperson ...' We should be aware of the various mechanisms by which the Government releases information (lobbying by political correspondents, news conferences, briefings on and off the record, leaks, press releases), of the ever-increasing importance of the Government press secretary, of the roles played by public relations agencies and special advisers, of the kinds of understandings that exist between journalists and politicians, of the functions of 'handlers' and 'sound bites'. Do you see any cause for concern in the fact that a number of recent Government press secretaries were recruited from news broadcasting?

TASK 15.3.6 A

The front page

Here are 'digests' or outlines of four news stories as they appeared in a side column on the front page of the *Irish Times* on 8 July 1995. In each case, what *sources* might have supplied the story?

Dunne's workers expected to accept strike settlement

Dunne's Stores strikers are expected to vote by a considerable majority to accept the settlement terms proposed by the Labour Court to end the three-week-old dispute. Mandate's general secretary, Mr Owen Nulty, said yesterday he would be arguing for acceptance of the terms and was optimistic that they would be accepted ...

Roy Keane defamation case dismissed

A claim for damages against the Irish international and Manchester United soccer star Roy Keane was dismissed at Cork Circuit Court yesterday after a day-long hearing in which it was alleged that he used an obscene remark. Judge Patrick Moran said he was sure Mr Keane had said something rude, but whether it was defamatory was another question ...

West to stand trial

Defence lawyers failed in a bid to stop the prosecution of the alleged mass murderer Rosemary West (41), accused on ten murder charges ...

Six new hotels for north

An American hotel chain is to announce a multi-million-dollar plan to build six three-star hotels in Northern Ireland, which would create hundreds of new jobs ...

15.3.7 AUDIENCE

The next section deals with audience as a concept. Here we need to ask what power audiences have to determine the nature of media output.

It is tempting to see audiences (or users) as the all-powerful element in the four-way relationship between technologies, regulators, providers, and users. If the audience gives the thumbs-down, as it did for example to the BBC's notoriously costly soap 'Eldorado', won't the providers have to cut their losses (e.g. sell up the multi-million-pound village set) and move on? Don't Hollywood providers sometimes radically alter films having tried them out on guinea-pig audiences?

The belief that audiences exercise ultimate control, getting from providers the products they want, is known as *consumer sovereignty*. But there is a long tradition in public broadcasting in Ireland as in Britain that audiences should be given some of *what they should have* alongside what is widely popular. The question then is, who has the right to decide what is 'good for' mass audiences?

TASK 15.3.7 A

Who's boss?

You've spent a considerable time thinking about *control* of the media. Now decide: in normal peace-time circumstances, who has *most* power to decide what we read, listen to, and watch? Big-wigs in the Government? Big-shots in the advertising world? Big deals in sponsorship? Big stars? Big bucks? Big egos? Big, *very* big audiences? Some 'big' that hasn't yet been mentioned? Big players in the world media market? In groups of no more than five, discuss the question, 'Who's boss?' Appoint a recorder and reach consensus. Discuss the findings of the various groups.

15.4 AUDIENCE

Audiences clearly have a role to play in the economics of media production. Does the role extend beyond that of paymaster?

Here are two extreme views:

(1) The hypodermic needle theory: A mass audience is a passive body injected with the hypodermic wielded by media providers. The syringe may be filled with beliefs, attitudes, values, longings, fears etc. To counter possible abuse of the needle by provider or user, *inoculation* is necessary: hence media studies!

(2) The uses and gratification theory: Mass audiences consist of alert, discriminating, active people who constantly make informed choices about books, films, television and radio programmes etc. and *use* the media to *gratify* such needs as escape, self-education, and group solidarity.

Those who subscribe to the second theory see audiences as makers of meaning rather than as passive *receivers*. Whether listening, reading, watching, or viewing, audiences are engaged in an *interactive* process. In the fiercely competitive battle for audiences, broadcast media personnel may resort to such clever scheduling ploys as 'hammocking' (placing a programme with low ratings between two very popular ones) or the 'inheritance factor' (scheduling a popular programme early in the evening in the hope that viewers will stay with the channel for the rest of the night); but audiences will, in the end, suit themselves.

Slightly undermining the view of the audience as all-powerful is another theory: that audiences and their purchasing power are *for sale*. For example, a new magazine may be launched and rapidly build up a large middle-class readership with high disposable incomes (ABC1s in socio-economic terms). The magazine owners then *sell* this highly desirable audience to advertisers. In return for advertising revenue, the owners position a captive audience to receive the advertiser's sales pitch.

Audiences are also sold by data-base companies *to the media*. The mail shot that drops into your letterbox singling you out as the lucky 'winner' of a subscription offer and the chance to win the car of your dreams isn't entirely random!

Some commentators have little confidence in the judgment of mass audiences. They worry that the media—especially television—are *trivialising* public discourse. In their view, media providers have low opinions of the audience's intelligence and powers of concentration and pitch their work for the lowest common denominator. Television has adopted the techniques of the tabloid press. Broadcasters work on the assumption that audiences have a three-minute attention span. Sensationalism and superficiality are replacing serious analysis. Worst of all, given the *globalisation* of media products, the *lowest* values *globally* will become the universal norm. Very small audiences, such as those in Ireland, will be increasingly subjected to a flood of media products originating in the United States or Australia, and minority interests will cease to be catered for. In this gloomy scenario, small nations will be 'colonised' by a few dominant media owners.

If you wish to explore further the concept of audience, some possible approaches are:

(1) The numbers game: A great deal may be learned by researching audience statistics: how many watched/attended/listened to/read/bought/complained about, etc. Just remember that the numbers are only the *beginning* of the story. Try to *account for* the figures.

(2) The crystal ball: Look at current trends in audience choices (e.g. the decline in newspaper readership) and try to predict what will happen in the new millennium. Perhaps concentrate on one medium—for example the book.

(3) How they see us: Pick a media product (e.g. a magazine, a radio serial, a suite of advertisements) and work *back* from the nature of the product to what you imagine might have been the producer's view of the target audience. What assumptions does the product seem to make about the user's life-style, needs etc.?

TASK 15.4 A

Watching television, seeing a film

From an *audience* point of view, what *differences* are there between the ways we experience television and films? List as many differences as possible. Here are three to start you:

(1) A television screen *reduces* most things from life size; a film screen *expands*.

(2) Films are watched in *darkness*, television in *normal light*.

(3) Television personnel sometimes talk directly to us; rarely does this happen in films.

When your list is complete, discuss what effects the differences produce as far as the audience is concerned.

15.5 ACCESS

Access means entitlement to *send* messages to an audience via the media rather than the right to *receive* them. How easy is it for 'ordinary people' to have their views represented in the media? Is it easier to gain access to some media than to others? Are some 'ordinary people' more likely to get a hearing than others? On what grounds? Are deserving groups and causes excluded because they are ignorant of the rules of a game that involves press releases, stunts, PR hand-outs, packaged information, and sound bites? Are the media essentially *conservative* industries, deliberately denying access to *alternative* voices and life-styles or political opinions?

What happens to 'ordinary' voices when they gain access? How are they allowed to represent themselves? Do the media always make room for violence?

Those who control access to the media are known as **'gatekeepers'**. Any piece of news must be allowed through several 'gates' before it is admitted to a newspaper's pages or the main news bulletins. Selection is inevitable, given the great volume of raw information pouring into media organisations; what concerns us is the basis on which gatekeepers decide who or what is worthy of access.

Sometimes access is barred for fear of legal repercussions. Sometimes gatekeepers fear that material won't prove commercially successful. A gatekeeper's preferences or prejudices might influence his or her decision. In England, trade unionists have often complained that news of industrial relations has traditionally favoured the management view, perhaps because media personnel share similar backgrounds to those of managerial status.

Access is important—just how important has been shown time and again in political coups over the second half of the twentieth century. The first target of the modern revolutionary is usually the national broadcasting station.

> **TASK 15.5 A**
>
> **A modest proposal**
>
> Assume that a new national television channel has come into being. Spare hours of transmission capacity are available. The suggestion has been floated that this might be taken up by increased coverage of Oireachtas proceedings. Devise a counter-proposal, making a case for providing access to interests not normally represented. Be innovative and specific in nominating interests and groups or activities and in suggesting *how* they might make use of the available time.

15.6 SELECTION

Media texts are always the result of selection. This book's cover, dimensions, typeface, paper quality etc. were all *selected* from a range of possibilities. The front pages of today's newspapers are the result of selections, starting with estimates of newsworthiness. The pictures selected to accompany the selected stories were almost certainly chosen from a range, all illustrating the same event. The photographers who took the pictures made selections of range, angle etc. The selected photographs may have been cropped, enlarged, or reduced; decisions were taken on positioning and captioning.

When reading any media text, we must always remember that it was *constructed*. A magazine advertisement is constructed with models, locations, sets, lighting, costumes, props and make-up to ensure that the product appears as attractive as possible. A film poster selects those elements of the film that will catch the public's attention, such as names of stars or director. In these instances it is easy to be aware of selection.

But sometimes the medium seems to be offering *unmediated* reality, to be giving us an unretouched, warts-and-all view of how things *really* are. When the media are, apparently, most innocently transparent we need to be most on guard. 'These scenes come to you direct, live, exactly as the camera sees them,' promises the television screen, and isn't it a *fact* that the camera never lies?

It doesn't—but neither does it tell the full truth. It doesn't record the context; it provides just one perspective, which may be so ambiguous that an anchoring caption is needed to explain the meaning; and sometimes it may be computer-enhanced to distort, as when *Time's* cover picture of O. J. Simpson was touched up to make him look blacker (more sinister?). Can you imagine how two caption-writers might produce quite different meanings from this photograph of the British Prime Minister, John Major?

The next time you watch demonstrators clashing with police on your television screen, ask yourself if it is possible to re-present violent scenes neutrally. What effect is given if the cameras are positioned behind the demonstrators? And if they're behind the police? What further alternatives exist? Would the cameras have been present if there hadn't been the possibility of violence? Do protesters exploit the media's apparent weakness for violence? A very basic question: do some newsworthy stories fail to reach us simply because *there are no accompanying pictures*?

Selection is important because it seems to justify the claim that the media set the agenda and play a key role in determining our perception of the items on it. By selecting an item to feature on the agenda, the media make it seem newsworthy. But is it? Is it more worthy of our attention than some stories that were rejected?

TASK 15.6 A

The making of a president

The accompanying photograph of Abraham Lincoln was taken by Mathew Brady on 27 February 1860. It's an early example of deliberate media construction—in this case, a photographer making selections to convey an image. Lincoln had a long neck, a very prominent nose, notoriously unruly hair, and cheeks deeply furrowed with wrinkles. What selections has Brady made to construct the image of an imposing president?

15.7 IDEOLOGY

This is the most fundamental and also most problematic of the five concepts we've chosen to study. Definition is tricky, because specialists in a number of areas use the word in different senses. The *Shorter Oxford English Dictionary* defines ideology as 'the manner of thinking characteristic of a class or an individual.' 'Class' here means any kind of group, such as a race, a social class, a profession, or a sect. To belong to the class that practises Christianity means sharing a manner of thinking that places belief in Christ at the centre of being. A Christian holds to a set of beliefs that follow from love of God and love of neighbour.

Our manner of thinking becomes apparent in the way we make meanings to others—in the most casual words we choose to express ourselves. In a predominantly Christian culture, people characteristically introduce God into their most mundane utterances: 'Soft day, thank God,' 'See you on Tuesday, please God,' 'It's true, God knows.' In

Ireland we accept such references as *natural*, part of the way things are, so familiar that we don't even notice them. A visitor to Ireland might wonder why city church bells ring out at noon and at 6 p.m. and why the national broadcasting service pauses at these times; to us, the occurrences are as familiar as rain.

In this context, ideology refers to the process of making meanings in terms that seem neutral and innocent but that in practice reinforce the dominance of a particular group's manner of thinking, values, ideas, or customs. This is *not* suggesting that anything sinister or underhand is intended. Members of dominant groups assert their dominance without, generally, being aware of doing so. They see it as the *accepted norm*, a matter of common sense, how things are, always have been, and always will be.

In a patriarchal society or culture, therefore, an invitation may be sent to 'Surgeons [or Lecturers, or Councillors] and their wives ...' the assumption being that surgeons etc. are invariably male. (What other assumptions does this invitation make?) No insult or bias was *intended* by the wording, as no insult is intended by 'male nurse' or 'Billy Murphy's widow'. (Have you ever heard a man described as, say, 'Jean Murphy's *widower*'?) Ideological meanings come from deep inside us, showing how we make sense of the world and how we see our place within it.

Our ideas of what is physically attractive are rooted in ideology. The wearing of high-heel shoes by women is regarded as normal and natural in our culture. But is this not another example of a dominant group imposing its manner of thinking on a subordinate group? 'Wearing them accentuates the parts of the female body that patriarchy has trained us into thinking of as attractive to men—the buttocks, thighs, and breasts. The woman thus participates in constructing herself as an attractive object for the male look, and therefore puts herself under the male power (of granting or withholding approval). Wearing them also limits her physical activity and strength: they hobble her and make her move precariously; so wearing them is practising the subordination of women in patriarchy. A woman in high heels is active in reproducing and recirculating the patriarchal meanings of gender that propose masculinity as stronger and more active and femininity as weaker and more passive' (John Fiske, *Introduction to Communication Studies*, p. 175).

Like the casual references to God in everyday conversation, high heels are non-controversial, everyday wear. We don't stop to question them.

Ideologies are 'taught' by—or caught from—society's principal institutions, such as schools, churches, courts, and, of course, the media. At school we absorb beliefs about authority, success, sex roles, and social behaviour. The appointment of prefects, for instance, sends ideological messages to the student body about what it takes to achieve power and status. If year after year the cup for Sportsman of the Year is the final award, preceded by the cup for Sportsgirl of the Year, what message will students take?

In a school, the teaching staff control assemblies, prizegivings, textbooks, blackboards, videos, and the substance of lessons. They have a dominant role in determining the school's ideology. In the wider society, the media—and those who control them—play a key role in reproducing the dominant ideology. They may not tell us what to think but they control the vital information that we need to form our opinions. The greater the reach of the media, the more powerfully they may act as ideological agencies.

Much media output makes no secret of the fact that it is trying to *persuade* us to buy this product or to use that service or to avail of those facilities. Our ideological bias towards thinness is to be detected not in the advertisement for the latest Hollywood star's fitness video but in the health column of a magazine where the medical expert writes, 'If you *suffer* from cellulite ...' Or it may be deduced from the fact that we see so few fat people on our television or cinema screens. To judge by what the media show us, thinness is the norm in our society.

Ideology speaks to us in the stereotypes that are, for understandable reasons, the stock in trade of the media. Stereotypes (see section 2.2.2) are part of the ideological baggage we all carry round with us, evidence of deep-rooted beliefs about the *categories* into which people, behaviour etc. fit. The 'dumb blonde' is stupid and naïve, curvaceous, materialistic, vain, vulgar, seductive, exhibitionistic, and often sexually voracious. Women, no matter what their hair colour, could see this caricature as evidence of a continuing power struggle between the sexes.

A national population (such as the Irish) might consider their international stereotype (as depicted, for example, in British cartoons, television programmes, and joke books) as evidence of a dominant group imposing its manner of thinking on a subordinate racial or national group. (Liz Curtis has an interesting account of the long British tradition of stereotyping the Irish as drunken, moronic, illiterate, illogical and violent in *Ireland: the Propaganda War*, p. 222–8.)

Ideology is important because it is unobtrusive and all-pervasive. It informs our commonest utterance: 'Wait till your father gets home!', 'Stop crying—only girls cry!', 'What a machine—she goes like the wind and she'll give you fifty to the gallon!' The media, with access to millions, have immense ideological power. We need to examine critically what they invite us to accept as 'pure common sense' or 'the natural order of things'. What group stands to benefit if we accept unquestioningly?

TASK 15.7 A

'it's good to talk'

Study the following advertisement carefully in all its aspects. What ideologies can you detect underlying its various appeals? Does it make assumptions? Is it common sense that 'it's good to talk'? Discuss your findings.

Why can't men be more like women?

In a single chapter it's impossible to do more than hint at ways you might study an enormous and highly controversial subject. The issues this chapter has touched on are arguably among the most important for the future well-being of democracy. To isolate one final example: are we, as some predict, headed for a future where there will be two classes: those who 'don't know' and those 'in the know'? Citizens in the first category will have dieted on tabloid press and television while those in the second will have consumed quality press and whatever remnants of television are devoted to serious analysis. Does it matter *for society* if there is a serious imbalance in the quantity and quality of information reaching citizens? Is the imbalance a matter of dear and cheap providers? Should the Government have an information policy?

One thing seems certain: the issues surrounding the media are unlikely to be resolved for a considerable time to come. Government policy is just beginning to respond to the vast and rapid changes in the field of mass communication. If you have a view on what the future of the media might be, you should have plenty of opportunity to air it!

Ten supplementary tasks

1. Media personnel and organisations have to be constantly alert to the *legal* implications of their choices and actions. Sensitive areas include copyright (remember the fuss about Ireland's 1995 Eurovision song contest entry?), libel, and slander. Research the laws that media producers have to be careful not to break. What exactly is defamation etc.? How far can a programme go? The best place to begin is RTE's *Broadcasting Guidelines for RTE Personnel.*

2. Investigate the work of the Advertising Standards Authority and prepare a short report on the body. Read the Code of Advertising Standards for Ireland. Obtain and study copies of recent ASAI case reports.

3. Examine and report on one or more of the famous advertising campaigns of recent years. Assemble as much documentary evidence as possible, and in your study include consideration of the cost of the campaign, its reach, the regulations governing it, its appeal, its commercial success, and its principal techniques. Examples might include the Benson and Hedges Special Filter 'surreal gold' campaign, the Marlboro cowboy sequence, or the notorious Benetton shock posters.

4. Carry out a media survey within the group, perhaps restricting your questionnaire to either print or electronic media, or even concentrating on a single under-researched medium (e.g. a form of popular music or cartoons). Note the advice on questionnaires in section 14.2. Centre your survey on the *uses* people make of the medium or media and on the *gratification* they derive from it or them. Summarise your findings in a report.

5. Research the career and current ownership of *one* of the international media moguls (e.g. Rupert Murdoch, Ted Turner, Tony O'Reilly, Silvio Berlusconi). Has the mogul in question a record of hands-on control (e.g. dictating editorial policy)?

6. A British newspaper once featured an entertaining survey of visual clichés in advertising. This is how one cliché was described:

BIG HAIR

Let's not move from this business of objectifying bits of people yet because women's hair-treatment ads — particularly shampoos — are quite gloriously, spectacularly and uncomplicatedly cliché'd in a way that's getting rare elsewhere.

The "let down your hair" shot recurs endlessly. Gorgeous thick shiny bouncy hair is let down in Rapunzel slo-mo like bungee ropes. Research-driven directors' contracts from hair care companies must specify one such shot per commercial. The research must demonstrate that intelligent women can no more resist this particular image than dogs can resist aniseed. It must, or else why would advertisers expose themselves to universal sniggers?

The variant on this is the "wet hair art" — a girl in a stream shakes her head with such energy as to create a huge arc of hair dispersing drops in a post-hippie, late Pre-Raphaelite image.

We've seen the hair from L'Oréal, at its more aggressively and absurdly bouncy in last year's Elseve Care Mousse Conditioner commercial, and the arc started, I think, with Timotei.

Independent on Sunday, 29 January 1995

Find three further examples of overworked visual images in advertising and show how they are typical. Analyse any ideological implications the advertisements may contain.

7. The *selective process* operates interestingly in the images used to promote Irish tourism abroad.

Four aspects of Ireland are represented here. How are we presenting ourselves to foreigners? Make an illustrated study, using postcards, Bord Fáilte promotional literature, posters, souvenirs, etc., of the imagery used in 'selling' Ireland abroad.

8. Here is an analysis of a successful television series:

Long Runners

'Baywatch'.

Age: four-and-a-half. First broadcast: January 1990.

Frequency: early Saturday evenings, twenty-two weeks a year, plus repeats—that's almost a hundred hours so far.

Formula: flesh. Pneumatic male and female lifeguards strut, pose and pout on Malibu Beach, California, rescuing drowning children, foiling criminals, pacifying gang members, resolving their own inner conflicts, but mostly just running around in inadequate red swimsuits. The perfunctory plot lines fade in the glare of body-worshipping close-ups that are half way between *Playboy* and Leni Riefenstahl.

Hallmarks: oddly vacant characters; happy endings—no-one ever dies; actors filmed from the neck down.

How do they get away with it? They don't always. In 1992 the Broadcasting Standards Council declared its 'unease about the nature of some of the camera angles used in shots of young women' after viewers complained about the notoriously voyeuristic second series, widely known as 'Crotchwatch'. Consequently, the third and fourth series have upped the lifeguarding and general do-gooding and cut back on the full-frontals. A bit.

Audience: around eight million for the current series—good for the slow slot between 'Grandstand' and Jeremy Beadle. Mostly watched by young men, in groups, fired up by an afternoon's sofa sport and waiting to go to the pub.

Who's responsible? A Los Angeles lifeguard called Gregory Bonnan had the idea at the beach one day (lifeguards spend a lot of time doing nothing), roped in David Hasselhoff, of 'Knight Rider' fame, as star, and sold it to NBC in 1989. LWT took it up two years later and have stayed loyal ever since.

Obscure facts: real lifeguards have to stand by at all times to protect the actors when they shoot the sea-rescue scenes. The filming of series 5 starts this week and will continue until December, when the water's cold enough for Hasselhoff to have to stuff his trunks to avoid on-screen embarrassment. All this happens on a public beach (just north of Santa Monica, if you want to go and watch) right beside the busy Pacific Coast Highway.

Cultural sub-text: like the similarly vacuous 'Beverly Hills 90210', 'Baywatch' can be seen as an important text about contemporary America. Its soft-porn elements co-exist uneasily with a carefully PC mix of non-white characters and an emphasis on the lifeguards 'serving the community' (which the producers claim is the point of the show). This in turn clashes with the show's obvious nostalgia for the hedonistic Aryan utopia that the Beach Boys sang about. If all this seems like reading too much into a 55-minute chunk of kitsch, consider the recent episode called 'Rescue Bay'. In this, a sleazy Hollywood mogul visited the lifeguards' beach and got the idea of making a television series called 'Rescue Bay' about ... heroic lifeguards in bikinis. For half an hour 'Baywatch's' lifeguards vied with each other to 'play' lifeguards in 'Rescue Bay'—with implications tailor-made for cultural studies essays with titles such as 'The difficulties of reality in the post-modern world'—only for the evil mogul to cast his own actors instead. The episode climaxed with these actors having to be rescued by the 'real' 'Baywatch' lifeguards. Quite bewildering, except for the swimsuits.

Does the cast ever escape 'Baywatch'? Hasselhoff was briefly a teen pop-idol in Germany four years ago. Pamela Denise Anderson, a blonde ex-volleyball-player who plays the busty lifeguard C. J. Parker, recently posed for *Playboy*. The current *Hello!* features a four-page interview with her proud mother.

Anything that makes you want to kick the set in? The lack of actual sex: like most American shows, 'Baywatch' eagerly and degradingly ogles the bodies but prudishly keeps real action limited to mere snogs.

The bottom line: is it any good? Not really. You need to watch it with other people to avoid getting bored or feeling pathetic. Lifeguards aren't very interesting, and the flesh becomes an aerobicised, asexual blur on repeated viewing. But it fulfils a basic need and, like Benny Hill, is easily exportable, watched in over a hundred countries. A fifth series has just started shooting, and the Baywatch Production Company is planning a spin-off, 'Baywatch Nights'. Wait for the *Modern Review* to canonise it.

(Andy Beckett, *Independent on Sunday*, 26 June 1994.)

Using the above approach as a guide, write a review (illustrated if possible) of another popular and long-running series from either television or radio.

9. Television soaps make constant use of stock characters. One example might be the gossipy neighbourhood nosy-parker: Audrey in 'Coronation Street', Nellie in 'East Enders', Myna Killeen in 'Glenroe', Eunice Phelan in 'Fair City'. Pick three instantly recognisable stock characters that appear in a range of soaps and describe the 'variations on a basic theme'. Possible choices might include the Tough Businessman, the Salt of the Earth, the Token Gay/Traveller/Protestant/Racial Minority, the Heartless Seducer.

10. Write an open letter to the Minister for Education arguing that media studies should be treated as a core subject at secondary level and allowed at least as much time as Irish or English in the curriculum.

Chapter review

1. In your own words, define
(*a*) mass communication
(*b*) mass media
(*c*) access

(d) ideology
(e) consciousness industries.

2. List three good reasons for studying the media.

3. Briefly explain

(a) the hypodermic needle theory
(b) gatekeeping
(c) subliminal advertising
(d) hammocking
(e) sound bite
(f) consumer sovereignty.

4. What is meant by

(a) public service broadcasting?
(b) state regulation?
(c) concentration of ownership?
(d) norm?

Bibliography

Advertising Standards Authority for Ireland, *Code of Advertising Standards for Ireland* (fourth edition), Dublin: ASAI 1995.

Argyle, M., *The Psychology of Interpersonal Behaviour*, London: Penguin 1983.

Astley, Helen, *Get the Message!*, Cambridge: Cambridge University Press 1983.

Bormaster, Jeffrey, and Treat, Carol Lou, *Building Interpersonal Relationships through Talking, Listening, Communicating* (second edition), Austin (Texas): Pro-Ed 1994.

Bostock, Louise, *Speaking in Public*, London: Harper Collins 1994.

Bowskill, Derek, *Acting and Stagecraft Made Simple*, London: W. H. Allen 1973.

Bryson, Bill, *Mother Tongue: the English Language*, London: Hamish Hamilton 1990.

Buzan, Tony, *Speed Reading*, Newton Abbot (Devon): David and Charles 1971.

Cameron, Ellen, *Understanding Graphology*, London: Aquarian 1995.

Carey, G., *Mind the Stop: a Brief Guide to Punctuation with a Note on Proof-Correction* (second edition), Cambridge: Cambridge University Press 1958.

Carver, Raymond, *The Stories of Raymond Carver*, London: Picador 1985.

Cleese, John, and Booth, Connie, *The Complete Fawlty Towers*, London: Methuen Mandarin 1989.

Corner, J., and Hawthorn, J. (editors), *Communication Studies: an Introductory Reader* (fourth edition), London: Edward Arnold 1993.

Coward, Rosalind, *Female Desire*, London: Paladin 1984.

Crystal, David, *The Cambridge Encyclopedia of the English Language*, Cambridge: Cambridge University Press 1995.

Curtis, Liz, *Ireland: the Propaganda War*, London: Pluto 1984.

Department of Arts, Culture, and the Gaeltacht, *Green Paper on Broadcasting*, Dublin: Stationery Office 1995.

Department of Education, *Charting our Education Future: White Paper on Education*, Dublin: Stationery Office 1995.

Doctorow, E.L., *Billy Bathgate*, London: Picador 1990.

Durcan, Paul, *A Snail in my Prime*, London: Harvill 1993.

Ellis, Richard, and McClintock, Ann, *If You Take My Meaning: Theory into Practice in Human Communication* (second edition), London: Edward Arnold 1994.

Fiske, John, *Introduction to Communication Studies* (second edition), London: Routledge 1990.

Friel, Brian, *The Communication Cord*, Dublin: Gallery Books 1989.

Gration, Geoff, et al., *Communication and Media Studies*, London: Nelson 1992.

Hargie, Owen, Saunders, Christine, and Dickson, David, *Social Skills in Interpersonal Communication* (third edition), London: Routledge 1994.

Hawking, Stephen, *A Brief History of Time*, London: Bantam 1988.

Hawkins, Eric, *Spoken and Written Language*, Cambridge: Cambridge University Press 1983.

Hussey, Gemma, *Ireland Today*, Dublin: Town House 1993.

Institute of Public Administration, *Administration Yearbook and Diary*, Dublin: IPA [annual].

Lusted, David (editor), *The Media Studies Book*, London: Routledge 1991.

McClave, Henry, *Communication for Business in Ireland*, Dublin: Gill & Macmillan 1986.

Masterman, Len, *Teaching the Media*, London: Comedia 1985.

Morris, Desmond, *Manwatching*, London: Jonathan Cape 1977.

Morris, Desmond, *Bodywatching*, London: Jonathan Cape 1985.

O'Connor, Joseph, *The Secret World of an Irish Male*, Dublin: New Island Books 1994.

O'Meara, Aileen, and O'Meara, Kathleen, *Headlines and Deadlines*, Dublin: Blackwater 1995.

Orwell, George, *Inside the Whale and Other Essays*, London: Penguin 1962.

O'Sullivan, Tim, Hartley, J., Saunders, D., and Fiske, John, *Key Concepts in Communication*, London: Routledge 1993.

Peel, Malcolm, *Improving Your Communication Skills*, London: Kogan Page 1990.

Pinker, Steven, *The Language Instinct*, London: Allen Lane 1994.

Pinter, Harold, *Plays 2*, London: Eyre Methuen 1981.

Postman, Neil, *Amusing Ourselves to Death*, London: Methuen 1987.

Radio Telefís Éireann, *Broadcasting Guidelines for RTE Personnel*, Dublin: RTE 1989.

Radio Telefís Éireann, *Annual Report*, 1993, Dublin: RTE 1993.

Rainey, Patricia Ann, *Illusion: a Journey into Perception*, Hamden: Linnet 1973.

Rigney, Geraldine, *English for the Office*, Dublin: Folens 1992.

Sadler, R., and Tucker, K., *Common Ground: a Course in Communication*, London: Macmillan 1981.

Sassoon, Rosemary, and Briem, G., *Better Handwriting*, London: Hodder and Stoughton 1984.

Scher, Anna, and Verrall, Charles, *100+ Ideas for Drama*, London: Heinemann Educational 1975.

Scher, Anna, and Verrall, Charles, *Another 100+ Ideas for Drama*, London: Heinemann Educational 1987.

Scott, John, *English for Secretarial and Business Students* (second edition), Dublin: Gill & Macmillan 1990.

Temple, Michael, *Get It Right!*, London: John Murray 1984.

Trevor, William, *Excursions in the Real World*, London: Penguin 1993.